Praise for *I Am Troy Davis*

"Here is a shout for human rights and for the abolition of the death penalty. This book, *I Am Troy Davis*, should be read and cherished. It will inspire courage in the hearts of those who are willing to use their efforts to save lives and increase the quality of life for all people."
—Dr. Maya Angelou, author, *I Know Why the Caged Bird Sings*

"Like Trayvon Martin's monumental murder, the execution of Troy Davis was a historic awakening for this country—an awakening of the deadly consequences of white supremacy. Don't miss this book!"
—Cornel West, professor of philosophy and Christian practice,
Union Theological Seminary

"Martina and Troy are heroes from a family of heroes. This story of their lives is also a call to action. It asks each of us to pick up where they left off by ending the death penalty once and for all so the risk of executing an innocent person is finally eliminated in America."
—Benjamin Todd Jealous, president and CEO, NAACP

"Read this book, about Martina Davis-Correia and Troy Anthony Davis. The lives of this sister and brother were tragically cut short, one by cancer, the other through a cruel injection of a lethal, chemical cocktail in the final act of a profoundly unjust criminal justice system. This book captures their unflagging courage in confronting the challenges thrust upon them. More than history, more than eulogy, *I Am Troy Davis* is an urgent call to action."
—Amy Goodman, host, *Democracy Now!*

"*I Am Troy Davis* is heart-stopping proof that the death penalty didn't just kill an innocent Troy Davis and break and bury his gorgeous family, but it charred the soul of America. This book will devastate you, piss you off, and then inspire you to work with your life to end the death penalty forever."
—Eve Ensler, playwright and activist

"*I Am Troy Davis* is a painful yet very important book, one that will bring you face to face with the human impact of the death penalty system, prompt you to think deeply about the flaws in our criminal justice system, and inspire you to stand with all those who have been wrongfully placed on death row."
—Susan Sarandon, actor and activist

"In this moving and intimate portrait of Troy Davis and his courageous family, Jen Marlowe restores to Troy his humanity, and reminds us why every life matters, and why capital punishment makes this country a pariah among the world's democracies."

—Gloria Steinem, author and activist

"Martina Correia's heroic fight to save her brother's life while battling for her own serves as a powerful testament for activists."

—Liliana Segura, the *Nation*

"*I Am Troy Davis* takes readers on the journey of a remarkable family whose faith, love, integrity, and convictions propelled their fight for their loved one and a larger cause. Jen Marlowe's careful and sensitive collaboration with the Davises has yielded a narrative that will surely inspire readers to pick up the torch that Martina Davis-Correia so bravely carried for social justice and human dignity with every ounce of her being and every day of her life."

—Laura Moye, Amnesty International USA
former death penalty abolition campaign director

"A must-read book—the searing, heartbreaking story of a strong and loving family caught in the vortex of a dysfunctional criminal justice system."

—Anne Emanuel, Georgia State University law professor
and ABA Georgia Death Penalty Assessment Chair

I Am
Troy
Davis

✧

Jen Marlowe and Martina Davis-Correia
with Troy Anthony Davis

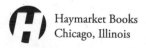
Haymarket Books
Chicago, Illinois

Published in 2013 by
Haymarket Books
P.O. Box 180165
Chicago, IL 60618
773-583-7884
info@haymarketbooks.org
www.haymarketbooks.org

ISBN: 978-1-60846-294-0

Trade distribution:
In the US through Consortium Book Sales and Distribution, www.cbsd.com
In the UK, Turnaround Publisher Services, www.turnaround-uk.com
In Canada, Publishers Group Canada, www.pgcbooks.ca
In Australia, Palgrave Macmillan, www.palgravemacmillan.com.au
All other countries, Publishers Group Worldwide, www.pgw.com

Special discounts are available for bulk purchases by organizations
and institutions. Please contact Haymarket Books for more information
at 773-583-7884 or info@haymarketbooks.org.

Cover design by Ragina Johnson. Cover image shows Troy Anthony Davis
entering Chatham County Superior Court in Savannah, Georgia, Aug. 22, 1991,
during his trial in the shooting death of off-duty police officer Mark MacPhail.
(AP Photo/ *The Savannah Morning News*, File)

This book was published with the generous support of the Wallace Global
Fund and Lannan Foundation.

Printed in Canada by union labor.

Library of Congress CIP data is available.

10 9 8 7 6 5 4 3 2 1

For all those who have been impacted by our country's failed death penalty policy;

For those currently on death row;

For those who have been executed, for those who have been exonerated, and for their families and loved ones, as well as for the families and loved ones of murder victims and for the murder victims themselves;

For all those who have been in the trenches for years, struggling to replace the death penalty with a more humane, more effective form of justice;

For the young people in our lives whom we love deeply: De'Jaun, Kiersten, Renée, Alex, and Maya—your futures are the reason we all must continue to struggle for a more just world;

To the memory of the Davis family's three angel-warriors for justice: Virginia, Troy, and Martina, your presence is with us each and every day

The Davis Family: A family full of faith

Troy with his family during visitation on Georgia's death row. Back row, left to right: Martina, Troy, Lester; middle: De'Jaun; front row, left to right: Ebony, Virginia, Kimberly. Courtesy of the Davis family.

Troy delights in holding his newborn niece, Kiersten.
Courtesy of the Davis family.

Contents

Foreword

I t's 1999 and I'm in the death house at Angola State Prison in Louisiana. In six hours, death row inmate—and my friend—Dobie Williams will be executed for a crime I believe he did not commit. A guard is standing near me. Behind us, Dobie and his family are saying a last, tearful farewell. The guard tells me he's been here for every one of the twenty or so executions since 1983. He jabs his thumb toward the visiting table and whispers, "We got to get rid of the death penalty once and for all, because look who's in here. It's always families like this."

I wondered then what he meant and I still wonder now. Was he talking about families of color? Was he talking about poor families? Or was he simply talking about the grief common to all families who have seen their beloved children killed at the hands of others?

As Dobie was being executed, another family was fiercely defending their son on Georgia's death row, though I hadn't yet learned about this family's struggle. I first met Martina Davis-Correia, sister of death row inmate Troy Anthony Davis, at the National Coalition to Abolish the Death Penalty conference in 2008 and was immediately struck by her fierce love for her brother. When she asked me if I would help Troy, there was no way I could refuse. Over the three years I knew Martina, her son De'Jaun, and the rest of the Davis family, I was touched not only by their unflappable faith in Troy but by their deep love for one another and their tough-as-nails determination in going up against the US justice system.

This is a system plagued by institutionalized racism, with an evident bias against poor defendants, defendants of color, and those convicted of murdering a white victim. This is a system that rewards "tough on crime" district attorneys who seek the death penalty, even in the face of exculpatory evidence and incompetent state-appointed defense lawyers. This is a system that causes violence to families—both of the victims and of the condemned.

In my thirty years of working on death's threshold I have seen firsthand how the families of murder victims suffer during the drawn-out appeals process. This may be the quietest, most pernicious legacy of the death penalty: the irreparable harm it inflicts on families, a pain made all the more unjust by its arbitrary application.

✧

The death penalty has a history of capricious application. In the 1972 case *Furman v. Georgia*, the US Supreme Court enacted a moratorium on the death penalty. The court not only found the imposition of the death penalty to be characterized by arbitrariness and racial bias but ruled that it constituted cruel and unusual punishment on moral grounds.

"These death sentences are cruel and unusual in the same way that being struck by lightning is cruel and unusual . . . the Eighth and Fourteenth Amendments cannot tolerate the infliction of a sentence of death under legal systems that permit this unique penalty to be so wantonly and so freakishly imposed," wrote Justice Potter Stewart, as one of the majority.

The landmark decision of *Furman*, however, was reversed only four years later in *Gregg v. Georgia*, in which the Supreme Court ruled that so long as states proved that their methods of execution followed humane guidelines, it was legal to impose the death penalty. The issue of capital punishment's arbitrariness—its racial bias, among other concerns—was addressed by mandating sentencing and appeals-process reforms. But no matter the extent of the tinkering that the death penalty has undergone during the thirty-six years since *Gregg*, there exists to this day wide regional variation in the application of the death penalty as well as vast disparities in capital sentencing along racial and economic lines.

It is not a fluke that some of the death penalty's most stalwart supporters and the states that execute the largest numbers of prisoners are in the historically slave-owning South. Over 40 percent of prisoners sentenced to death are black, despite the fact that African Americans make up only 13.6 percent of the population at large.[1] Moreover, an October 2012 study examining Delaware's death penalty showed that black defendants who kill white victims are more than six times as likely to receive the death penalty as are black defendants who kill black victims. Meanwhile, black defendants who kill white victims are three times more likely to be sentenced to death than white defendants who kill white victims.[2] While these data by no means tell the whole story of racial bias, they do point to a deeply disturbing trend in a justice system that acknowledges, but neglects to address, serious evidence of racial prejudice in death penalty sentencing. I don't see it as mere coincidence that anti–death penalty advocates are known as "abolitionists."

Troy Davis's case bears some of the classic marks of racial prejudice. As a black man convicted of killing a white policeman, he was statistically much more likely to receive the death penalty than a white man convicted of the same crime.[3] And the atmosphere of heightened racial tension and fear that surrounded the Savannah Police Department's investigation of his case undoubtedly contributed to an investigation that was later discovered to be replete with problems.

As the death-row adage goes, "Capital punishment means them without the capital get punishment." Or, to put it another way, the death penalty differentiates between "the O. J.'s and the No-J's"—those with the means to hire a capable attorney and those without. Over 90 percent of the men and women on death row are indigent: they cannot afford to hire competent, dedicated attorneys who are often the only barrier between those accused of first-degree murder and the death penalty, and must instead rely on state-appointed counsel and poorly funded, overworked public defenders. Troy's family was able to hire a lawyer for his trial, but post-conviction, Troy's case was turned over to the Georgia Resource Center, which provides counsel to indigent death row inmates. The Resource Center lawyers represented Troy throughout the appeals process to the best of their ability, but that ability was hampered by an overwhelming caseload and a budget that was cut by 70 percent right before a critical period in Troy's habeas process.

Poor people's inability to obtain effective representation should alone be enough reason to abolish the death penalty. If the accused do not have defense competent enough to challenge the prosecution's evidence at trial, wrongful convictions are inevitable. Supreme Court Justice Ruth Bader Ginsberg, in a 2001 statement in support of a moratorium on the death penalty, noted that she had "yet to see a death case among the dozens coming to the Supreme Court on eve-of-execution stay applications in which the defendant was well represented at trial."[4] This lack of adequate legal representation contributes to the high numbers of exonerations: between 1976 and 2012, for every ten persons executed, one wrongfully convicted person has been released from death row.[5] And those are only the ones whose wrongful convictions were discovered. It is a certainty that we have executed innocent people in the name of justice.

Though *Gregg* was meant to reform the appeals process, appellate courts, which function largely to protect convictions, have never been able to address issues of innocence adequately. Troy's situation was a case in point: The 11th Circuit Court of Appeals denied Troy's petitions, even after new, possibly exculpatory evidence came to light. Time and again, process and procedure took precedence over fairness and a desire to get to the truth.

In the face of these seemingly insurmountable odds, the Davis family—particularly Martina—rallied in a remarkable way around their imprisoned son, brother, and uncle. Even while suffering from aggressive breast cancer, Martina engaged the support of leaders around the globe. South African archbishop Desmond Tutu, Amnesty International, former president Jimmy Carter, and even death penalty supporter and former FBI head William Sessions spoke out on behalf of Troy. Martina's son De'Jaun began speaking to large audiences about his uncle's case starting in middle school. The entire family contributed their time, paychecks, and earnest prayers to proving Troy's innocence and to fighting the system that was trying to kill him.

✧

There is still much for us to do, as the California electorate's narrow failure to abolish the death penalty in 2012 demonstrated. During my thirty years of dialogue with Americans on this issue, I've learned that support for capital punishment is a response that arises more from the spleen than from the brain. The cure for this knee-jerk reaction, I've seen time and again, is heightened public awareness of the death penalty's true costs to society—financially, emotionally, and ethically. When given concrete information about the death penalty, the public's support for this draconian measure drops.

One certainty I hold: The death penalty will be abolished. Due to the sustained efforts of courageous men and women such as Martina Davis-Correia and the entire Davis family to educate the public about the real horrors of state-sanctioned killings, we have made much progress. As of this writing, six states in the past six years—New York, New Jersey, New Mexico, Illinois, Connecticut, and, most recently, Maryland—have abolished the death penalty and one— Oregon—has enacted a moratorium. American support for the death penalty has fallen precipitously since its 80 percent peak in 1994. A Gallup poll conducted shortly after Troy's execution showed the lowest American backing for the death penalty since its reinstatement, indicating the extent to which Americans were deeply disturbed by his death.[6]

✧

I Am Troy Davis is a book for everyone who has ever been the victim of injustice at the hands of the US judicial system. It belongs to all death row inmates, to their families who suffer alongside them, and to those who have already been executed.

But it is more than that. The story at this book's heart is one of a family's courage, heartbreak, and undying struggle. A family whose members love each other fiercely and are determined not to let one of their own fall victim to injustice or the dehumanization of death row. *I Am Troy Davis* is a story is for all of us who have loved a brother, a sister, a mother, an uncle, a son or daughter.

All of us have, I suspect, moments of illumination in our lives that revealed disturbing realities that we had long ignored, moments that pushed us to question and, ultimately, to act. May the light provided by Troy and Martina's powerful story represent one of these epiphanies. The tragedy that Troy, Martina, and the Davis family endured should push us all to think deeply about the system that necessitates the telling of their story. And may their courage and indomitable spirits inspire us to act, for as long as it takes, to change that system.

Sister Helen Prejean, CSJ
April 2013
New Orleans, Louisiana

Notes

1. Deborah Fins, *Death Row USA* (New York: Criminal Justice Project of the NAACP Legal Defense and Educational Fund, Inc.,Winter 2011), www.naacpldf.org/files/publications/DRUSA_Winter_2011.pdf; Sonya Rastogi et al., *The Black Population: 2010* (US Census Bureau, September 2011), www.census.gov/prod/cen2010/briefs/c2010br-06.pdf.
2. Sheri Lynn Johnson et al., "The Delaware Death Penalty: An Empirical Study," *Iowa Law Review* 97 (2012).
3. According to a 2001 study conducted in North Carolina, even when only cases that are "death eligible" are examined, cases involving nonwhite defendants who murder whites have a capital sentencing rate of 11.6 percent, while cases involving white defendants who murder whites have a capital sentencing rate of 6.1 percent. "Death eligible" cases include the murder of a police officer or murder while attempting to escape from prison, among other factors. Isaac Unger and John C. Boger, *Race and the Death Penalty in North Carolina* (Chapel Hill: University of North Carolina, April 2001), www.unc.edu/~jcboger/NCDeathPenaltyReport2001.pdf.
4. Associated Press, "Ginsberg Backs Ending Death Penalty," April 9, 2001.
5. "Innocence: List of Those Freed from Death Row," Death Penalty Information Center, accessed October 1, 2012, www.deathpenaltyinfo.org/innocence-list-those-freed-death-row.
6. "Death Penalty," Gallup, November 26, 2012, www.gallup.com/poll/1606/death-penalty.aspx.

Timeline of Events

Below is a chronology of some of the most significant events in the book, intended to help the reader navigate the back-and-forth in time.

August 18, 1989, 11:45 p.m.: Michael Cooper is non-fatally shot in the jaw outside a pool party in the Cloverdale neighborhood of Savannah.

August 19, 1989, 1:04 a.m.: Sherman Coleman is shot in the leg outside the Cloverdale pool party.

August 19, 1989, 1:10 a.m.: Officer Mark MacPhail is fatally shot in the parking lot of the Burger King/Greyhound bus station.

August 19, 1989, 7:55 p.m.: Sylvester "Redd" Coles enters the police station and gives Troy's name. A manhunt for Troy Davis ensues.

August 23, 1989: Troy turns himself into the Savannah Police Department (SPD).

August 24, 1989: Chatham County DA Spencer Lawton announces he is seeking the death penalty in Troy's case. The SPD holds a reenactment of the crime with witnesses.

August 24–29, 1989: Eyewitnesses identify Troy from a photo lineup, having already seen the identical photo or footage of Troy on wanted posters, in the newspaper, or on television.

November 15, 1989: Troy is indicted by a grand jury for shooting Michael Cooper, assaulting Larry Young, and murdering Officer MacPhail. He enters his plea: not guilty.

August 19, 1991: Jury selection for Troy's trial begins.

August 22, 1991: Troy's trial begins.

August 28, 1991: Troy is found guilty of all counts.

August 29, 1991: Troy's sentencing hearing begins.

August 30, 1991: Troy is sentenced to death.

September 1991: Troy is moved to death row.

February 3, 1992: Joseph Davis dies of a diabetic coma.

June 22, 1994: Martina's son, Antone De'Jaun Correia, is born.

1995: Troy's first state habeas petition is filed in the Superior Court of Butts County. Troy is now represented by the Georgia Resource Center.

1995: US Congress votes to defund all federally funded legal resource centers across the nation. Georgia Resource Center's budget is slashed by 70 percent.

April 24, 1996: President Bill Clinton signs the Antiterrorism and Effective Death Penalty Act (AEDPA) into law.

September 9, 1997: The Superior Court of Butts County, Georgia, denies Troy's appeal.

March 28, 2001: Martina is diagnosed with advanced breast cancer and is given six months to live.

2002/2003: The Georgia Resource Center, with a reconstituted budget, is finally able to do serious investigative work on Troy's case.

May 2004: A federal judge refuses to grant Troy a hearing, citing AEDPA statues as one reason. Arnold & Porter begins to represent Troy.

September 26, 2006: Troy's final *habeas corpus* appeal is denied by the 11th Circuit Court of Appeals.

February 1, 2007: Amnesty International releases a report about Troy's case entitled *Where Is the Justice for Me?*

June 29, 2007: Troy's first execution date is set for July 17, 2007.

July 16, 2007: Troy is granted a ninety-day stay of execution by the Georgia State Board of Pardons & Parole.

August 7, 2007: The Georgia Supreme Court agrees to hear arguments on Troy's extraordinary motion for a new trial (a motion that had been denied by the Chatham County Superior Court and appealed).

November 13, 2007: The Georgia Supreme Court hears arguments on Troy's extraordinary motion for a new trial.

January 6, 2008: Kiersten Herron (Troy's niece, his sister Ebony's daughter) is born.

March 17, 2008: The Georgia Supreme Court denies Troy's extraordinary motion for a new trial. Troy appeals the decision with the US Supreme Court.

March 22, 2008: De'Jaun wins Georgia's statewide social science contest for his project entitled "How Does the Troy Anthony Davis Case Impact Georgia?"

September 3, 2008: Troy's second execution date is set for September 23, 2008, at 7 p.m.

September 12, 2008: Troy has a clemency hearing in front of the Georgia State Board of Pardons and Parole. Clemency is denied.

September 23, 2008, 5:30 p.m.: The US Supreme Court grants Troy a one-week stay of execution so that the court can rule on his appeal for an extraordinary motion for a new trial.

October 15, 2008: The US Supreme Court declines to review the Georgia Supreme Court's denial on Troy's motion for a new trial.

October 20, 2008: Troy's third execution date is set for October 27, 2008.

October 21, 2008: Troy's attorneys file a petition with the 11th Circuit Court of Appeals requesting the court's permission to file a new federal habeas petition, which would allow him to petition the US District Court for an evidentiary hearing.

October 24, 2008: The 11th Circuit Court of Appeals stays the execution in order to consider Troy's petition.

December 9, 2008: The 11th Circuit Court of Appeals holds a hearing.

April 16, 2009: The 11th Circuit Court of Appeals denies Troy's petition.

May 19, 2009: Troy files a petition directly with the US Supreme Court for a new evidentiary hearing.

August 17, 2009: The US Supreme Court orders a Georgia federal district court to grant Troy an evidentiary hearing.

January 2010: Contact visits are revoked on Georgia's death row.

June 23–24, 2010: Troy's evidentiary hearing takes place, presided over by Judge William Moore.

August 24, 2010: Judge Moore denies Troy's petition for habeas relief in federal court. Troy appeals the decision to the 11th Circuit Court of Appeals.

November 5, 2010: The 11th Circuit Court of Appeals denies Troy's appeal. Troy appeals the decision to the US Supreme Court.

March 15, 2011: Georgia's supply of sodium thiopental, used for lethal injection, is confiscated by the Federal Drug Enforcement Agency. Executions are temporarily on hold.

March 28, 2011: Troy's appeal is denied by the US Supreme Court, clearing the way for Georgia to set a new execution date.

April 12, 2011: Virginia Davis passes away of "natural causes."

May 20, 2011: The Georgia Department of Corrections announces that it will substitute pentobarbital for sodium thiopental, thereby permitting executions to resume.

September 6, 2011: Troy's fourth execution date is set for September 21, 2011.

September 19, 2011: Georgia State Board of Pardons and Parole holds a clemency hearing.

September 20, 2011: Clemency is denied.

September 21, 2011: Troy Davis is executed by the state of Georgia. The time of death is 11:08 p.m.

December 1, 2011: Martina Davis-Correia passes away.

Martina and De'Jaun gather petition signatures in Savannah with a team of supporters on behalf of Troy Davis. Left to right: Natalia Taylor Bowdoin, Ellen Kubica, Lisa Potash, Kathryn Hamoudah, Sahil Khatod, Laura Emiko Soltis, James Clark, Loretta Vanpelt, Jenell Holden, Roberto Gutierrez, De'Jaun Davis-Correia, Andrea Folds, Martina Davis-Correia. Courtesy of Kathryn Hamoudah.

Glossary of Characters

There are many people to keep track of in the pages of *I Am Troy Davis*. The below list consists of those who are mentioned multiple times, in order to help prevent confusion.

Anneliese MacPhail: Mother of slain police officer Mark MacPhail

Antione Williams: Eyewitness to the murder of Officer MacPhail; implicated Troy at trial, but later recanted via affidavit and testimony at Troy's 2007 parole board hearing and 2010 evidentiary hearing

April Hester: Host of the Cloverdale pool party; testified at Troy's 2008 parole board hearing and 2010 evidentiary hearing

Benjamin Gordon: Attended the Cloverdale pool party and was in the car with Michael Cooper when he was shot. Testified at Troy's trial and the 2010 evidentiary hearing

Benjamin Todd Jealous: President and CEO of the NAACP

Brian Kim: Martina's initial oncologist

Danielle Garten: One of Troy's attorneys from Arnold & Porter

Darrell "D.D." Collins: Eyewitness to the events leading to the murder of Officer

MacPhail; implicated Troy at trial, but later recanted via affidavit and testimony at the 2010 evidentiary hearing

David Lock: Chief assistant district attorney for Chatham County from 1986 to 2008

De'Jaun Davis-Correia: Martina's son; Troy's nephew

Dorothy Ferrell: Eyewitness to the murder of Officer MacPhail; implicated Troy at trial, but later recanted via affidavit and testimony at Troy's 2008 parole board hearing

Ebony Davis: Troy and Martina's younger sister

Edward DuBose: President of the Georgia Conference of the NAACP

Elijah West: Valerie West's son, Aunt Mattie's grandson

Earl/E.Red: Hip-hop artist who knew Troy growing up

Gemma Puglisi: American University professor of journalism; close friend of Troy and the Davis family

Dr. George Negrea: Martina's second oncologist

Harriett Murray: Eyewitness to the murder of Officer MacPhail; implicated Troy at trial, but later signed an affidavit contradicting her trial testimony

Jason (Jay) Ewart: Troy's lead attorney from Arnold & Porter

Jeff Walsh: Investigator with the Georgia Resource Center

Jeffrey Sams: Went to the pool hall with Troy and D.D. the night Officer MacPhail was shot

Jeffrey Sapp: Troy's childhood friend; implicated Troy at trial but later recanted via affidavit and testimony at Troy's 2007 parole board hearing and 2010 evidentiary hearing

Joan MacPhail: Widow of slain police officer Mark MacPhail

John Hanusz: An attorney with the Georgia Resource Center assigned to Troy's case in 2002

Joseph Davis: Martina, Troy, Kimberly, Lester, and Ebony's father

Kathleen (Kitty) Behan: Attorney at Arnold & Porter who initially agreed to take Troy's case pro bono

Kevin McQueen: Testified at Troy's trial; later recanted via affidavit and testimony at the 2007 parole board hearing and 2010 evidentiary hearing

Kiersten Herron: Ebony's daughter; Troy and Martina's niece

Kim Manning-Cooper: Amnesty UK's death penalty abolition campaign manager

Kimberly Davis: Troy and Martina's younger sister

Larry Chisolm: Chatham County district attorney at the time of Troy's execution, replacing Spencer Lawton

Larry Cox: Executive Director of Amnesty International USA (AIUSA) from 2006 to 2011

Larry Young: Homeless man harassed and pistol-whipped on August 19, 1989; implicated Troy at trial, but later recanted via affidavit and testimony at Troy's 2007 parole board hearing

Laura Moye: Amnesty International USA's death penalty abolition campaign director from 2009 to 2012, previously deputy director of AIUSA's Southern Regional Office

Ledra Sullivan-Russell: Close friend of Troy and the Davis family

Lester Davis: Troy and Martina's younger brother

Madison MacPhail: Daughter of slain police officer Mark MacPhail

Mark Allen MacPhail: Off-duty police officer fatally shot in the early hours of August 19, 1989

Mark MacPhail Jr.: Son of slain police officer Mark MacPhail

Martina Davis-Correia: Troy's older sister

(Aunt) Mattie Simmons: Older sister of Virginia Davis; Troy and Martina's auntie

Michael Cooper: Teenager shot non-fatally in the jaw while in a car driving away from the August 18, 1989, Cloverdale pool party

Quiana Glover: Testified at the 2010 evidentiary hearing

(Reverend Dr.) Raphael Warnock: Senior pastor of the historic Ebenezer Baptist Church, where Martin Luther King Jr. once preached

Robert T. Falligant: Troy's trial lawyer

Scott Langley: Photojournalist and grassroots organizer against the death penalty

Spencer Lawton: Chatham County District Attorney from 1981 to 2008

Stephen Marsh: One of Troy's attorneys from Arnold & Porter

Steve Sanders: Implicated Troy at trial; never recanted

Sue Gunawardena-Vaughn: AIUSA's death penalty abolition campaign director prior to Laura Moye

Sylvester "Redd" Coles: The man who argued with Larry Young over a can of beer, which triggered the series of events that led to the fatal shooting of Officer MacPhail

Terry Benedict: Documentary filmmaker who was working on a film about Troy

Tonya Johnson: Testified at Troy's trial and at the 2007 parole board hearing

Trevor Ferguson: Martina's long-term partner

Troy Davis: Executed by the state of Georgia on September 21, 2011, for the killing of off-duty police officer Mark MacPhail despite a strong case of innocence

Valerie West: Aunt Mattie's daughter; Troy, Martina, Kim, Lester, and Ebony's cousin.

Virginia Roberts Davis: Martina, Troy, Kimberly, Lester, and Ebony's mother

Wende Gozan Brown: Media relations director for AIUSA until 2011

Glossary of Organizations

Below is a list of organizations that are mentioned multiple times in *I Am Troy Davis*. The following descriptions come (edited for style) from the websites of the organizations themselves.

American Civil Liberties Union (ACLU): The nation's guardian of liberty, working daily in courts, legislatures, and communities to defend and preserve the individual rights and liberties that the Constitution and laws of the United States guarantee everyone in this country

Amnesty International (AI): A global movement of more than three million supporters, members, and activists in more than 150 countries and territories who campaign to end grave abuses of human rights

Amnesty International USA (AIUSA): The US branch of Amnesty International

Campaign to End the Death Penalty: National grassroots organization dedicated to the abolition of capital punishment

Change.org: World's largest petition platform, empowering people everywhere to create the change they want to see

Coalition for the People's Agenda: Organization with a mission to improve the quality of governance in Georgia and help create a more informed and active electorate and responsive and accountable elected officals

Color of Change: Organization seeking to empower members—Black Americans and allies—to make government more responsive to the concerns of Black Americans and to bring about positive political and social change for everyone

Correctional Emergency Response Team (CERT): CERT teams receive extensive training on managing noncompliant offenders in day-to-day facility operations as well as advanced training in cell extractions, chemical munitions, and less lethal escorts and transports, offender searches, interview and interrogation techniques, and security threat groups

Democracy Now!: A national, daily, independent, award-winning news program hosted by journalists Amy Goodman and Juan Gonzalez

Fraternal Order of the Police (FOP): World's largest organization of sworn law enforcement officers, with more than 325,000 members in more than 2,100 lodges

FTP Movement: Mission is to raise political awareness and engage and inspire people to take an active role in building the community

Georgians for Alternatives to the Death Penalty (GFADP): Statewide coalition working to end the death penalty, build power in communities targeted by the criminal justice system, protect the rights and dignity of those on death row and their families, and transform Georgia's broken public safety system

Georgia Bureau of Investigation (GBI): Mission is to provide the highest quality investigative, scientific, and information services and resources to the criminal justice community

Georgia Resource Center: Small, nonprofit law office providing free representation to indigent death-sentenced prisoners in Georgia

Interracial Interfaith Community: Offers a variety of educational and cultural programs to promote appreciation of our diversity and sameness; takes an active role in exposing and confronting both personal and institutional racism

MoveOn.org: A community of more than eight million Americans from all walks of life who are using the most innovative technology to lead, participate in, and win campaigns for progressive change

National Action Network (NAN): Founded by Reverend Al Sharpton, one of the leading civil rights organizations in the nation, with chapters throughout the United States

National Association for the Advancement of Colored People (NAACP): Organization that works to ensure the political, educational, social, and economic equality of rights of all persons and to eliminate race-based discrimination

National Coalition to Abolish the Death Penalty (NCADP): Nation's oldest organization dedicated to the abolition of the death penalty

People of Faith Against the Death Penalty: The mission of People of Faith Against the Death Penalty is to educate and mobilize faith communities to act to abolish the death penalty in the United States.

Police Athletic League (PAL): An organization that works to prevent juvenile crime and violence by building the bond between cops and kids

Rainbow/PUSH Coalition: A multiracial, multi-issue, progressive, international membership organization fighting for social change

Southern Center for Human Rights (SCHR): Provides legal representation to people facing the death penalty, challenges human rights violations in prisons and jails, seeks through litigation and advocacy to improve legal representation for poor people accused of crimes, and advocates for criminal justice system reforms on behalf of those affected by the system in the southern United States

Southern Christian Leadership Conference: In the spirit of Martin Luther King Jr., SCLC renews its commitment to bring about the promise of "one nation, under God, INDIVISIBLE" together with the commitment to activate the "strength to love" within the community of humankind

US Human Rights Network: National network of organizations and individuals working to build and strengthen a people-centered human rights movement in the United States

Davis family warriors for justice: Virginia, Troy, and Martina
Courtesy of the Davis family.

Introduction

Writing this book may very well be the most difficult task I have undertaken. The difficulty was partially emotional—I was diving into the painful details of the story of two people I loved after having so recently lost them. But there were other challenges as well: how to complete a manuscript when both of my coauthors were now gone?

It was Troy who, after learning that I was a filmmaker, first put the idea into my head that I might be a part of helping his family tell their story. "You should consider doing a documentary about Martina," he wrote to me on April 21, 2008, during the early months of our correspondence. "That's a story of love, tribulation, survival, strength, and determination that everyone can be moved by."

Having seen Martina on *Democracy Now!* (which is what led me to begin corresponding with Troy), I more than agreed with Troy. Martina was clearly a force of nature, and I instinctively felt that her double struggle (for her brother's life and her own) was a powerful window into Troy's story and to the violent impact that the death penalty has on innocent families.

The following year, I met Martina when she came to speak at the International Longshore and Warehouse Union Convention in Seattle. "Everyone keeps telling me I should write a book," she mentioned in an offhand comment. "And I'd really like to, but I don't have the time—I'd need somebody to write it with me." Over the next days, I couldn't get the idea of working with Martina on her book out of my mind. I wrote her an email, asking if she'd like to embark on this partnership together. "I would love for you to work on my book with me, please go forward," Martina wrote back, and the project began.

The bulk of *I Am Troy Davis* comes from intensive interviews with Martina conducted between February 2010 through November 2011. Much of the hardest work—talking about the months leading up to Troy's execution and the execution itself—we did over the phone and Skype during what would be the last two months of Martina's own life.

"We can wait until more time has passed and the memories are not as raw," I said to Martina before we plunged into the trauma of the recent events.

Martina responded with her usual grit and determination. "I'd rather do it now while it's still fresh." Completing this book had become her highest priority, she told me. I wonder now if Martina realized she didn't have much time left.

Troy participated directly in the book as well. In my first visit to him on death row, we devised a system where he could contribute his memories and thoughts to the manuscript through letters and phone conversations. I tried to include in the book as many as possible of the anecdotes and details Troy shared with me.

I also interviewed many other members of the Davis family, including Virginia, Kimberly, and De'Jaun. I spoke in depth with attorneys and investigators who worked on various aspects of Troy's case, with advocates and activists who were entrenched in the campaign to prevent his execution, and with close friends and allies who stood by the family's side at crucial moments. Video footage of certain rallies and vigils often permitted me to offer detailed descriptions and exact quotes. Kimberly Davis (Troy and Martina's sister) pored through three different drafts of the manuscript, consulting with other family members to fill in gaps and correct mistakes.

The details of Troy's case that are described in the book, as well as the details of the crimes for which he was convicted and ultimately executed, are based largely on documents that are in the public record: trial transcripts, hearing transcripts, and decisions from the 11th Circuit Court of Appeals and the Georgia Supreme Court; the transcript from Troy's June 2010 federal evidentiary hearing; police reports; witness affidavits and recantations. Martina's and Troy's own memories of those events, as well as the recollections of others who were present, including my own, fleshed these out. There are no transcripts available of parole board hearings, so I had to rely on the notes and memories of those who were in the room, filling in some details using witness affidavits. Several of Troy's attorneys were invaluable in helping me piece together the "behind the scenes" stories related to the twists and turns of the case.

I Am Troy Davis is not an investigative book, nor is it an effort to expose all perspectives about Troy's case. It is the unapologetic story of Martina Davis-Correia, Troy Anthony Davis, and the Davis family. Still, as the manuscript neared completion, I felt compelled to reach out to Anneliese MacPhail, the mother of Mark MacPhail, the Savannah police officer who was murdered in the early hours of August 19, 1989. I wanted to invite the MacPhail family to share with me some details about Mark as a person, so that his family's loss would be keenly felt. Mrs. MacPhail declined to participate, telling me that her family felt the same way. Though missing his family's contribution, I tried to render Officer Mark MacPhail with respect and humanity, and hope that this book treats the MacPhail family's tragic loss with compassion. We should never forget, as the Davis family is always the first to remind us, that the events that were set in motion, ultimately leading to Troy's execution, were triggered by the brutal murder of a police officer who heroically answered a cry for help from a man being attacked.

I have made every effort to be as accurate as possible in these pages. Kimberly Davis and others informed me of instances where I strayed, allowing me to correct errors. Though dialogue and details often had to be reconstructed, *I Am Troy Davis* reflects, as honestly as possible, the essence of Martina's experience.

One thing that struck me while writing is the intrinsically ephemeral nature of memory. Often Martina, Troy, and other witnesses described to me the very same event with slightly different details. As criminology research informs us, and as Troy's case itself highlights, memory is not a perfect science. Recalling the past is far more complicated than replaying a videotape in one's mind—memory is invariably subject to various factors and influences. This is precisely why eyewitness testimony should always be regarded with caution and why Troy Davis—and so many others—should never have been sentenced to death on its basis.

Writing *I Am Troy Davis* was the fulfillment of a sacred promise, a weighty responsibility, and an extraordinary privilege. This book is what I could do for Martina, for Troy, for their mother Virginia (all three of whom I miss dearly), and for the Davis family. My deepest hope is that these pages reflect Martina's and Troy's courage, spirit, and humanity in all of their beautiful complexity. I hope the book is a worthy tribute to them and does justice to their story and their struggle. By telling Martina's and Troy's truth, I hope that *I Am Troy Davis* provides an alternative form of justice for them and for the Davis family.

Jen Marlowe
April 2013
Seattle, Washington

Virginia Davis sits in her home, surrounded by family and supporters.
Clockwise around Virginia, starting from the bottom left: Amina "Rocky" Brown on
the lap of her mother Wende Gozan Brown, Jen Marlowe, Kim Manning-Cooper,
Laura Tate Kagel, Laura Moye, Martina with Kiersten on her lap, De'Jaun.
Courtesy of Nicolas Krameyer.

Prelude

*L*ate at night on Friday, August 18, 1989, an unknown assailant shot a teenager named Michael Cooper non-fatally in the jaw as Cooper and his friends were driving away from a pool party in the Cloverdale neighborhood of Savannah, Georgia.

About an hour later, in the early hours of Saturday, August 19, a group of young men were playing pool at Charlie Brown's pool hall, located near Savannah's Yamacraw housing project and across the street from a combined Greyhound bus station and Burger King restaurant. A homeless man named Larry Young went to a convenience store next to the pool hall to buy some beer. Sylvester "Redd" Coles came out of the pool hall and asked Young for a can of beer. Young refused. Coles began arguing about the can of beer with Young, following him across the street to the parking lot of the Greyhound bus station/Burger King. Two other youths, Darrell "D.D." Collins and Troy Davis, came out of the pool hall and followed Coles and Young to the dimly lit parking lot as Coles continued to harass Young.

Suddenly, Larry Young was pistol-whipped on his temple. Bleeding profusely, Young yelled for help, banging on the hood of a van filled with Air Service personnel at the Burger King drive-through. Police officer Mark Allen MacPhail, working an off-duty job as night security, rounded the corner of the bus station, running to Young's assistance.

Officer MacPhail was shot once, and then, when he was down, shot again.

27

The police arrived on the scene minutes later and tried unsuccessfully to resuscitate their slain colleague. They rounded up scores of people in the vicinity, yet they had no idea who the perpetrator was. The identity of the gunman remained a complete mystery until 7:55 p.m., when Redd Coles and his lawyer walked into the police barracks and Coles provided a name to the Savannah Police Department. The name Coles gave was Troy Anthony Davis . . .

October 8, 2011

Martina sits on her bed, childhood photos spread on her lap. It's one week after Troy's funeral and her first quiet moment since his execution date was set. She lifts Troy's second-grade school picture from her lap and stares at it, smiling at the white milk ring around his mouth. School pictures were taken after lunch; Troy always drank milk at lunch, and when the goofball drank milk, he stuck his entire lip into the cup. "Couldn't someone at least wipe my child's mouth before taking his photo?" Mama would mutter when Troy proudly presented her with his school picture. Mama did not have to endure these last weeks—that's one blessing.

What went through Troy's head during those final minutes? What was he feeling? Jay Ewart, Troy's lead attorney, told Martina that Troy spoke his final words and then went peacefully, the life draining from his eyes. As if God helped him with the transition. Martina trusts Jay—he would not lie to her. But how can she be sure that her brother did not feel any pain?

Martina fought with every ounce of her strength to prove Troy's innocence and keep him alive, even when she was weakened by cancer and chemotherapy. For years, no one wanted to listen. Now everyone keeps reminding her that she is the reason the world knows the name Troy Anthony Davis. But what does that matter? Her brother is still dead.

She traces the fading edges of an even older photo. Martina must have been three years old. Mama had dressed her that Easter morning in a ridiculous frilly white bonnet, white sleeveless dress with a poufy skirt, and lacy white leggings. Toddler-aged Troy had on a light gray three-piece suit with the jacket removed. Little Tina clutched baby Troy's hand protectively as they both squinted solemnly into the camera.

What more could she have done?

It's too painful to stare at the photos any longer. She tucks them behind a stack of condolence letters: cards from death-row inmates in San Quentin telling her they are with her during her time of struggle; crayon-drawn pictures from the kids of filmmaker Terry Benedict, who was making a documentary about Troy; letters from Troy's friends with messages from Troy that he had asked them to relay to her—"Keep your faith strong, and take care of your health."

She pulls a yet-unopened letter from the bottom of the stack and strokes it, as she has every day since its arrival. It's postmarked September 21, the day Troy was killed. Her name and address are written in his careful, looping, almost childlike cursive with "Mr. Troy Anthony Davis" on the return address—he always wrote "Mr." to force the prison officials who handled his mail to think of him in respectful terms.

Carefully, so as not to tear any part of the envelope with Troy's handwriting on it, Martina opens the flap and gently pulls out the lined paper, smoothing the creases as she unfolds it. Her eyes fall on one sentence within this final letter: "Make sure you finish writing your book."

Martina and Troy, Easter, 1971
Courtesy of the Davis family.

Davis family kids in the front yard of their home in Cloverdale.
Back row, from left to right: Kimberly, Martina, Troy. Lester in front.
Courtesy of the Davis family.

Part One

June 29, 2007

The phone was ringing when Martina returned home from her chemotherapy treatment.

"Hello?"

"Hello. This is Global Tel Link with a collect call from Troy Davis at Georgia Diagnostic and Classification Prison." Martina punched through all the buttons required in order to accept the call.

"Tina?"

She could hear something in his voice.

"What's the matter?"

"I just got this paper that I have to fill out, and I need you to help me."

"What is it?"

Warden William Terry had called Troy to his office. With his deputy present and surrounded by Correctional Emergency Response Team (CERT) officers, the warden began reading. "The Court having sentenced Defendant, Troy Anthony Davis, on the 3rd day of September, 1991, to be executed by the Department of Corrections at such penal institution as may be designated by said Department . . ." The date, time, and method were all spelled out: July 17, 7 p.m., with a three-drug cocktail to first numb him, then paralyze him, then stop his heart. The warden had told him to sign the document,

Troy told Martina, but he refused to sign his own death warrant, as if he agreed to those terms. Next, the counselor had entered and had given Troy a form. Troy then had thirty minutes to fill it out and return it.

"I have to decide who my final visitors will be. I have to tell them if I want my organs donated."

If Troy elected to have his body returned to his family, he continued, it would have to go first to the state crime lab in Atlanta. His family would have to pay for an autopsy to determine the cause of his death.

"Cause of death?" Martina echoed, dumbfounded. After killing her brother, the state would require an autopsy to determine the cause of his death?

"If you all don't want to pay to bring my body back to Savannah, they'll bury me on the prison grounds in a pine box for $25. Those are our options."

Martina could hear her brother's words but could not quite grasp their meaning. She felt as if she were in the Twilight Zone.

"We'll give them this information, Troy, but they're not going to need it," Martina finally said, jaw clenched.

They went through the questions one by one: Did he want to record any final words? Did he want a last meal? Troy's voice cracked only once or twice as he and Martina drew up the list of the last twenty-four people who would see him alive. Cradling the landline receiver with Troy on it on one shoulder, Martina called friends and family members from her cell phone.

"Troy has an execution date for July 17," she informed each stunned person. "Would you like to visit him on one of the two final days?"

She updated Troy on who could visit and on which day as he filled out the information on his form. As family was not permitted to be inside the execution chamber with him, his attorney, Jay Ewart, would witness the execution.

When Troy's phone time was over, Martina hung up, allowed herself exactly five minutes to cry, and then sharply pulled herself together. She hoped nobody would ask her about the details of that thirty-minute phone call, planning with Troy his death and funeral. She did not think she would ever be able to repeat that conversation.

The walls in her house were thin. Martina could hear Mama in the next bedroom late that night, crying and praying. What possible comfort could she offer her mother? She lay awake in bed, listening to her mother's desperate plea throughout the long, sleepless night: *Please don't let them kill my child. Please don't let them kill my child.*

♦ ♦ ♦

Virginia Roberts Davis, mother of Martina, Troy, Kimberly, Lester, and Ebony, was born on May 19, 1945, in a house on Myrtle Street in Savannah, Georgia, that her father, Screven Eugene Roberts, built himself.

When Virginia was twelve years old, her mother took sick with pneumonia and passed the following week. Screven, blind in one eye from an untreated steel-mill injury, did his best to care for his three daughters, but Mattie, the eldest, Annalee, the middle sister, and Virginia mostly had to fend for themselves. By the time Virginia reached high school, her father had lost sight in his second eye as well. Annalee contracted polio shortly after her mother died and gradually grew weaker. She finally passed on the sofa with her head in fourteen-year-old Virginia's lap. Mattie got married soon after, leaving Virginia at home with her father, who remarried shortly after.

When Virginia finished high school, she found a job at a coffee shop next to the Chatham County Courthouse. A man named Joseph worked in the courthouse as a deputy sheriff and frequented the coffee shop regularly, chatting with Virginia. One day, Joseph casually asked Virginia where she lived. Next thing she knew, Joseph rode out to her house on his bicycle. He started coming by more often and, although Joseph was quite a bit older and had previously been married with children, Virginia was certain she was in love.

Virginia was eighteen years old when she married Joseph. Martina arrived after five years of marriage in the early hours of May 13, 1967. Mama, ecstatic, bought Martina all the things that a baby girl should have: a sweet little bassinet, a stroller, pretty clothes. But Martina was Daddy's little girl from the start. Joseph took his infant daughter everywhere with him.

"Where have you been at with that baby?" Virginia demanded, hand on hip, when Joseph opened the front door late one night with little Martina tucked contentedly into the crook of his arm.

"We was down there to the pool hall, shooting pool," Joseph answered.

"You took the baby to the pool hall? Who was holding her while you was shooting pool?"

"Oh, we had her sitting up on the pool table," Joseph grinned as Virginia shook her head.

Troy was born less than seventeen months later on October 9, 1968. "Two peas in a pod," Virginia said about her pair of little ones as she pushed them together in the stroller. Kimberly came along two years after Troy, providing Mama with two little girls to dress in frilly outfits with matching bonnets and Shirley Temple curls tight enough for Troy to pull them taut and watch them go *boing* back into place on their heads. Martina had no use for Shirley Temple. She wanted to play half-rubber and run with the boys.

Martina and Troy were always thick as thieves. "T & T," they called themselves, Tina and Troy. Together they could accomplish any feat. They felt quite sure of this as they hatched an ambitious plot one Christmas Eve—they would catch Santa Claus in action. They lay in their beds that night, eyes screwed tightly shut as they feigned sleep until the murmur of Mama's and Daddy's voices subsided and the house fell still. Silently, making sure not to wake Kimberly, Martina crawled on her hands and knees out of the bedroom and met Troy on his hands and knees at their rendezvous point in the hallway, poking each other and stifling their giggles as they settled onto their pajama-clad bellies for their Santa Stakeout.

Martina sat up abruptly when she heard Mama and Daddy's simultaneous cry of "Merry Christmas!" Rubbing sleep out of her eyes, Martina saw shiny bicycles and gleaming roller skates under the Christmas tree. She and Troy looked at each other in a mixture of excitement and incredulity. How was it possible they had both fallen asleep when they hadn't been even a little bit tired? How had Santa managed to assemble the bikes without waking them?

"Come on, everyone, Christmas breakfast is ready," Mama called as Martina, Troy, and Kimberly inspected their goods and Baby Lester joyfully scattered pieces of wrapping paper around the living room. Martina was too eager to play to be hungry, but she knew she had better get to the table right away. Mama always insisted that her family eat together, pray together, and make fellowship together. Virginia considered breakfast so crucial that, though she began work at Candler Hospital Food and Nutrition Services at 3 a.m. each morning, she took her break at 6 a.m. in order to dash home and prepare a hot breakfast for her children before school, just as Joseph was leaving the house for work.

Martina swallowed Mama's eggs, bacon, pancakes, and biscuits as quickly as she could, eager to strap on her white skates with red wheels and to help Troy fasten his white and blue ones. Martina and Troy alternated all morning between precariously teetering on the sidewalk and squarely landing on their rumps. Martina, whose skating legs kicked in after lunch, spent the afternoon picking up Troy off the ground, while Daddy and Mama helped Kimberly and Lester ride on their new toy inchworms.

Martina and Troy were knit as tightly together at Butler Elementary School, where they were just one grade apart, as they were at home. If something happened to one, the other was right there to console. Frequently, they banded together to protect each other from Kimberly—the tattletale of the family. "Kim can't hold ice water," Martina would say scornfully. Martina and Troy's little sister leaked whatever she was told.

Mama came home from running errands to find all four of her children on the couch, watching television.

"Have you done your homework?"

"Yes, ma'am."

"Everything's fine?"

"Yes, ma'am!"

Kim lasted less than twenty seconds before blurting out what Martina and Troy had paid her a quarter not to reveal. "Mama! Tina broke a glass and Troy hid it in the trashcan!" Martina glared fiercely at Kimberly. Later, when the spankings were over and the incident was far behind them, Kim was going to get it.

The next day, Martina made a lovely cake in her Easy-Bake oven.

"Troy, you want some cake? Oooh, let me get you some extra icing, Troy." She turned to preschool-aged Lester. "Here's some for you, Lester." She handed him a generous portion. "Your piece, Kim? Ooh, sorry, Kim, it's all eaten up."

Grudges between Martina, Troy, and Kim never lasted long, nor did fights between the Davis kids and the other kids in the Cloverdale neighborhood. If any of Virginia's children scrapped with other kids on the block, Mama made them come to the chain-link fence surrounding the yard, apologize to one another, and hug.

"Come on, Mama, what kind of fight is that?" Martina protested, objecting especially strongly to the hug. But Virginia, known for being gentle yet strict, insisted, and peace reigned among the younger inhabitants of the predominantly black, working and middle-class Savannah subdivision. Cloverdale was only a few miles from some of Savannah's most notorious projects, such as Yamacraw Village, and was not completely immune from the drugs and violence that plagued Yamacraw. But Cloverdale was the kind of neighborhood where parents knew that all the adults were looking after all the young ones, no matter whose they were. Even so, the Davis children knew that if they could not hear Daddy or Mama calling their name, it meant they were playing too far from home, and that they had better be inside the house—not en route or in the yard—by the time a streetlight so much as flickered.

Summers in Cloverdale brought a Bookmobile—and the Bookmobile led to a reading club. Martina, Troy, and Kim sat themselves in the driveway each summer Monday with their fresh stack of books and began reading. The other kids on their block did the same, everyone eager to be awarded the gold star for completing the greatest number of books. The summer book club was eventually replaced by Uptown, the teen dance club. Joseph had gone to great lengths to make sure his children knew how to dance, and teenaged Martina and Troy won every contest with ease. When breakdancing became all the rage, the dancing moved outside to the Cloverdale streets. A crowd of kids would gather round, watching Troy and the other Cloverdale breakers compete against b-boys from Liberty City. Cloverdale always won because Cloverdale could lay claim to Troy, and Troy could do the Worm.

"T & T" remained inseparable when Martina entered Windsor Forest High School, with Troy following a year later. "Are y'all twins?" people asked them regularly. Yet, although they were so close that they often completed each other's sentences, their temperaments were starkly different. Martina took after feisty, argumentative Joseph. Troy, like Virginia, was the peacemaker.

✦ ✦ ✦

August 19, 1989

It was after 2 a.m. when Troy finally got home. He shook his head as he climbed into bed. He didn't know the source of the gunshots he had heard as he was leaving the Greyhound bus station/Burger King parking lot, but whatever had gone down, it was messed up. Mama and Daddy had warned him about hanging out with the wrong crowd and spending time at places like the pool hall across from the bus station. Maybe it was time to start listening to them.

It seemed to Troy that his head had barely hit the pillow when Mama was knocking on the door and calling him to breakfast. He checked the clock. Just before ten. "Five more minutes, Mama," he groaned, pulling the pillow over his face. Mama would have none of it. "You all get up!" she hollered, knocking more vehemently on his door and the girls' door. After breakfast, Virginia asked Troy to do the dishes.

"Ma, that's a girl's job!" Troy protested. Mama raised her eyebrows. "That's what your daddy fed to y'all, that men don't wash dishes. Boys can wash dishes!" Troy pushed his plate away and stood up. "I'll take the trash out, Mama." He hoisted the garbage bag onto his shoulder and headed to the front door. "Clean the whole yard while you're at it, since you won't do the dishes!" Virginia called after him good-naturedly.

Spending the day cleaning the yard and bathing the puppies had been Troy's intent anyway, since his morning ride to Atlanta with his cousin Valerie had fallen through. Martina agreed to drive him, but she was hosting a dinner party and could only leave in the late evening. Troy was eager to get to Atlanta to look for some better-paying work than what he had in Savannah, but there was no real rush. He couldn't ask his cousin Skippy about a job at his construction company until Monday anyway.

At 9 p.m., Virginia, nineteen-year-old Kimberly, and eight-year-old Ebony got in the car and drove Troy to Martina's apartment just as her guests were leaving. Shortly thereafter, Troy, Martina, and Martina's husband Louie were on the road to Atlanta and Virginia, Ebony, and Kim were on their way back home to Cloverdale. Louie took a wrong turn on the highway and by the time they arrived in Atlanta, it was too late for Troy to call his cousin Abdus, with whom he would be staying.

"We'll wait with you until morning," Martina decided, and Louie found a spot to park so they could try to stretch out in the car to get some sleep. As pink light began to streak the Atlanta sky, Troy tried to extricate his backpack from underneath his sister's head without waking her.

"You alright?" Martina murmured heavily.

"Yeah, I'm good."

"You got money? You have Abdus's phone number?"

"Yeah."

Troy climbed out of the car with his backpack, yawning and stretching after the cramped night. Martina and Louie waved goodbye and began the four-hour return journey to Savannah.

The answering machine was blinking twice when Martina and Louie walked inside the apartment. Martina hit play and heard Mama, anxious.

"Tina, call me when you get home."

The second message was from Mama as well, the panic in her voice heightened.

"Tina, come in here!" Louie called from the living room.

"What?" Martina responded, as she dialed Mama's number.

"Troy's on TV!" Louie called to her again, louder.

Martina went into the doorway. "He's on TV for what?"

"Just come in here!"

Martina sank onto the sofa beside her husband. Why was the television station displaying a photo of her brother wearing the New York Yankees jacket that Louie had given him? Martina could only make out a few disjointed words from the anchor: *murdered police officer, Troy Davis wanted dead or alive.*

What on earth were they talking about? They must have the wrong Troy. If Troy had been involved in anything, Martina would have sensed it on the drive to Atlanta. Troy would have been apprehensive or jagged. Did that anchor really say *dead or alive*? Were they going to kill her brother? What was going on?

"Take me to Cloverdale," she said to Louie. She needed to talk to Mama.

It wasn't easy to understand what had happened—Mama was more agitated than Martina had ever seen her—but slowly, in bits and pieces, Martina managed to piece together the story.

Virginia had returned to Cloverdale after dropping Troy off at Martina's, but both entrances to the U-shaped Sylvester Drive were blockaded. Police cars were everywhere, with officers swarming around her red-brick house. Virginia parked her car before the blockade, seeing neighbors peeking from their doorways or windows. "Stay in here until I know what's going on," she instructed her daughters.

She got out of the car and approached her neighbor, Craig Young.

"What's going on? Why do they have the street blocked off?"

"They're looking for Troy," Craig told her.

Virginia's heart skipped a beat. "Looking for Troy for what?"

Craig shrugged. Police and SWAT teams were lying down in the grass, Virginia began to observe, and on her roof, in her backyard, across the street, on her neighbors' roofs. Rifles were pointed at her house from every direction. Several officers were at her front door, and it appeared as if they were about to kick it down.

Virginia quickly approached an officer at the blockade.

"Why are you looking for my son?"

"Hey!" The policeman called out to the other officers. "I got his mother over here!"

"Why do you want my son?" Virginia pressed. "Why do y'all have all those guns pointed at my house?"

"We have orders to shoot to kill," the officer said.

"Shoot to kill?" Virginia could feel hysteria rising. "What? He's not in there! I can open my door and show you he's not there!"

"We can't let you enter," the policeman told her. "We have to go in there and see."

"I have another son, and I don't know if he's home or not," Virginia said. "I'm going to go in there with you." What if they saw fifteen-year-old Lester and shot him by mistake?

"No, you can't go in. If we move anything, we will put it right back."

What choice did she have? If she didn't give the police her house key, they would kick down her door. It did not occur to Virginia to ask about a warrant.

"You be careful. Don't point those things at my younger boy if he's inside!"

Virginia clutched her purse and whispered prayers for ten agonizing minutes before the police officers came out and returned her key.

"He's not in there," the policeman said.

Virginia's fear began to turn to anger. "And if he was, y'all would gun him down like a dog in the street?"

"Ma'am, we're just looking for him," the police officer said. "If you know where he's at, the best thing is to turn him in."

The SWAT team and police officers piled into their vehicles and pulled away as Virginia ran inside her house, Kimberly and Ebony behind her.

"Lester? You there, baby?"

Thankfully, he wasn't. Virginia went from room to room, trying to assess what they had done. The board covering the attic door had been pushed back, so they had clearly been inside the attic. Items normally stored under the beds were strewn about and they had taken a pair of shorts out of her washing machine, but nothing else seemed terribly amiss. Then she looked at the living room wall, covered with photos of her children. There was a blank space in the middle of the wall. They had taken a photograph of Troy.

On Sunday morning, after a night filled with tossing and turning, Virginia pulled out the telephone book and started looking through the Yellow Pages to find a lawyer. She came across a name that was familiar to her from television commercials—John Calhoun. Virginia dialed his number with trembling fingers and explained the situation.

"I'm sorry, ma'am," John Calhoun said. "I cannot represent you at this time because I'm already involved in the case." Virginia did not ask what he meant; she hung up and tried another lawyer, Robert T. Falligant. He agreed to meet with her first thing Monday morning.

Virginia had finished updating Martina on all this when a neighbor slipped inside the house.

"The entire force has got to be in Cloverdale," the neighbor said. "All the subdivision is under siege. Anybody resembling Troy, any black boy from fifteen to fifty, is getting slammed on the concrete. If the cops catch Troy, Ms. Davis, it's gonna be a problem."

The cops were kicking in black folks' doors, the neighbor reported, threatening young black men that they would lock them up and throw away the key if they didn't give information about Troy's whereabouts.

One lady had a developmentally disabled son who slightly resembled Troy. The cops had thrown him up against the wall. "We got Troy Davis!" the cops had called out. "Where's your identification?"

Martina listened to the neighbor in horror and disbelief. Apparently, this wasn't just taking place in Cloverdale. There were Troy Davis sightings going on all over town. The police had the black residents of the city terrorized. Racial tensions in Savannah were inflamed.

All Virginia, Martina, and the rest of the family could do now was lock the door and wait until the appointment with Falligant, trying not to let their flooding anxiety overwhelm them. The Savannah news, which they watched against their better judgment, was focused entirely on the manhunt for Troy. Why on earth did they think that Troy had killed that police officer?

✧

Martina snatched the phone before the end of the first ring. "Hello?"

"Hey, it's me, just wanted to let you know that I'm alright. Abdus and I went around South Atlanta today, looking for places that are hiring. Hey, you got Skippy's number?"

"Do you know that they're looking for you for killing a police officer?"

"You can stop playing, you play on the phone too much!"

"Troy, I'm not joking. They have your picture all over TV."

"What are you talking about?"

Virginia grabbed the phone out of Martina's hand. "We can't talk on the phone long because they might have already bugged it."

"Oh, Mama, I didn't kill no police officer! Where did it happen?"

"Near the Greyhound bus station. In the Burger King parking lot."

Troy was silent for a moment. Then: "I'm taking the next bus back to Savannah."

"Stay where you are, baby, don't move."

"I'll answer their questions and explain to them whatever I know, and then they'll let me go."

"No! Lord, if they see you anywhere, then they're going to kill you . . ."

Virginia was in Robert Falligant's office by eight o'clock Monday morning. Falligant agreed to represent Troy, provided, of course, that Troy gave his consent—and provided, of course, that Virginia could pay.

The hours and details of Monday and Tuesday passed in a blur. Martina could focus only on how to get Troy back to Savannah safely. Everything else was just a fog.

✦ ✦ ✦

July 9, 2007

The realization gnawed at Martina before she was fully awake—Troy's execution date, July 17, was one day closer. Martina's eyes flew open and she raced into action, grabbing her cell phone and laptop before her feet hit the hotel floor.

She was typing furiously on her keyboard, straining her brain to come up with something new they could try, when Troy called.

"How you doing?"

"I'm hanging in, how are you?"

Five minutes into the conversation, an idea suddenly sprang up. She could almost see the smile on Troy's face as she passed it by him. Troy would call her back, they agreed, so that she could notify Wende and Laura.

Wende Gozan Brown, media relations director for Amnesty International USA (AIUSA), was a short, dark-haired, energetic woman whose warmth and direct, no-nonsense approach suited Martina perfectly. Martina had known Laura Moye, the deputy director of AIUSA's southern regional office, for eight years and had always found her to be a clear-headed, strategic thinker. Martina and Laura had been two of the founding members of Georgians for Alternatives to the Death Penalty (GFADP) in 1999 and also worked together in Martina's capacity as one of the AIUSA death penalty abolition coordinators for the state of Georgia.

Amnesty International (AI)'s role in Troy's campaign had solidified just a few months earlier, on February 1, when AI released a report about his case entitled *Where Is the Justice for Me?* Martina had been speaking for years about Troy as part of her volunteer work with the organization, always careful not to focus on her brother but to emphasize the broken system. But when Troy's final habeas petition had been denied by the 11th Circuit Court of Appeals on September 26, 2006, the clock had begun to tick in earnest. Martina consulted with members of the AIUSA team. Might Amnesty initiate an urgent action on Troy's behalf? If so, it would have to happen soon. Waiting until there was an execution date would be too late. Rob Freer, a London-based researcher for AI, had contacted Martina soon thereafter. He had procured Troy's files from Jay Ewart, the attorney at the DC-based law firm Arnold & Porter, who had been representing Troy pro bono since 2004, and had just finished reading them. The picture he was piecing together, he had told her, was a travesty of justice. He started working on *Where Is the Justice For Me?* that very day.

The recantations from the eyewitnesses, the new witnesses who had come forward and implicated Redd Coles, the allegations of police coercion and intimidation . . . they could all be found in the nearly forty-page report. For years, Martina and her family had been shouting in the wilderness about Troy's innocence. But now, with the AI report, the significant problems in Troy's case had finally been laid out in empirical black and white for everyone to see, and by a reputable, third-party source.

The expressions of outrage and offers of support began piling up as soon as the report hit the Internet. Exhausted yet exhilarated, Martina had answered emails late into the night, letting people know how they could get on board. Troy's case was finally growing legs. Martina was no longer shouting alone.

Now, five months after the release of the report, AIUSA's Atlanta office was serving as the nerve center for a full-out campaign to urge Georgia's five-member Board of Pardons and Parole to grant clemency to Troy. Wende, Laura, and Martina were working closely together on Troy's campaign. Laura and Sue Gunawardena-Vaughn, AIUSA's death penalty abolition campaign director, were organizing a rally in downtown Atlanta, a press conference, and the delivery of letters and postcards to the board from people all over the world. Wende, who was responsible for the media outreach, had been pitching Troy's story as widely as possible, updating Martina with the discouraging responses that she was receiving: *It's just another innocence case. You don't have any DNA evidence. There's no way my editor will let me cover this.*

Martina's fingers flew across the cell phone as soon as she hung up with Troy. This had to get rolling immediately. "Wende, it's Martina. Can you set up a conference call with reporters? Troy's calling me back in fifteen minutes and I can patch him through on my cell phone."

It was a risky venture, and Martina knew it. If the warden found out that Troy had spoken to reporters, he might take away Troy's phone and visitation privileges. Martina did not want to even contemplate how excruciating it would be if Troy and her family could not say goodbye to each other, should the parole board hearing go the wrong way.

The proposition contained other risks for Troy as well. Prison officials who already resented the attention that Troy was receiving could harass him. The parole board might view his defiance of prison regulations negatively. Jay, his attorney, would surely be extremely cautious about a move like this, especially at such a sensitive juncture. But Martina let her instinct guide her. She wanted the reporters to hear how honest and genuine Troy was: when they did, she knew they would tell his story. Wende hesitated for just a moment. "Okay. Let's do it." Martina hurriedly got dressed, imaging the scene at the Amnesty office. Wende would be frantically calling reporters to pitch the idea, while Laura would be calmly setting up the logistics of the conference call.

Wende called Martina back ten minutes later. "Every single reporter who told us they couldn't cover the story said they would like to talk to him on the phone!"

"Great. I'm on my way."

Martina briskly crossed the street from the Georgian Terrace Hotel to the Amnesty office, trying to ignore a small twinge of nerves. Troy had been pressing for years for an opportunity to tell the world he was innocent. In the short span of time that he'd have on the line with reporters, would he be able to convey the essential information with the poise and clarity on which his life depended?

Martina had scarcely sat down with Wende and Laura when her red Razr cell phone rang.

"Troy, can you hear us?" Martina asked, after patching him through to the journalists waiting on the conference call.

"Hi, everyone. Yes, I can hear just fine."

"OK, go ahead."

"I want my innocence proved one way or another." Troy spoke calmly, clearly, and with conviction. "I don't want to die, especially for a crime I didn't commit. I want to make sure the MacPhail family has justice, but accurate justice. I think it's a sad day in Georgia that they're willing to try and kill an innocent man."

Martina took a deep breath when the conference call ended. No matter the outcome, Troy had finally been given the chance to speak his truth.

Early the following morning, Martina's cell phone woke her.

"Did you see the news yet?" came Wende's breathless voice on the other end.

"Not yet," Martina said, reaching to the nightstand to get her laptop and fire it up.

"We got the Associated Press, Martina! And the AJC, NPR's *All Things Considered* . . ."

The *Los Angeles Times* ran an article the following day, and the *New York Times* and the *Washington Post* in the days that followed. Martina scanned the coverage on site after site: "Execution of Ga. Man Near Despite Recantations" from the *Washington Post*. "As Execution Nears, Last Push from Inmate's Supporters" from the *New York Times*.

Not only had Troy been given the chance to finally speak—he had actually been heard.

◆ ◆ ◆

August 23, 1989

Troy stood on a preappointed street corner in Atlanta, waiting for the car. They should be here any minute now. Nothing to be nervous about, Troy convinced himself. He would get back to Savannah, walk into the police station, and clear up this whole mess.

Troy had been stunned when Martina told him there was a manhunt for him. The information circulating on the news was that he was armed and dangerous. In addition to the murder of the police officer, there was the earlier shooting at the pool party in Cloverdale. As Troy had been walking home from the party, he had seen a car speeding down the street and heard some commotion followed by a shot, but hadn't known who had done the shooting or why. Now, Martina was telling him, they were trying to pin that shooting on him as well. According to Martina, Savannah was out for blood.

Troy was suspicious about the ministers who had orchestrated his return to Savannah. Reverends LaBon and Johnson had called Mama a few days earlier, claiming to be from Jesse Jackson's Rainbow Coalition and to have handled cases like this before. They said they could bring Troy back to Savannah safely for questioning. But how had they gotten Mama's unlisted phone number? Martina and Mama put the ministers in touch with Robert Falligant, whom Mama had hired as Troy's attorney, and with Major Pendergraph of the Savannah Police Department, who was the uncle of a friend. At Troy's suggestion, Martina had also contacted Louis Tyson from Cloverdale. Tyson, a rookie on the Savannah police force, had gone to school with Martina. Troy had played for the Police Athletic League (PAL) with Tyson's little brother.

The car pulled up to the corner—Troy knew instantly that it was an unmarked police car—and Martina emerged from the back seat. Relief spread over him as his sister wrapped her arms tightly around his neck. Everything was going to be okay. Then Martina took her arms off Troy's neck and gripped his shoulders hard. The others were still in the car. This was her only chance to ask.

"Troy, did you have anything to do with the shooting of that police officer?"

"Of course not!" Martina's vice-like grip did not loosen. "Look at me, Tina. Look at my face. You know me better than anyone else in the world does. I did not shoot any police officer."

Martina stared at Troy for a long moment. Her brother met her gaze without flinching. Troy was her other half. They could finish each other's sentences.

"I believe you," Martina said. "You don't have to say another word." She removed her arms from his shoulders, all business now. "Okay, get in the car," she directed, opening the back door for him. "In the middle, away from the window."

Troy slid in between Martina and Reverend Johnson. Louis Tyson was driving and Major Pendergraph sat up front next to him. Tyson pulled the car around and started to make his way back to the interstate to begin the four-hour return to Savannah. Troy craned his neck to see if anybody was following the car, then leaned over the front seat.

"Man, there's no way I would have killed that guy," Troy said to Tyson. "What kind of monster do they think I am?"

"You gotta remember, I'm a police officer," Tyson replied awkwardly, adjusting his glasses and merging the car onto highway traffic. "Save that for your lawyers."

Troy took a good look at Pendergraph before settling back into his seat. He was a tall man, sixty-something, with light brown skin. Troy could not read the expression on his face. Troy took a sideways glance at Martina, who was staring straight ahead. She said she believed him. But still . . .

"Tina, you know I didn't do it."

"I know."

"All I got to do is go back and they'll question me and see that I'm innocent."

"Let's just get you in safely. The only thing I'm worried about is this shoot-to-kill business."

Martina told Troy about the "message" that had been anonymously delivered to various Savannah media outlets. It was a photocopy of Troy's picture alongside the slain officer's, with a sketch of the Grim Reaper added. *An eye for an eye, a tooth for a tooth* was penned, followed with: *but in your case, a death for a death.*

The moment Officer MacPhail had been killed, Martina said, the city began to divide along racial lines. Martina had never before witnessed this level of inflamed hatred and bloodthirsty calls for vengeance. Black mothers were keeping their sons inside the house. Troy said little, trying to digest the information about the hostile environment he was returning to.

Reverend Johnson broke the silence first. "Why did you decide to come back?" he asked Troy. "You were already in Atlanta. Why didn't you run?"

"I'm not running from something I didn't do," Troy answered. "If I run, they will take that to mean that I'm guilty. And I'd have to keep on running. I'd never be able to see my family again. No. My daddy always taught us to tell the truth and that's what I'm going do. I'm going to tell the truth, stand and face it."

Troy's stomach tightened as Tyson pulled off the highway and drove past a tree-lined park in a residential Savannah neighborhood. White men with combat boots and long trench coats lined the streets around the park. Trench coats in August? Martina felt certain they were undercover cops who were making sure that Troy's surrender would go smoothly. But who had informed them that Troy would be driven through this neighborhood?

Tyson pulled up at Reverend LaBon's tightly shuttered house. Martina, Reverend Johnson, Tyson, and Pendergraph surrounded Troy from all sides and ushered him onto the sunporch and into the two-story house as quickly as possible. Before Troy had the chance to look around the parlor, Virginia was hugging him and holding his face between her hands.

"Are you okay, baby?"

"I'm fine, Mama. Are you okay?"

"Get down on the floor now," Pendergraph instructed him, not unkindly. "Lie on your belly."

Pendergraph handcuffed Troy's hands behind his back and read him his rights. Then Troy sat on the sofa with Robert Falligant, his attorney. They would be turning Troy into the sheriff's department rather than directly to the police station, Falligant explained to Troy. It would be safer for him that way.

"Let's go," Pendergraph said after a few minutes. "We have to bring you in."

Troy got back in the unmarked police car with Pendergraph, Tyson, Johnson, and Falligant. Martina and Virginia followed them to the prisoner's intake area of the sheriff's department. They were not able to accompany Troy further, but watched as Falligant, Tyson, and Pendergraph escorted him safely inside the back door. He would be brought to booking and then, in the custody of the sheriff's department, to the police for questioning. Martina breathed deeply for the first time in days. The police couldn't get away with shooting Troy if he were already in custody. The worst, she thought, was over.

✦ ✦ ✦

July 15, 2007

Thirteen-year-old De'Jaun picked at his dinner at the restaurant, barely speaking. Martina knew her child was worried about the next day's clemency hearing. The family was trying not to speak about it, but it was all any of them could think about. Georgia had executed forty people since the death penalty had been reinstated in 1976. The Georgia State Board of Pardons and Parole had granted clemency only six times during that same period. The parole board was made up of former prosecutors, investigators with the Georgia Bureau of Investigation, and law enforcement officers, all appointed by governors. Their jobs had been to arrest and convict—they were not likely to give a fair shake to someone convicted of killing a police officer.

Yet there was good reason to be hopeful. Witnesses who had implicated Troy at trial in 1991, and then later recanted, would testify for the first time about what they had seen—and what they had not seen—the night that Officer MacPhail had been murdered. They would explain why they had given false witness against her brother.

Plus, momentum for Troy's campaign had started to build in the past week, especially after the media coverage following the telephone conference call. Larry Cox, the executive director of AIUSA, had delivered four thousand postcards to the Georgia Board of Pardons and Parole in support of Troy's clemency bid on July 10, and countless others had faxed or emailed their letters directly. Afterward, AIUSA had held a press conference outside the Sloppy Floyd building in downtown Atlanta, where the board met. A prestigious coalition of individuals and organizations attended, including Dr. Joseph Lowry of the Georgia Coalition for the People's Agenda, representatives from the US Human Rights Network, Southern Christian Leadership Conference, Rainbow/PUSH Coalition, ACLU, Southern Center for Human Rights (SCHR), Georgia State Conference of the NAACP, and GFADP, and religious leaders of multiple stripes and denominations. An exonerated death-row inmate from Louisiana spoke as well.

The following day, William Sessions, a pro–capital punishment former FBI director, had penned an op-ed in the *Atlanta Journal-Constitution*. "It would be intolerable to execute an innocent man," Sessions wrote. "It would be equally intolerable to execute a man without his claims of innocence ever being considered by the courts."

On July 12, fifty activists had gathered on a downtown Atlanta street corner passing out leaflets and holding signs. The Atlanta-based musical duo the Indigo Girls was also getting the word out about Troy's case.

And just the night before, Kalonji Jama Changa from the FTP Movement in Atlanta helped to get folks out to a protest vigil at Sacred Heart Church in Savannah. Alete Toure, a community activist from Interracial Interfaith Community, had an idea inspired by the ending scene of Spike Lee's *Malcolm X*, when schoolchildren stand up on Malcolm's birthday and shout out, "I Am Malcolm X!" Alete took De'Jaun's cousin Elijah and a group of his friends aside in the church. When they returned to the center of the vigil, they were wearing white T-shirts on which Alete had written in black Sharpie using bold, large capital letters:

I AM TROY DAVIS
THIS IS TROY DAVIS
TROY DAVIS IS MY NAME

It caught on quickly, and before long, dozens of young black men, as well as some young women at the church, had written variations of *I AM TROY DAVIS* on their shirts. Martina loved it, and Laura and Wende were equally enthused when she told them about it. It was exactly the slogan Amnesty had been looking for. *I Am Troy Davis* resonated strongly for black folks who were routinely targets of an unjust system and at the same time commented on the universality of human rights, publicly elevating Troy's humanity.

It wasn't until Martina went to say goodnight to her son that De'Jaun finally blurted out, "Why do we kill innocent people? Why do they want to kill Uncle Troy?"

Martina sat down on the edge of the hotel bed, speechless for a moment.

"I am praying and believing that it won't come down to that, De'Jaun," she finally answered. "But if it does, maybe it means that Uncle Troy is meant to be a catalyst of change."

It was not an adequate response to her son's question, or to the pain that had prompted it. But at that moment, it was all that she could manage to say.

◆ ◆ ◆

August 23, 1989

Martina and Mama stood inside the police barracks as Troy was led in from an underground tunnel by the sheriff's deputy, his hands still cuffed behind his back. Just moments ago, Police Chief Gellatly had reassured Virginia that Troy would be shown the utmost respect from the officers, and that Gellatly personally would ensure Troy's safety. Everything would take place discreetly.

Troy briefly made eye contact with Martina before being brought face-to-face with the police chief.

"Where is your gun?" Gellatly asked Troy.

"I don't own a gun," Troy responded.

"Where is your gun?" the police chief repeated.

"I don't have a gun, I don't own any weapon," Troy insisted.

Gellatly informed Troy of his arraignment date and when he would need to appear in front of a grand jury.

"That's all for now," the police chief told him.

Was anybody from the police department going to ask Troy about his involvement in the crime? Weren't they going to take him to an interrogation room to question him?

Officers from the Savannah Police Department took hold of Troy's arms and began leading him toward the main entrance of the barracks rather than back to the tunnel.

Martina pushed through the door behind Troy, and then froze in astonishment. The street was lined with police officers in Kevlar riot gear, holding shotguns. Media were swarming outside as well, satellite trucks and all. This had clearly been orchestrated in advance.

A police officer abruptly herded Martina and Virginia down the steps and across the street just as the cameras starting flashing. Police officers shouted and jeered at Troy, who stood on the top step in bewilderment.

"Nigger, you won't make it to the jail because we're gonna kill you and throw you in a hole!" Martina heard one call out.

"We're gonna kill you execution style, just like you killed Mark MacPhail!" Martina heard another policeman say.

Wasn't anybody going to stop them? What about Chief Gellatly's promise that Troy would be treated with respect?

"Run, nigger! Go on, run!" a beefy, blond officer taunted, patting his weapon.

Please, Troy, Martina, panic-stricken, tried to communicate to her brother wordlessly, *don't make any sudden move. Don't give them any excuse to gun you down.*

Troy looked as stunned as Martina felt. And then Troy looked up, and he smiled. Martina, who could finish her brother's sentences, knew exactly what the smile meant: *Your threats and insults will not intimidate me.*

Troy's photo, smiling, was in the morning paper. The footage of her brother being led out of the police station was splashed all over the news. The *Savannah Morning News* stated that "an aborted smile, almost a smirk, crept across his face." The coverage went on to imply that the police were certain they had their man. As far as Martina could ascertain, no one else was even being investigated as a suspect.

The eyewitnesses to the murder were apparently reading the same news accounts. At Troy's September 8 preliminary hearing, eyewitness Harriett Murray described the shooter as having "a little smirky smile on his face" as he gunned down Officer MacPhail.

✦ ✦ ✦

July 16, 2007

Marshals led the Davis family through the Sloppy Floyd building to the waiting area outside the parole board hearing room. The last time Martina had felt this kind of terror and lack of control was when her family had begged for Troy's life during the sentencing phase of his trial. Now they were preparing to plead for Troy's life a second time, one day before his scheduled execution. Martina was not sure where the prosecution and Officer MacPhail's family were waiting, but she did not expect to see them. The two "sides" of parole board hearings were kept strictly separate.

The hearing room was small, with pale yellow walls, fluorescent lights, and a table in front for Troy's attorneys, Jay Ewart and Danielle Garten. Martina was glad to see GFADP and AIUSA folks, including Bob Nave, a death penalty abolition activist who had flown in from Connecticut, sitting on the four rows of smooth wooden benches. Their support was needed and appreciated.

Journalists entered to photograph and film as the board members took their seats on an elevated platform behind white panels in the front of the room. *Three of you*, Martina thought as she looked squarely, one by one, at the face of each board member. Buddy Nix. Gale Buckner. Robert Keller. Garfield Hammonds. Garland Hunt. *Three of you need to decide that my brother's life has value.*

Virginia, strong and stoic on the outside, sat down next to Martina, but out of the corner of her eye, Martina saw Mama silently mouthing, "Please, Jesus." The media exited, and the proceedings began.*

John Lewis, sixty-seven-year-old Georgia congressman and civil rights movement icon, took the witness stand first. "I will not speak long, because what I have to say is very simple," he began. "I do not know Troy Anthony Davis. I do not know if he is guilty of the charges of which he has been convicted. But I do know that nobody should be put to death based on the evidence we now have in this case." Representative Lewis outlined Troy's innocence claim: no physical evidence; no murder weapon; no fingerprints; no DNA; just the testimony of

---

* There are no available transcripts from parole board hearings. The descriptions of testimonies from parole board hearings come from the recollections and detailed notes of those present, including attorneys, with some specifics informed by affidavits that witnesses had previously signed. Congressman Lewis's remarks were later made public.

a few frightened and confused people, most of whom later recanted. Congressman Lewis spoke slowly and with conviction. "I am here now, because I could not stay away. As a fellow public servant, I believe I know what you should do. And as a man of faith, I am sure I know what God wants you to do. Do justice. Commute the sentence of Troy Anthony Davis." Martina leaned back on the bench and sent a silent message of gratitude to Congressman Lewis.

Next, Kevin McQueen, a muscular forty-year-old man with a wide forehead, took a seat in front of the parole board, and, prompted with questions from Jay, began speaking. Kevin and Troy had engaged in a verbal confrontation consisting mainly of name-calling while inmates together at Chatham County Jail where Troy was held while awaiting trial, and Troy had spit in Kevin's face. Kevin, who was in jail for robbery by force, theft by receiving stolen property, and giving a false name, had already been jealous of the instant notoriety granted to Troy in the joint as a cop-killer and wanted revenge. Kevin called his girlfriend that night and asked her to contact Detective Ramsey, with whom he had "worked" in the past as a paid informant. At the back of his mind was the hope that he would receive money and preferential treatment—in the form of a reduced sentence—in exchange for snitching. He told Ramsey that Troy had bragged to him about killing the cop, filling in some of the details of the invented confession from courtyard chatter about the incident. Kevin claimed that Troy had told him he had shot some dude at a party in Cloverdale, and because he didn't want to go down for what happened in Cloverdale, he panicked when the police officer told him to freeze and shot the officer. He couldn't leave him alive, so he shot him again.

No part of that conversation with Troy was true, Kevin now stated in front of the parole board. He had lied about the entire confession and had gotten the benefits he had been hoping for.

"Why did you come to this hearing?" one parole board member asked Kevin when he had finished.

Kevin was quiet for a moment before answering. "My sister heard that the execution was coming up. The guilt was killing me. I went to talk to my mom. She told me I needed to come forward and that I wouldn't be able to live with myself if I didn't. I know I perjured myself and if I need to take my punishment now, I will. But I've cleaned up since my twelve-year stint. I got my GED last year, and I have a job as a mechanic and I have custody of my son. I really don't want to be here and it's not easy. I'm here because of the guilt I feel."

Kevin was calm and respectful, even when someone on the board suggested he was being paid for his testimony. But when a board member asked him what he had been convicted for, Kevin bristled. "I done my time, so don't ask me about that!" he retorted. "I'm not on trial here. I lied against this man and I came here to tell the truth!" Kevin turned directly to the Davis family. "I want to apologize to you all," he said. "There's no excuse for what I did."

Martina wanted to respond to Kevin McQueen that yes, there was no excuse for the role he had played in wrongfully convicting her brother. She wanted to thank him, as well, for having the courage to listen to his conscience, come forward, and tell the truth. But Kevin had already left the stand, and Jeffrey Sapp, wearing a tracksuit and carrying a washcloth as if it were a handkerchief, had taken his place. Jeffrey, who had grown up in Cloverdale with Troy, appeared frightened as he quietly answered Jay's and Danielle's questions in as few words as possible.

Though Jeffrey had not been in the Burger King parking lot and had not been a witness to the crime, two police officers had awoken him at two thirty or three the morning after the murder of Officer MacPhail. Jeffrey had thought he was being busted for selling drugs until the officers said they had heard that Jeffrey had some information about the killing.

"I don't have no information about killing no police officer," Jeffrey had answered. "I wasn't even there." The policemen had left, but returned the next afternoon and took Jeffrey down to the precinct. There, several officers interrogated him further: one shouting in either ear, one in front of him and one behind. Jeffrey could smell their breath.

"We got information that Troy confessed to you!"

"Who told you that?"

"Don't worry about that," they retorted harshly. "We got information, though."

The police's narrative unfurled as they barked questions at Jeffrey, spit flying in his face: Redd Coles and a homeless man were arguing, right? Didn't Troy intervene and pistol-whip the homeless man? Officer MacPhail came to assist and Troy shot him twice, didn't he?

Jeffrey had been terrified and worn out after being there for hours. All he wanted was to get out of there and to be left alone. He gave the police the statement they wanted to hear: that Troy had approached him in Cloverdale the afternoon of August 19 and had confessed that he had shot the officer. Jeffrey's statement about Troy's confession was based entirely on the details that the officers themselves had provided while interrogating Jeffrey. District Attorney Spencer Lawton instructed him to stick to his statement at trial, and so Jeffrey had.

Jeffrey finished speaking and twisted his washcloth in his hands as the board questioned him with skepticism about why he would have signed a false statement against his friend. Martina was flabbergasted: could the board members truly not understand the role that fear might have played for a young black male surrounded by angry police officers whose colleague had just been gunned down?

"What were your and Troy's reputations in those days?" Garland Hunt, the board chairman, asked Jeffrey. Hunt was a slender African American lawyer and minister with an aggressive style.

"We didn't have any bad reputations—we were just normal kids."

Hunt wanted to know what kind of weapons Troy carried.

"Troy didn't carry a gun, or knives, or anything like that," Jeffrey answered. "He carried a baseball bat in the trunk of his car. If there was a problem, Troy would open his trunk and get his bat."

"But what about this 'RAH'?" Robert Keller, a white former prosecutor pressed. "Everyone knows that Troy was known as Rough As Hell."

Martina's heart dropped. They had used this Rough as Hell nonsense at trial in order to suggest that Troy had been some hooligan terrorizing the neighborhood.

"Troy's car was called 'Rough as Hell' because it turned colors and had rims. Nobody had a nice car like that," Jeffrey said. "Troy's mom bought him that car to take care of his sister when she was paralyzed."

Martina sat straight up. She hadn't realized Jeffrey even knew what Troy had done for Kimberly. RAH was also short for Raheem, Jeffrey continued. As teenagers, Troy and his friends had connected to Malcolm X and the empowerment rhetoric of the Nation of Islam. "We all took Muslim names, we all stopped eating pork. I don't even think Troy eats pork to this day."

The board chairman wasn't buying it. Whether it was Troy or Troy's car with a nickname like Rough as Hell, Hunt pressed, if he was driving a "gangsta car" like that, if he was running around the pool hall at that time of night, Troy must have been packing heat.

Jeffrey, who had been soft-spoken throughout, started to get angry. "I told you he didn't carry a gun. I know you're fishing for the gun, but it wasn't there!"

"What do you have to gain by coming clean now, Mr. Sapp?"

"Nothing," Jeffrey said without a moment of hesitation. He squeezed his washcloth for emphasis. "It's a matter of honor—it's the right thing to do."

Larry Young hesitantly made his way to the witness stand. Wearing a simple button-down shirt, Larry looked proper, neat, and very nervous. At trial in 1991, Larry had testified that the man who had been arguing with him, standing directly in front of him wearing a yellow T-shirt, was not the one who had assaulted him in the Burger King parking lot. The man who had struck him, he had testified, had been slightly behind him, on his right, wearing a white T-shirt.

Jay asked Larry to show the parole board his scar from having been pistol-whipped. The board members peered over the edge of the bench to get a good look. Though the attack had occurred nearly eighteen years prior, the scar was easily visible, running down the right side of his forehead against his dark skin and shaved head.

"Can you please explain exactly what happened on August 19, 1989, in the Burger King parking lot?" Jay asked Larry.

Larry politely and earnestly explained what he could, but he had never been able to make sense of what had happened that night. It was as much a blur now as it had been then. At that time, he had been homeless and had already been drinking all day before going to the convenience store next to the pool hall to buy more beer. When he emerged with the beer, a man approached him and asked for a can. Larry refused and the man started harassing him. Larry walked toward the Greyhound station and Burger King across the street and the man followed, cursing and threatening him. By the time Larry got to the parking lot, the guy who was shouting at him was in front of him and two others were slightly behind him, on either side. The one to his left made a sudden movement and when he turned in that direction, he was struck on the right side of his head by a heavy object.

Contrary to what he had testified at trial, Larry now stated that he assumed it was the man in front of him who had attacked him, but he couldn't be certain.

His head bleeding, he stumbled to the drive-through, beating on the hood of a van filled with Air Force personnel and hollering for help. This is when he heard "one pop"—the officer being shot. His girlfriend Harriett Murray grabbed him at that point and dragged him inside the bus station so he could go into the bathroom and clean off the blood that was streaming down his face.

When he came out of the bathroom, overcome with pain and pressing a handful of paper towels against his wound, Larry said, he was grabbed by police officers, thrown onto the hood of a police car, and handcuffed. They locked him in the back of the police car where he was trapped for an hour, bleeding profusely from the gash in his head and calling out that he needed medical attention.

The police took him to the station and interrogated him for hours about what had happened in the parking lot. Larry kept telling them he didn't know what exactly had happened; it had all taken place so quickly. He couldn't tell who did what or remember what anyone looked like or the clothes they were wearing. His state of intoxication, not to mention his head wound, contributed to his lack of clarity.

But the cops kept pressing him to give answers, Larry told the parole board. He kept asking them to treat his head, but they wouldn't. They made it clear that he wasn't leaving until he told them what they wanted to hear. They suggested answers and he gave them what they wanted. They put typed papers in his face and told him to sign, which he did without reading them. Finally the police took him to the hospital, where the gash required fifteen stitches and two subsequent brain surgeries due to blood clots that resulted, Larry believed, from lack of immediate medical attention.

A detective visited him on a daily basis while he was in the hospital, repeatedly reviewing with him what had happened in the parking lot until the detective's narrative began to shape Larry's memory of what had taken place. With every visit from the detective, Larry grew more and more certain that the man who assaulted him was Troy Davis. Since that night, Larry has suffered from post-traumatic stress disorder and depression.

Antione Williams was almost shaking on the witness stand as he revisited the traumatic night of the murder. In August 1989, Antione, an eighteen-year-old African American, had just parked his car in the Burger King lot to start working his graveyard shift when, through the double layer of dark tint on his car window, he saw a police officer chase a young man, heard a shot, and saw the police officer go down. Scared for his life, he ducked down, trying to peek above the dashboard, and heard a few more shots. He waited until the gunfire stopped and then ran into the Burger King to try to get help.

Late that night, the cops asked him to describe the shooter and what he was wearing. Antione told them he did not know; it was dark out, the shooter was black, his car windows were tinted. It had all happened so fast, and he had been frightened. Sitting in the police station, he was still frightened and wanted only to get out of there. He had no idea what was in the statement the police told him to sign. He did not read it, he said—because Antione could not read.

On August 30, an investigator asked Antione to identify the shooter from a photo spread. Antione picked the photo of Troy from the spread, a spread that did not include Redd Coles or anyone else who had been in the parking lot that evening, saying he was 60 percent certain that this was the shooter. Antione had already seen that same photo of Troy on a wanted poster at Burger King.

Antione began having nightmares about the murder and moved to New York to try and get away. But the state subpoenaed him to testify at trial and so he returned to Savannah. The district attorney prepped Antione before the trial: there were going to be two sides, Troy's side and their side. When it came down to it, the prosecution wanted him to point out Troy Davis.

They had brought him all the way from New York for the trial, Antione said, had told him that he was the lead witness, and had drilled into him repeatedly that Troy Davis was the perpetrator. When Chief Assistant District Attorney David Lock had asked Antione at trial if he could point out the shooter in the courtroom, he fulfilled what he saw as his duty and pointed to Troy. But even as he had, he hadn't known whether or not Troy had shot the police officer. To this day, Antione had no idea what the man who shot the police officer, or his gun, looked like.

Antione, who remained on anti-depressants and anti-anxiety meds, still had nightmares about the officer getting shot. He had spent all these years trying to get it out of his head—trying to forget.

At Troy's trial, Tonya Johnson had testified that she had been at her home in Yamacraw, just across the street from the crime scene when the shooting took place, and had gone outside to see what was going on. Redd Coles and a guy named Terry had approached her nervously. Redd, who she had testified was wearing a white T-shirt, had instructed Tonya to go to the Burger King parking lot to check out what had happened to the police officer; when she had reported that he was dead, Redd's agitation had increased.

Tonya, now a short, heavyset woman with long cornrows, added new information in front of the parole board. After the shooting, Redd Coles and Terry not only had asked her to check out what had happened to the cop, they also had asked her to hold their guns. When she had refused, Redd opened the screen door of the vacant house next door, set the guns inside, closed the screen door behind him, and left. He returned shortly afterward and retrieved the guns.

Tonya had been too frightened to ask Coles if he had killed the policeman, though everyone in Yamacraw was saying that he had, and she had been too intimidated to disclose this additional information about the guns at trial. Redd, who had a reputation for being violent, had already warned her that she "talks too much." But, she told the parole board, she finally felt that she had to come forward. She didn't want to see an innocent man get killed for something that he didn't do.

As Jay and Danielle made their final statements to the board, emphasizing the tunnel vision that the police investigation had on Troy from the moment Coles had given the police Troy's name, Martina thought about the troubling dynamics she had just seen at play. The parole board was taking its task seriously, yet it felt to Martina as if some of them were perhaps taking a perverse pleasure in the power that they wielded. It made Martina appreciate the courage of the witnesses all the more. Most of them had experienced a lifetime of marginalization, and, in Larry Young's case, severe brutalization, yet here they were, trying to take a stand in a system and in front of individuals who were intimidating at best and hostile at worst.

Martina slipped out the side door of the Sloppy Floyd building, imagining DA Spencer Lawton ushering Officer MacPhail's mother, wife, and nearly grown children into the room her family had just exited. What arguments would they use to convince the parole board that Troy should be killed? Was Spencer Lawton proclaiming that Troy had murdered the officer execution-style, wearing a smirky smile? Martina would never know. The Georgia State Board of Pardons and Parole was the final body determining who lived and who died, and it operated with no transparency.

"Tina, it's almost four o'clock," Mama said urgently. The parole board hearing had lasted so long that one of the final two visitation days for friends and family to say goodbye to Troy was now over. Martina called her cousin Valerie, who had spent the day visiting Troy with her mother Aunt Mattie (Virginia's sister) and her children, Elijah and Toiwanna.

"How did he seem? Is he holding up okay?"

Valerie laughed. "Troy was up there teaching the kids his dance moves, and they were showing Troy the 'Bus Stop.' He was telling them stories about us when we were little!"

Martina felt somewhat better. Troy had been cracking jokes, laughing, swapping dance moves with the kids. He had been surrounded by family. As Martina spoke to Valerie, Troy was receiving a physical and an enema. When the call ended, Troy was being stripped of all his belongings, including clothing, belt, shoes—anything that he could use to harm himself—and was being issued a brand-new uniform, flip-flops, and a radio. Martina entered the Georgian Terrace Hotel as Troy entered the death-watch cell next to the execution chamber. As the Davis family stationed themselves in their hotel suite to await the parole board's decision, two guards were stationed outside Troy's death-watch cell to observe his every move. From this point on, Troy would be under constant surveillance. The countdown to execution had begun.

✦ ✦ ✦

August 24, 1989

The day after Troy turned himself in, DA Spencer Lawton announced that he would seek the death penalty in Troy's case. That same day, Martina learned that Reverend LaBon, who had identified himself to Mama as being from Jesse Jackson's Rainbow PUSH Coalition, was actually a chaplain with the Savannah Police Force. Fury rose in Martina's stomach when she discovered the deception. That explained why she thought she saw undercover agents lining the streets outside the park near LaBon's house. They could have gotten her brother killed!

As August turned into September, Troy sat in downtown Savannah's Chatham County Jail, segregated from the other inmates in an isolation cell, waiting for police investigators to come and interrogate him, but aside from Police Chief Gellatly's asking about the whereabouts of his gun the day he turned himself in, he was never questioned. He had no idea why.

The solitary confinement was difficult to endure. Whether alone in a heavily guarded yard call or on the way to visitation, which was also kept separate from visitation for the general population, he was handcuffed, shackled, and escorted by a team of officers.

Other inmates pounded on his cell door as they walked past, calling out their encouragement. "What's up, Troy? We're behind you!" The segregation was for his safety, he was told, but being isolated made it easier for guards to target him with abuse. Guards clanged metal cups on the bars of his cell door throughout the night, waking him with a start every time he managed to drift off to sleep.

"Don't close your eyes, nigger, or you'll be dead before you know it," Troy heard one guard growl.

Troy was afraid to eat, though a kind guard or fellow inmate always managed to slip him a warning when guards had tampered with his food tray. He wasn't so concerned about the instances in which he was told that guards had spit in his food, but it was more alarming when he was surreptitiously notified that feces had been mixed into his dinner. Another time, he was warned, it was rat poison.

Troy resolved to keep the torment to himself, so as not to worry his family, but after three harrowing months, the prison chaplain informed Virginia about the treatment that Troy had been forced to endure. The words had scarcely left the chaplain's mouth before Virginia was in the office of the jail administrator to complain. The administrator assured Virginia that the problem would be dealt with swiftly.

"If it doesn't stop, I'll have their jobs," he told Virginia. "They are supposed to be jailers, not judges."

Troy was moved into the general population and the abuse ended. His food was no longer separate and vulnerable, and he felt safe eating once again.

Troy called home as often as he could, but he and his family could never talk openly.

"We hear you!" Martina snapped each time she heard the little click that signified their conversation was no longer private. "Hope you get an earful!"

Relieved and joyful as the Davis family was each visitation day, the experience was frustrating. It was impossible to hear Troy clearly over the decrepit phones that were installed on either side of the thick plastic barrier. Martina hated not being able to touch her brother, to hug him. More than anything, she despised seeing Troy locked up in a place where he did not deserve to be, awaiting a trial in which he should not have been a suspect.

✧

On November 15, 1989, Troy was indicted by a grand jury for shooting Michael Cooper, assaulting Larry Young, and murdering Officer MacPhail. Five months later, Troy entered his plea: not guilty.

Robert Falligant, Troy's attorney, only returned Mama's calls, it seemed, after she had dropped off a sizeable chunk of her paycheck. As the months wore on and legal costs mounted, Virginia was forced to take a second mortgage on the family's home.

On Fathers' Day in 1990, the media was filled with stories about the young, fatherless MacPhail children. Officer MacPhail's daughter, Madison, was not quite two years old when her twenty-seven-year-old father was killed and his son, Mark Jr., was only seven weeks. The little ones would never know their father, who, by all accounts Martina read, had been an honorable man, as his actions coming to the rescue of a homeless man who was being assaulted illustrated. Mark MacPhail had grown up in Columbus, Georgia (his own father had died of a heart attack when he was young), and had joined the Savannah Police Department after serving in the military. Martina had nothing but compassion for toddler Madison, newborn Mark Jr., and their widowed mother Joan. She could only imagine the agony of Mark's mother Anneliese, who had already lost a three-month-old baby boy to double pneumonia and had been widowed at a young age.

But regardless of the legal presumption of innocence until proven guilty, the Savannah public was being spoon-fed by the media a narrative that portrayed Troy as the monster who had deprived those children of their daddy. According to the rumors, Troy had always been a no-good hoodlum, though he had no previous record of violent crime. There were insinuations that Troy hated police officers, though Cloverdale was populated with the homes of police officers, Troy had played ball his entire childhood for the Police Athletic

League, and Daddy had been a deputy sheriff during a time period when black law enforcement officers were not permitted to arrest whites. That piece of information never seemed to make the news, nor did the fact that Joseph was a decorated Korean War veteran. By the time the trial approached, after two long years, white Savannah had been whipped up into a frenzy of hatred and fear. The black community was too scared to challenge any of the distortions. In Savannah, black people learned not to rock the boat.

Martina was tense as the trial grew near. Falligant had requested a change of venue based on the amount of media there had been about the murder of Officer MacPhail, much of it already seeming to have convicted Troy, but the judge denied the motion. Troy would be tried in Savannah.

Martina was also concerned about Troy's representation. According to Troy and Mama, Falligant met with Troy only occasionally and only after Troy called Mama and asked her to get him to come—which usually involved Mama having to bring the attorney more money, which was in scarce supply. Troy sometimes complained in frustration that Falligant was not listening to his suggestions or following up on the leads he offered. Falligant hadn't spoken to any of the state's witnesses—though he told Troy that he had tried unsuccessfully to reach them—and he wouldn't be calling a single expert witness to the stand. The few times that Martina met him, she found Falligant to be smart and polite; he seemed to truly believe in her brother's innocence. Her instinct was that he would perform well on his feet with the witnesses on the stand. But she was worried that he had not done the investigative work necessary to demonstrate Troy's innocence.

Troy tried to put his parents, sisters, and brother at ease in the days before the trial. Daddy had always taught them to speak the truth and stand up for what is right, Troy reminded Martina through phones on either side of the thick bulletproof glass.

"It's all going to work out," he said confidently. "I just need to tell the truth."

✦ ✦ ✦

Joseph used to line his children up on the couch once or twice every month. It was never too early to begin to prepare them. "No matter how smart you are, how rich you are, or how many friends you make, there will be times when the color of your skin will get in the way," he lectured his little ones.

Martina understood that Daddy was trying to protect them, though from what, she was not certain. But as the monthly sessions continued and her age and experience mounted, Daddy's talks began to make more sense.

"In certain instances, people will see you only as a nigger. You have to let folks know that you won't stoop down to their level of ignorance," he instructed them. "You rise above it, you get your education, and you do what you need to do." For good measure, he usually added, "Always tell the truth—don't lie, cheat, or steal."

Young Martina, Troy, Kimberly, Lester, and Ebony sat wordlessly on the couch as Daddy described lying in muddy trenches in the Korean War with his white brothers-in-arms, sharing food out of the same tins and inhaling from communal cigarettes.

Upon his return to the United States, he walked into the mess hall of his Kentucky base to have lunch with his platoon-mates.

"Nigger, where you going?" a white private whom Joseph had never before seen called out to him. "The darkies gotta go around the back. And y'all don't eat till 7:00." Joseph waited for his friends to stick up for him, but those with whom he had pledged eternal brotherhood—crouching in the same foxholes and sleeping side by side in the same tents—kept their heads down and continued eating. One tried to stammer out an apology to him later that evening, but Joseph understood perfectly. He had to go back to his place; they went back to theirs.

"You can't allow anybody to hurt you," Joseph told his children repeatedly, determined to educate them to stand up for themselves. Virginia, in contrast, encouraged her brood to avoid confrontation.

"Turn the other cheek," Mama regularly advised Martina or Troy if they had a problem with a classmate or friend. Virginia's counsel irritated Joseph to no end.

"Hell, woman, you only got two cheeks! What do you do after you've turned them both?"

✦ ✦ ✦

August 20, 1991

Martina and Darrell "D.D." Collins stood outside the elevators at the Chatham County Courthouse waiting for Robert Falligant to arrive. D.D. had contacted Martina just a few hours before to tell her he needed to talk with Troy's lawyer. It was important, D.D. had insisted.

Falligant arrived at the courthouse a few minutes later and Martina introduced him to D.D. Falligant already knew who D.D. was, of course—D.D. would be called by the prosecution as a witness at Troy's trial in a few days.

"Mr. Collins, you wanted to talk to me?" Falligant asked the young man once they were settled on the second-floor lobby, where they had more privacy.

"Yes." D.D. was eighteen, but his round baby face made him look more like the sixteen-year-old he had been the night the murder took place.

"What do you want to talk to me about?"

"About the shooting over at Cloverdale."

"What do you want to tell me about the shooting?"

D.D. and Troy had been together that night, both at the Cloverdale pool party and at the pool hall and Burger King parking lot.

D.D. had signed two police statements in the days following Officer MacPhail's murder, swearing that he had seen Troy packing a black, short-barreled gun with a brown handle and that he had witnessed Troy shoot at the car in Cloverdale outside the pool party.

"I didn't see Troy shoot at the car. I didn't see Troy with a gun that night," D.D. now told Troy's attorney.

"Then why did you make those statements?" Falligant asked him.

D.D. fidgeted, clearly nervous. "I was pressured into it," he said.

Three police officers had interrogated the terrified sixteen-year-old boy without his parents present, he told Falligant. If he didn't cooperate with them, the officers threatened, he would go to prison for ten to twelve years as an accessory to murder.

Troy had a black, short-barreled gun with a brown handle, Detective Ramsey told D.D.

It had a brown handle and the gun was black with a short barrel, D.D. parroted back.

He told them whatever they wanted to hear.

✧

August 22, 1991

The Davis family entered the imposing Chatham County Courthouse in Savannah's tree-lined historic district. Troy was being tried on five counts: murder with malice aforethought; obstruction of justice; aggravated assaults against Larry Young and Michael Cooper; and possession of a firearm.

Troy had tried to reassure the family that he was not nervous. It had been two hellish years in the Chatham County jailhouse, but this whole mess would soon be behind him. He would finally have the opportunity to publicly explain what had happened the night Officer MacPhail was murdered. Martina tried to hold onto a fraction of Troy's optimism as she sat down on the bench between Kimberly and Mama, who was clutching her Bible.

Just as the proceedings were about to begin, a courtroom official began calling out names. Joseph Lester Davis. Virginia Roberts Davis. Martina Correia. Kimberly Davis . . . Martina looked around. What was going on? A deputy approached the bench where the family was seated.

"You have to leave the courtroom," the deputy told them. "Witnesses can't observe the proceedings."

"I'm the only one from the family supposed to testify on Troy's behalf!" Virginia clarified.

The deputy checked the paper in his hand. "You're all listed as witnesses for the state."

"But we don't know anything about the crime!" Martina protested.

The deputy shrugged and made it clear that they needed to leave the courtroom regardless. Martina was fuming as she and her family exited and took seats in the hallway. The DA, Spencer Lawton, must have put the entire Davis family on the witness list so that the jury would not view Troy as a human being with a devoted, loving family. The courtroom was filled with members of the MacPhail family and their supporters, and her brother was in there all alone.

Martina got on the phone the moment she walked into her apartment.

"Can you sit in on the trial?" she asked a litany of friends and relatives, lining them up for the coming days. "Troy needs to feel some encouragement in there. And we need reports on what's happening."

Friday, August 23. Monday, August 26. Tuesday, August 27. Wednesday, August 28. Virginia, Martina, and Kimberly entered the Chatham County Courthouse together each day, impeccably dressed. Joseph, who had been separated from Virginia for eight years, entered alone. Mama, Martina, and Kimberly sat for hours on the hard stone bench outside the courtroom as Daddy stood slightly apart from the rest of the family, staring silently out the window.

After each of the state's thirty-four witnesses, the Davis family huddled around whichever friend or cousin slipped into the hallway to report in hurried whispers what had just transpired. Many of the witnesses were law enforcement officials who had arrived at the scene after MacPhail was down or had worked on the investigation. Seven of those testifying were eyewitnesses.

Martina grew increasingly disconcerted as the whispered updates progressed. Harriett Murray pointed Troy out in the courtroom as the man whom she saw shoot Officer MacPhail and testified that he did so with "a little smirky-like smile on his face." Antione Williams, Steve Sanders, and Dorothy Ferrell identified Troy in the courtroom as well. D.D. Collins testified that he saw Troy slap Larry Young, and others testified that the same man who struck Larry shot Officer MacPhail. Some witnesses testified that the shooter had on a white T-shirt and dark pants, and then other witnesses put Troy in the white T-shirt and dark pants. Multiple witnesses described the gun as being a snub-nosed .38 with a brown handle and black barrel. Kevin McQueen and Jeffrey Sapp both testified that Troy had confessed the murder to them.

A slew of other witnesses were trundled out to try to pin the Michael Cooper shooting on Troy. Benjamin Gordon, who had been in the car with Cooper when he was shot, testified that he had signed a police statement stating that the Cloverdale shooter had had on a white Batman T-shirt and dark jeans, though on the stand he testified that he did not remember saying that and didn't know who shot Michael Cooper.

The state brought in a ballistics expert to try to link the two shootings. The bullets recovered from Michael Cooper's jaw and MacPhail's body were very possibly shot from the same .38 caliber gun, Roger Parian from the state crime lab testified, though the murder weapon itself had never been recovered. Shell casings found near both scenes matched as well.

D.D. Collins, however, testified to exactly what he had told Falligant in the courthouse lobby: he had not seen Troy with a gun, nor did he see Troy shoot anyone in Cloverdale; he had made those statements to the police under duress.

Craig Young's testimony suggested similar police coercion. According to the police statement that Craig had given Detective Ramey, Troy had told Craig at the Cloverdale pool party that he had gotten into a confrontation with a guy named Mike-Mike and, right before the shots were fired at the car, Troy had said: *I feel like doing something, doing anything.*

But now, Craig testified that Detective Ramey, a short, heavy-set black man with a round face, had told Craig, hollering, that Craig knew these things. Ramey had led him through, telling him what to say, step by step. Craig and Troy had gotten into a fight the week before and, still angry, Craig had complied with the detective. He was not, however, going to lie on the stand. He had never heard Troy say anything about a confrontation with someone named Mike-Mike. Troy had not said: *I feel like doing something, doing anything.*

Martina sat stiff as a board as she received the report on the testimony of Sylvester "Redd" Coles. Redd testified that he had been the only one picking a fight with Larry Young, a man he did not know, over a can of beer. He also testified (as did others) that he had been carrying a chrome long-barreled .38 gun and that he had first put the gun in some bushes near the pool hall, then given it to Jeffrey Sams to hold. He carried the gun for protection, he said, admitting that he already had a felony record for carrying a concealed weapon.

According to Redd's testimony, he had followed Larry up Oglethorpe Drive toward the Burger King parking lot, each man still cursing the other. Troy and D.D. were behind him at first and then they cut through the bank, arriving at the parking lot moments later. While Redd was arguing with Larry, Redd testified, Troy came up and blindsided Larry on the right side of his face with a .38 snub-nose pistol. Troy and Redd both started running. Redd said he didn't see the police officer until he heard the words *Hold it!* Redd turned around and the police officer ran past him. Redd heard the first shot, turned and ran, heard two more shots, and kept running to his sister's house in Yamacraw. He changed shirts at his sister's place—after all, he had been at the scene of a shooting. According to Redd, Troy showed up at the sister's house around a half-hour later, topless and asking for a shirt. Redd said he gave him the yellow Turtles T-shirt he had just taken off—and Redd's sister, Valerie, corroborated that in her testimony.

There were so many aspects of Redd's story that made no sense to Martina. Why would Troy have assaulted Larry Young when, by Redd's own admission, Redd was the one picking the fight with Larry? Why would Redd pick a fight with someone unless he had reclaimed his weapon, which he carried "for protection?" How could it not be obvious that Redd and his sister might have coordinated their testimony?

But one detail of Redd's testimony bothered Martina most of all. Redd claimed that he had started to flee after Larry Young was struck, stopping and turning when the police officer came around from the side of the Burger King and shouted *Hold it!* Then, Redd testified, Officer MacPhail ran past him in pursuit of Troy and/or D.D. Martina believed that no police officer in his right mind would run right past the closest suspect and turn his back toward that suspect in order to pursue two others. Martina was certain that Redd Coles was lying.

✧

Six witnesses testified on Troy's behalf, with Troy himself providing the final testimony. Martina ached at not being able to support her brother when he took the stand, though she had heard every detail of the story from Troy and knew exactly what he would testify:

The night of August 18, 1989, Troy had gone to a pool party in Cloverdale with D.D. and Eric. He heard shots as he was leaving the party, but did not see the shooting.

Later that night, Troy, D.D., Eric, and Jeffrey Sams went to Charlie Brown's pool hall, near Yamacraw. Troy went inside to shoot some pool. Not long after, D.D. came inside the pool hall.

"Look at Redd, he's starting a fight with someone outside," D.D. told him.

"Man, just forget Redd," Troy responded. "Let's shoot some pool."

Just as Troy was about to break the balls, D.D. reported that the argument with Redd and the dude was escalating—it might be trouble. Troy stepped outside, observing Redd getting in some other guy's face, feuding with him over a beer.

"Why don't you leave the man alone?" Troy said to Redd.

"Shut the hell up," Redd snapped back.

"Man, this is stupid," Troy said, but the man had already taken off down Oglethorpe, with Redd in pursuit.

Troy and D.D. began to follow Redd and the dude to see what was going to happen.

"Motherfucker, I'll take your life, you don't know me!" Redd yelled to the man as they were approaching the Burger King parking lot.

"What the hell is wrong with him?" Troy muttered to D.D.

"I don't know, man," D.D. answered. "Redd's tripping."

By the time Troy and D.D. caught up to Redd, they were in the Burger King parking lot. Troy tried one more time to intervene.

"Why don't you leave that man alone?"

"Shut the fuck up!"

Redd struck the dude then, and Troy decided this was too messed up to stick around and watch. He started walking back toward the pool hall.

When D.D. ran past him, Troy quickened his pace, and when he heard someone say *Hold it!* followed by a shot, he ducked instinctively and began running. Was Redd—who was known to pack heat—shooting at him? He heard another shot, so he kept going, straight into the neighboring projects of Yamacraw.

A few moments later, Redd ran past him. Maybe it was Redd who had gotten shot?

"Redd, you all right?" Troy called out.

Redd kept running without responding.

Troy made his way back to Charlie Brown's pool hall just a few minutes later, but his ride was already gone. Damn. Now how was he going to get home? He tried to call Mama, but the payphone kept spitting his quarter back. Sirens began to wail and police cars started coming from the underpass. Troy didn't know what had just gone down, but his gut told him to get out of there. Cloverdale wasn't so far from Yamacraw. He could walk home in under an hour.

Lawton's closing statement laid out the narrative he had been trying to build throughout the trial. Redd Coles's version of the events, he said, was supported by a "small army of witnesses," witnesses who were credible and, furthermore, had no reason to lie against Troy. Troy shot Michael Cooper in

Cloverdale and then, out of "fear that he would be arrested and connected with the Cloverdale incident," also shot Officer MacPhail.

According to Lawton, the fact that Troy went to Atlanta the night of the shooting was evidence that he was fleeing from the scene of the crime. "He was going [to Atlanta] to get away from here, and he had a very good reason for getting away from here," Lawton said.

Falligant summarized in his closing statement what was so painfully obvious to Martina: as soon as Redd Coles walked into the police station and gave the name Troy Anthony Davis, the police bought Coles's story hook, line, and sinker, even though Redd Coles had been seen by several people with a .38-caliber weapon that night and was the one with the means and motivation to strike Larry Young.

It would have been difficult to see clearly in the dimly lit parking lot and easy to confuse identities. In fact, Larry Young had confused Troy and Redd just a few days after the shooting. At the police station on August 24, Larry Young had mistakenly identified Troy (from a photo spread that did not include Redd) as the man who had been arguing with him. Yet, minutes later, Redd had walked into the police station for a witness reenactment and, upon seeing Redd, Larry corrected his mistake, having realized that it was Redd who had been arguing with him, not Troy.

The photo spread itself was unduly suggestive. Eyewitnesses would have seen Redd, D.D., and Troy in the parking lot. Why was Troy's photo, then, the only one of the three in the photo lineup? The witnesses were never asked to view the three of them in a lineup and to pick out who had done the shooting or who struck Larry Young.

In addition, before ever seeing the photo spread, the witnesses had already seen Troy's photo splashed across the front page of the *Savannah Morning News*, on television, or on wanted posters all over town. Everybody in town knew who was wanted for the death of Officer MacPhail. He had been tried and convicted in the media.

Why was Redd never treated as a suspect? Because from the moment that Redd gave Troy's name to the police, the entire investigation focused on Troy—no other suspect was even considered. Rather than seeking truth, facts, and answers, the prosecution sought evidence to be used to convict Troy, even if they had to coerce or intimidate witnesses to get it.

The jury began deliberating at 7:53 p.m. In just under two hours, it reached its unanimous verdict. Troy Anthony Davis was guilty on all five counts.

The Davis family left the courthouse stunned, speechless, and numb. Troy was returned to his cell in the Chatham County Jail to await his sentencing hearing. Martina went to her apartment with Louie. Virginia and Kimberly went home to Lester and Ebony. And Joseph went to his residence, alone. If only they could at least deal with this reeling blow together as a family, as they had once been.

✦ ✦ ✦

Family trips were more comical than road-trip movies, with Daddy sitting at the wheel, lecturing his captive family about the ways of the world. Martina and Troy's silent eye-rolling in the backseat intensified as Daddy invariably popped one of his tapes into the eight-track player.

Joseph refused to admit when he was lost. "I know where I'm going!" he insisted vehemently if somebody tried to suggest that perhaps he should stop and ask for directions. A few wrong turns later, the family ended up in the wrong city. It was never Daddy's fault, of course; the Department of Transportation was to blame for altering the streets.

All five kids stayed with Mama and Daddy in one motel room.

"Dad, can't we kids have our own room, please?" Martina would beg him.

Daddy put his hands on his hips, raising his eyebrows at his eldest daughter. "Do you work?"

You own a construction company! Martina wanted to remind him. *You can afford a second motel room!*

But getting money out of Joseph had never been easy. Troy, in his preteen years, attempted now and again.

"Dad, can I have a quarter?"

"A quarter? What did you do to deserve a quarter?"

"Well, I cut the grass."

"It's your responsibility to cut the grass!"

Joseph always strove to be the hip, young dad. When the kids started strapping wheeled metal frames over their tennis shoes, Daddy also took up roller-skating. Joseph took Martina, Troy, and Kimberly to a roller rink, plunking down money to rent skates for his kids and himself.

"Daddy, these skates are a lot faster than the ones we use outside," Martina tried to warn him.

"I can skate as good as anyone out there!" Joseph boasted.

Daddy hit the rink with enthusiasm and went rolling around, doing his thing, moving to the music, until a small child whisked past him unexpectedly. Joseph lost his balance and fell right on his backside, viciously puncturing his buttock with his car keys. At breakfast the next morning, Martina, Troy, and Kim studiously examined their eggs and oatmeal in order to avoid laughing as Daddy emerged from the bedroom, rubbing his sore bum and grumbling about having to sleep on his stomach.

Martina was certain that Daddy viewed embarrassing his children to be part of his paternal responsibility. In the seventies, Joseph wore the requisite platform shoes and pink-and-lavender leisure suits. But, unlike the more compliant fathers, Joseph did not retire this wardrobe at the end of the decade— he continued to sport his platform shoes and leisure suits well into the eighties. Daddy looked like he had stepped out of a Frankie Avalon beach party movie when he wore his tight swim trunks, and his Kmart tube socks were pulled all the way up to his knees.

"Please take that off," teenaged Martina begged him each time he left home. Martina used her first paycheck from her after-school job to buy Daddy a suit.

Joseph Lester Davis was famous for his dancing. Daddy was serious about dancing. If a friend came over, especially a white friend, Joseph would turn on the music. "Come on, let's dance!"

They would start dancing, until, without warning, Joseph would lift the needle from the record and shake his head sternly.

"You've got to sit down, my friend."

The friend would sit.

"You can't dance unless you have a nickel's worth of soul. So you know what I'm going to do? I'm going to give you a nickel's worth of soul!" Joseph would turn toward the hallway. "Tina! Lester! Kim! Troy!" he roared. "Get in here!"

The kids staggered out of the bedrooms in their pajamas, half asleep.

"Get up on the furniture!" Daddy knocked on the table and turned to his friend. "This glass won't break! I made this table! And it's strong. It can hold a thousand pounds! Virginia! Get up here with the kids!"

Within seconds, the entire Davis family was stomping on the furniture, demonstrating its strength.

"All right, give 'em a nickel's worth of soul!"

Joseph would drop the needle back down onto the spinning record. But, just as the kids were getting warmed up, Daddy would snap the music off again.

"That's a nickel's worth—that's all you get! If you want more, you've got to pay for it!" Joseph's friend would be in stitches by then. "You want ten cents' worth of soul? Pay my babies! Pay my babies!!"

"Can we go back to bed now, Daddy?" Lester would groan.

But Joseph would have the music going again and drag the furniture to the edges of the living room, spinning around in his platform shoes, doing the split and popping back up as if he were James Brown.

"Ohh, y'all want some more?"

"Please, Lord, let it be over," Martina would whisper to Troy, both of them doubled over with laughter.

By then, Daddy would have his white friend up on his feet, coaching him.

"Come on now, put a little dip, put a little wiggle. Don't move your whole body, you're not fighting the song! You've got to caress the song!"

The height of Joseph's scorn was reserved for black folks who could not dance. "Where the hell did you come from? You need to sit down, you're a shame to the race."

Candler Hospital held a picnic each year for its employees and their families. Martina and Troy were in the pool when Daddy came running over.

"Come on! They got a dance contest! $100 to the winner!"

"Daddy, we don't want to dance right now," Troy protested.

"Get out of the pool and come on! Ain't nothing but white people entered, they can't dance, they don't got no soul! We got this! Come on!"

"What did you just say?" Martina asked, shocked and embarrassed. White people were all around and could hear every word that Joseph had bellowed.

"You heard me! Come on!"

Martina and Troy reluctantly climbed out of the pool and made their way dripping and shivering to the contest area.

"Shake it off!" Joseph commanded. "You better dance like you're dancing for $50 apiece, cause that's what we're taking home!"

Martina and Troy won the contest with ease. Daddy kept the $100.

✦ ✦ ✦

August 29, 1991

Martina had never begged for anything in all her twenty-four years. Now, as her family entered the courtroom for the first time since the trial had begun, it was to plead for her brother's life.

Mama spoke first, holding her head high and keeping her voice steady. When she and Joseph separated and then divorced, fourteen-year-old Troy had taken over as man of the house, she told the jury, taking care of the house and the younger kids when Virginia was at work. After Kimberly took ill, Troy got a job. Every two weeks, Virginia would come home from work and find seventy or eighty dollars on her dresser.

"Troy, you don't have to give me all this money," Virginia told him each payday.

"No, Mama," he said. "All I need is enough to get me a couple of hot dogs and gas for my car."

Virginia wanted to insist that her son take back his money, but there was the electric bill to pay and groceries to purchase, and the extra helped.

Virginia's voice wavered only slightly when she described the conversation she had had with her ten-year-old daughter the previous night.

"Mama, is it over?" Ebony had asked her.

"It's not over yet."

"Well, y'all came out of the court, is Troy coming home now?"

He can't come home now, Mama had explained gently to her little girl, but they were going to ask the Lord to put it in the jury's heart to spare his life.

Martina had struggled all weekend to determine how to make the jury understand the kind of human being her brother was. She decided to tell the story about Troy and the catbird.

As a boy, Troy was playing outside with his BB gun when he accidentally shot a little gray catbird. Troy was heartsick when he realized that the bird had been hit and was bleeding. Joseph had always taught his children to never harm any of God's creatures unless it was for food or other needs of life. Troy gently scooped up the injured creature and brought it into the house. He fashioned a small cage for it and tried to mend its wing. He sat next to the little bird for hours, coaxing it to eat and praying to God to let it live.

"My brother is the foundation of our family and we're all the house that's built around him," Martina told the jury, wiping away the tears that she had battled with and lost.

But no one could demonstrate better the central role that Troy played in the Davis family than Kimberly, who approached the witness stand with the help of a cane—but, thanks to Troy, walking on her own two feet.

✦ ✦ ✦

Kim, number three of the Davis children, had always struggled to fill the big shoes she was coming up after.

"Kimberly Davis?" successive teachers asked in elementary, middle, and then high school. "You related to Tina and Troy?"

Kimberly tagged along with her sister and brother everywhere, including Uptown, the teen dance club. The other kids dragged Kim onto the dance floor as Martina and Troy were bringing down the house.

"She's a Davis, she can dance!"

Kim couldn't dance to save her life (much to Joseph's shame)—but she loved basking in the glory of her older brother and sister.

Kim was the only freshman to make the varsity basketball team; she was never certain if she was really skilled or if it was because Martina was the team captain.

"Race you home!" Troy often shouted to Kimberly when they got off the bus from Windsor Forest High School. Kim and Troy took off toward the red brick house on Sylvester Street, sneakers pounding pavement as fast as legs could pump. Troy usually bolted into the house moments before Kim, slamming and locking the door behind him.

"Troy! Let me in!" Kim shouted, pounding on the door. "I have to go to the bathroom!"

It was a sunny morning toward the end of ninth grade. Kimberly was feeling off when she woke up, but she had not missed a single day of school since kindergarten and was determined to maintain her perfect attendance record. Exhausted, she forced herself out of bed and onto the school bus.

There was no racing Troy that afternoon. Kim could barely make it back to the house and, when she did, she collapsed in the driveway.

"I don't feel good," she moaned to Virginia. "My legs are giving me grief."

Kim started throwing up. Virginia immediately got her into the car and drove to Candler's emergency room. The next morning, Kimberly could not lift her hands or legs. Terrified, she realized she was paralyzed from the neck down. She was rushed to intensive care where she remained for weeks, and then months, as perplexed doctors ran a battery of tests. She became unable to breathe unless she was hooked up to a respirator. The doctors were uncertain if she would live to see her fifteenth birthday, a few months away.

"Why is this happening to me?" Kim cried to Mama repeatedly.

Kimberly, finally diagnosed with multiple sclerosis, was in intensive care for three months. Mama slept on a cot in Kim's hospital room, going directly to her early-morning shift at Candler's cafeteria. While Mama was at work, Lester sat by Kim's side, or Troy, or Martina, who came to the hospital from her basic training in the military as often as she could. There was always a family member to celebrate with Kim when she made improvements, like when she began breathing again without the respirator. There was always someone to distract her when boredom grew overwhelming and, when terror gripped her, there was always someone to provide comfort.

Troy, age sixteen, kept everything functioning at home. It was not the first time that Troy had stepped in when help was needed; he had been taking on that role ever since Daddy and Mama split up. Troy looked up to Joseph and it had hurt when he left, but he had understood what he needed to do. He had stopped playing sports so he could come straight home after school and do whatever Mama needed: cut the grass, feed the dogs, mind Lester and Ebony.

Now, with Kimberly sick and Mama at the hospital twenty-four hours a day, Troy also prepared dinner every night for twelve-year-old Lester and five-year-old Ebony, helping his younger brother with his homework and tucking his baby sister into bed. In the mornings, he dressed Ebony, combed her hair, fixed breakfast, got Lester off to school and Ebony to day care, and then went to school himself. After school, he fed the kids a snack and then took them to the hospital so they could see Mama and visit with Kim.

Kimberly finally made enough progress to move from intensive care to the occupational therapy floor. In painful, incremental stages, she gained limited use of her upper body. She learned to partially feed herself through a device on her wheelchair that lifted her hand to her mouth. But she still could not stand or walk. She might never walk again, the doctors had told Virginia.

With Daddy gone, Martina in the military, and Mama despondent over Kim's condition, Troy knew it was up to him to keep his family strong.

"Everything's going to be all right, Kim," Troy reassured his sister when he visited every day.

When Kim was especially gloomy, Troy lifted her into her wheelchair and wheeled her to the hospital chapel, where they prayed together for her full recovery.

After six months in the hospital Kimberly was able to go home, though she was wheelchair bound. Mama made arrangements for a special teacher to instruct Kim at home in the mornings. She would need to go to occupational therapy at 1 p.m. every afternoon.

Troy sat his mother down the night after Kim came home. "I know you got to work, Mama," he said. "I'll take Kim back and forth to therapy afternoons."

"How can you do that with school?" Virginia asked.

"I'll have to withdraw. But I can go to adult ed and still get my diploma. And I can get a job."

"Let me think about it."

Virginia stayed up most of the night wrestling with the decision. She didn't want her son to leave school. But she needed Troy's help. A few days later, Virginia went to the Windsor Forest High main office to withdraw Troy. What choice did she have?

Troy continued to get Lester and Ebony ready in the mornings and then went to his classes at the GED program at Richard Arnold School. He was home by early afternoon, ready to take Kim to physical therapy. Troy helped Kim use the bathroom, get dressed, and tie her shoes. He changed the sheets on her bed. He fed her until she could feed herself. He dialed the numbers of friends she wanted to talk to and held the phone to her ear.

Troy went to his job serving fast food at Captain D's after Virginia got home from work in the late afternoon. Initially Troy used Virginia's car, making sure his mother got to and from Candler as well, but that was not sustainable. Virginia had some money saved up, and there was Candler's credit union. She bought Troy his own car, a blue 1984 Cougar. It was a practical necessity, but it was also a thank-you to her seventeen-year-old son, who had put his life on hold for his sister and his family. Troy was proud of his car. None of his friends had a car as cool and as ruff as his.

After several months of intensive outpatient occupational therapy, Kimberly had improved enough to go back to school. Five mornings a week, Troy lifted Kim from her wheelchair, gently placed her in the passenger seat of his blue Cougar, and drove her to Grover High, the only wheelchair-accessible high school in Savannah. Every afternoon, Troy stood outside his car at Grover High waiting to bring her to therapy.

Kimberly continued to make progress, but every little task took so much effort. It was easier, sometimes, to ask her family to do things for her that she knew she should do herself, but Troy never let her get away with being lazy.

"Kim, if you don't do it for yourself now, you never will," he told her firmly, no matter how hard she pleaded with him to brush her hair or apply toothpaste to her toothbrush.

Whenever Kim permitted herself to wallow in self-pity, Troy was up in her face. "Why are you feeling sorry for yourself? You want to be able to do everything you used to? Then you have to get up and do it. It's your body. Faith without works is dead."

"Get up and do it? Troy, I can't walk," Kim said sullenly, pointing out what she thought was quite obvious.

"You used to play varsity basketball," Troy answered. "What's stopping you from playing basketball now?"

"Troy! I can't walk!"

"Can you move your arms?"

"Yes."

Without another word, Troy wheeled Kim outside to the driveway, a few feet away from the hoop that Joseph had installed, and tossed a basketball onto her lap.

"Okay, let's see you shoot."

The ball felt good in Kimberly's hands. But sitting in this chair . . . this was ridiculous. Troy stood next to the basket, his hands on his hips, looking at her expectantly. Kim tossed the ball half-heartedly. It barely brushed the bottom of the net.

"See? I can't do it."

"*Can't* is not a word in your vocabulary." Troy scooped up the ball and returned it to her. "Try again."

She shot with more effort this time and the ball bounced off the rim. Troy passed the ball to her again, giving her tips on how to get the necessary velocity and arc. Before the afternoon was over, Kimberly was sinking baskets.

"What else do you wish you could still do?" Troy asked Kim, once she had earned a spot on Grover High's Special Olympics basketball team.

"I miss playing in the marching band," Kim answered. There was no way she could maneuver her wheelchair on the football field while playing her clarinet.

Troy thought about it for a few minutes.

"You know what you need to do? You need to take up another trade."

"What?"

"You need to learn how to play another instrument that will work with the wheelchair."

By the time football season started, Kim was skillfully striking wooden keys with a rubber mallet as Troy or Lester pushed her wheelchair during halftime, her xylophone balanced securely on her lap.

Troy sat in on many of Kim's occupational therapy appointments so that he could watch the therapist work with her. Once they got home, Troy made sure his sister did the exercises that the therapist had assigned, no matter how much she resisted. After nearly a year, the occupational therapist told Kim it was time to start work toward using crutches.

That Saturday, Troy wheeled Kimberly to the driveway. "It's time for you to stand up."

She wasn't strong enough, Kim protested. She was not yet ready.

Troy would not tolerate any of her excuses. Slowly, with Troy's help, Kim lifted herself from the wheelchair. Troy wrapped one arm around Kim's waist to steady her and, with his other arm, pulled her wheelchair around so she could lean on it for stability.

Kim was almost in a daze by what she had just accomplished as Troy whooped and hollered in circles around her. She was shaky, she was holding onto the back of her wheelchair, but for the first time since the day she had collapsed in the driveway, she was standing up.

Troy wheeled Kimberly out to the driveway every Saturday and Sunday from then on, and continued to work with her on standing. Before long, Kim could balance on her own. It was time to start working with the crutches. Troy helped Kim stand up each Saturday and Sunday and handed her a pair of crutches. With great effort, they worked on crutching a step or two, and then a step or two more.

One Saturday, after helping Kim stand, Troy backed away a few steps, her crutches still in his hands.

"Okay, now walk to me."

"Give me my crutches, Troy!"

"You have to walk to me to get them."

"Troy, I can't do it."

"*Can't* is not a word in your vocabulary."

Kimberly sank back down in her wheelchair and began to cry.

"If you cry, you're gonna cry, but you're going to sit there until you walk."

Kim refused to get out of her wheelchair. She would not—she could not—walk.

The following Sunday, Troy helped Kimberly stand up in the driveway as usual, but this time, he pulled her wheelchair out of reach so she couldn't collapse back into it.

"What are you doing?"

Troy took several steps away. "I want you to walk to me."

Kim was rooted to the spot, furious. "Give me my wheelchair, Troy! I can't do it."

"*Can't* is not a word in your vocabulary."

Afraid that her knees would buckle underneath her if she stood much longer, Kim forced herself to thrust out her right leg in one, tiny, shaky movement toward Troy. She compelled her left leg to follow.

"Mama! Mama! Come here!" Troy bellowed.

The front door opened, and, from the doorway, Virginia saw her daughter standing on shaking legs with her wheelchair several feet behind her and her brother several feet in front of her.

"Tell Troy to give me my wheelchair, Mama!" Kim pleaded.

"No, you're going to keep walking. You're going to do this!" Troy said sternly.

Kim began crying.

"Troy, please!"

"Troy, maybe she's had enough . . ." Virginia began, but Troy interrupted her. "Mama, no, she's going to do it. She can do it."

Kim took one more step. Two steps. Three steps. She walked all the way across the driveway with her mother and brother cheering her on.

Every member of the Davis family applauded and hollered loudly as Kimberly walked unassisted across the stage at Grover High auditorium to receive her high school diploma.

✦ ✦ ✦

August 29, 1991

"I love you, Troy," Kimberly said, closing her testimony after telling the jury what Troy had done for her. "Troy, he means the world to me, and I just ask you to spare his life, because if you take Troy's life, you might as well take my life, too, because I can't go on without my brother."

Earl Coleman, deacon in the Savannah Temple Reformed Church, lived across the street from the Davis family and had known Troy since he had been a little boy. He had always found Troy to be friendly, respectful, and helpful, both to his own family and to all the neighbors, he testified. But what if Troy had a previous conviction for carrying a concealed weapon, Spencer Lawton asked Deacon Coleman on cross-examination? Would that change his opinion about him being a good boy? Deacon Coleman allowed that it might.

With a flourish, Lawton presented a legal document. Martina's stomach tightened when she realized what it was. It was a misdemeanor conviction against Troy from the Chatham County Superior Court for carrying a concealed weapon in 1988, over a year before the murder of Officer MacPhail.

Troy never would have signed the plea bargain, he testified, had he realized it would come back to haunt him.

In the summer of 1988, he had been out riding with a friend when they saw a guy Troy vaguely knew. The young man had gotten into the back seat of Troy's car and they had headed to a convenience store to get something to drink. The acquaintance had said that he needed to use the bathroom. After the young man had gotten out of Troy's car, police pulled up in front of the car. Troy had cut the engine and got out, and the acquaintance had taken off running.

The police had searched Troy's car, emerging from the back seat with a .22 pistol they had found on the floor. Troy had never seen the gun before.

"Is this your car?" the cops had asked him.

"It's my car, but it's not my gun," Troy had answered.

They had thrown him up against the hood of the car, slapped handcuffs on him, and took him to jail.

Sign this document, Troy's attorney Harris Odell had advised him, and you'll only pay a fine of $250. The charges will be dropped and you can go. If you don't sign, Odell had warned, and this goes to trial, you might get five or six years. Troy had never been in trouble before and he was afraid to do time. He signed the plea deal and paid the fine.

Spencer Lawton began his closing statement as Martina clenched her fists tightly by her side. First, the DA called Virginia a liar. She would beg for his life, Lawton continued, even if Troy had slaughtered an entire department of police. Her opinions and feelings should not influence the jurors. Lawton then proceeded to cry crocodile tears over Kimberly's affliction, insinuating that poor Kim, the most helpless member of the family, had been used as a vehicle for the entire burden of the defense. The DA was careful to acknowledge that the Davis family was a respectable family from a respectable neighborhood. "But their virtue can't obviate his evil," he hastened to add. Furthermore, if Troy was a mama's boy, as he had testified, how did he get the nickname "Rough as Hell"?

Lawton laid out with dramatic flair seven reasons why the jury should sentence Troy Davis to the electric chair. The heinousness of the offense was offered as reason number one. "This is a gruesome, calculated, cold-blooded murder," Lawton said. "It doesn't come any worse than this." Reason number two: Officer MacPhail had received no due process. Troy had been judge, jury, and executioner. Number three, according to Lawton, was that Troy had lied and denied responsibility all during the trial and continued to do so. Reason number four? "You haven't seen even the tiniest shadow of remorse pass over his face since this trial began," Lawton said. "Even by his own sister's testimony, if you accept that testimony, Troy Anthony Davis had more compassion for a wounded bird than he's got for a police officer, a fellow human being." Martina struggled to restrain herself. How dare Spencer Lawton manipulate her testimony like that? Lawton had already continued to reason number five: Troy's cowardice and brutality were compounded by a ruthless cynicism—Troy would have let Coles be executed in his place.

In attacking a police officer, the DA offered as reason number six, Troy had attacked an institution that functions as our first and last bastion against barbarism, our only assurance of a civilized society. Troy Anthony Davis killed the very embodiment of that defense and that assurance. "This is a case that cries out for the death penalty," Spencer Lawton concluded. "If not this case, then what case?"

Falligant and his team reiterated the mitigating evidence that had been offered by family, neighbors, and Troy's former boss. "If in your mind there's certain little nagging lingering doubts, I hope you'll consider those today," Troy's attorney said in summation. "It's your decision, irreversible, if you impose the death penalty. That would be very final, and you would hate to wake up some night and have those little lingering doubts come back into your mind."

Martina and her family waited in agony as the jury deliberated from 2:45 in the afternoon until 9:30 at night, only to find out they had not yet reached a decision and would continue the following morning.

At 11 a.m. on August 30, the jury came back in. Virginia, Martina, Kimberly, Lester, and Joseph sat behind Troy and his lawyers. Impeccably dressed, postures straight as boards, jaws set tightly, Mama clenching her Bible, they waited to hear.

"Mr. Foreman, has the jury reached a unanimous decision as to the defendant in this case?" the judge asked.

"We have, Your Honor."

"Give it to the sheriff, please."

The foreman handed the decision to the clerk, who read it aloud. "We the jury find that Troy Anthony Davis shall be punished by being put to death."

Troy was to be put by death by electrocution during the seven-day period commencing at noon on October 17, 1991, and ending on October 24.

I need to touch my brother, Martina thought desperately as court was adjourned, trying to push down the rising panic. Troy was going to be killed in the electric chair in just over a month and she hadn't been able to hug or touch him in more than two years.

✦ ✦ ✦

July 16, 2007

An unfamiliar number appeared on Martina's caller ID at 8 p.m.

"Hello?"

"Martina?"

"Yes."

"This is the *New York Times*. How do you feel?"

"How do I feel about what?"

"About Troy's stay?"

"What stay?"

"The parole board gave Troy a ninety-day stay of execution."

Martina threw the phone down and began to leap around the hotel room. "Troy got a stay! Troy got a stay!" she screamed.

Just then, Mama's cell phone rang. Virginia punched through the numbers as quickly as she could so that she could hear Troy's voice.

"Hi, Mama. How'd the hearing go?"

Virginia put her cell phone on speaker so Troy could hear Martina, who was still dancing and shouting ebulliently.

"You hear that, honey?"

The family huddled around Virginia's cell phone to hear Troy's reaction. For a moment, there was silence. Then an almost inaudible "Thank you, God," followed by another "Thank you, God," this time a little louder.

Troy did something he did regularly: Troy prayed. Then he did something he almost never did: Troy began to cry.

Warden Terry verified the news of the stay and two guards led Troy from the death house back to his cell block. Fellow death row inmates lined up at the doors of their cells, extending their arms through the iron bars to grasp Troy's hand as he walked down the row.

"Praise God, brother!" one man called out to him, tears in his eyes. "Maybe at least one of us will survive this place!" another cheered.

Troy's friends shoved small items through the bars for him to take back, items that Troy had bequeathed to them the previous day: a bottle of shampoo, some extra stamps, a few envelopes, his belt and shoes.

Troy, head high and a new spring in his step, walked into his cell. He heard the familiar clank of the cell door locking behind him, but at that moment he was not focused on his confinement. He was focused on his life. Georgia had intended to take it from him in less than twenty-four hours. He and his family and scores of supporters had fought—and they had prevailed.

De'Jaun and Martina with *Democracy Now!*'s Amy Goodman on July 16, 2007. Courtesy of the Davis family.

Troy poses outside his car for his prom picture.
Courtesy of the Davis family.

Troy holds his diploma from Richard Arnold School.
Courtesy of the Davis family.

July 24, 1994: Troy holds his nephew De'Jaun for the first time. Courtesy of the Davis family.

De'Jaun visits his uncle Troy on death row. Courtesy of the Davis family.

Uncle and nephew share a playful moment. Courtesy of the Davis family.

Part Two

August 7, 2007

As De'Jaun was getting ready to start eighth grade, Troy's case had a new, hopeful opening at the Georgia Supreme Court. After the July 2007 execution was stayed, his attorney, Jay Ewart, had filed an extraordinary motion for a new trial. Chatham County Superior Court judge Penny Haas Freesemann had flatly denied it, and Jay had appealed the decision to the Georgia Supreme Court. Unexpectedly, Georgia's highest legal body decided to hear oral arguments, a decision that superseded the parole board's ninety-day stay. Though the Court would not hear the arguments for several months and there was no predicting what the outcome would be, Troy was, for the time being, safe.

"I want to do my social science project on Uncle Troy's case," De'Jaun announced to Martina after his first week of school. De'Jaun had come to Martina the year before with the same idea and she had dissuaded him. At that time, De'Jaun had only just started to fully grasp the fate that Georgia had in store for his uncle. Given the political climate, she had not wanted her son to be exposed to the hostility that would surely accompany such a project. But De'Jaun was a year older now, understood more, and had lived through the stress of July's execution date. She could not discourage him again.

The thirteen-year-old boy delved into the details of his uncle's case. He worked for weeks on a display board with summaries of his hypothesis, procedure, materials, graphs, data, results, visual aids, and conclusion. His central thesis question was glued to the middle of the black posterboard: *How Does the Troy Anthony Davis Case Impact Georgia?* Running across the top were pictures of other African Americans who had had an impact on society: Sojourner Truth, Frederick Douglass, Harriet Tubman, Booker T. Washington, W. E. B. Du Bois, Jackie Robinson, Martin Luther King Jr.

De'Jaun appeared confident as he packed up his materials to bring into school. He would have to give an oral presentation of his uncle's case in front of his class, but he was prepared. That afternoon, De'Jaun bounded into the house. "Guess what?" he greeted Martina and Virginia with a broad smile. "I won first place in my class!"

The Mercer Middle School–wide competition was the following week. Martina saw the slump in De'Jaun's posture before he even uttered: "I scored a seventy-six."

A month later, Martina received a surprising call from Massey Heritage Center in downtown Savannah.

"Your son's social science project was a first-place winner in the district, and we want your permission to send his project onto regional."

There must have been some mistake. De'Jaun had only scored a seventy-six at the school—how had his project even advanced to the district level? Martina called Mercer Middle School and the principal explained what had happened. A teacher had heard the judge make a snide comment about the "cop-killer case" and, when she saw De'Jaun's score, she was concerned that the judge's assessment had been biased. She had told the principal, who then examined De'Jaun's work and agreed that something was amiss. The principal unilaterally awarded De'Jaun an honorable mention and sent his project to the district level.

And now, after being awarded first place at the district level, *How Does the Troy Anthony Davis Case Impact Georgia?* was on its way to the regional competition.

Martina hung up the phone and shook her head in amazement. It seemed like only yesterday that the family had been trying to adjust to the horrific reality of Troy being on death row. In those early days, they could not have imagined that Troy's case would have any larger impact at all.

✦ ✦ ✦

October 1991

The entire family left Savannah before daybreak to make the three-and-a-half-hour drive to Jackson, pulling off the highway onto Prison Boulevard at 9 a.m. It was their first opportunity to visit Troy since he had been moved to Georgia Diagnostic and Classification Prison, where Georgia's death row was housed.

They drove through pristine landscaping on the prison grounds. For whose benefit were these groves of pine trees and idyllic ponds, Martina wondered? Her brother and his new cellmates would not have the opportunity to appreciate their shade or beauty.

Sheaves of barbed wire and guard towers loomed into view. Somewhere behind all that steel, wire, and concrete was her brother. It was silent as Martina parked her car, aside from Mama's muttering prayers. Everything had to be left in the car, except for a plastic baggie of quarters for the vending machines and picture IDs, which would be deposited in a white bucket on a string that was lowered from a guard tower in exchange for a permission slip to enter the prison.

Virginia searched her purse and then searched it again. Her eyes grew wide behind her glasses as she realized that she had been so agitated leaving home that morning that she had forgotten to bring her driver's license. She would not be permitted to enter the prison without it.

"I'll drive you to Atlanta," Martina's cousin Valerie, Aunt Mattie's daughter, suggested quickly. "We'll get an ID made for you." Virginia and Valerie sped off to Atlanta as Martina, Kimberly, Lester, Ebony, and Aunt Mattie entered Georgia's death row for the first time. Martina scarcely registered walking through the tunnel, up the stairs, and through the metal detector or going through multiple layers of iron-barred locked gates. She was focused only on seeing her brother.

After having had no physical contact with Troy for the two years he had been at Chatham County Jail, restricted only to talking over the phones with glass between them, Martina was slightly overwhelmed just being in the same room as him. Yet, despite the concrete surrounding them and the guards standing directly outside the suffocating visitation room, Troy immediately made it feel like they were home. He clowned around with ten-year-old Ebony, getting her to giggle, got family updates from Aunt Mattie, Martina, and Kim, and took eighteen-year-old Lester aside for a man-to-man talk.

Virginia and Valerie breathlessly entered the visitation room. Mama hugged her son for the first time in two years and then visitation was over. The family gathered in a circle quickly to hold hands and say a prayer.

It took the entire drive back to Savannah for Martina to shake the cold and damp she had absorbed from the prison. It took even longer for the sound of the gates clanging shut to stop ringing in her ears.

✧

The Davis family was immediately thrust into the steep learning curve of the post-conviction process. Troy realized that the appeals process was going to be long and arduous and, though he was optimistic about the outcome, he knew he would be at the Georgia Diagnostic and Classification Prison for many years. He had decided on the very first day not to let death row break him and worked on building internal defenses in order to remain physically and emotionally intact. Troy understood from the start that the way to survive was to be respected; he set out to earn that respect by the way he carried himself and by how he treated the other 110 inmates on the row. Troy tried not to think about the fifteen he had never met: those who had been executed since the reinstatement of the death penalty in 1973. He trained himself to focus on living in the moment and to block out anything happening outside the prison walls. If he dwelt too much on family events he was missing, he would become depressed and lose hope. He put out of his mind whatever was out of his control and taught himself to shut down his feelings. He refused to let himself cry, even when friends were killed in the electric chair.

Troy clung to his blessings, which the starkness of prison life helped him recognize and appreciate. He had God, and he worked on strengthening his faith. He took comfort in knowing that no matter how restricted his physical self, his ideas and thoughts were always free. And he woke up with the sun every Saturday, knowing that his family was en route to visit.

"Mama, you don't have to come so often," Troy said during one visit. "It's too hard. You have your own lives." But Virginia insisted on coming every week. If her son had to do time, the family would do time together.

✧

Joseph used to smoke and drink, though Virginia always scolded him not to drink in front of the kids. Occasionally the drink got the best of him. He was never abusive to the kids, but from time to time there were, as Martina thought of it, little demons in the house. No one knew anything in those days about post-traumatic stress disorder and how Joseph's army days in Korea and Vietnam might have impacted him.

After Troy's arrest, Daddy's larger-than-life persona seemed to deflate, like a cartoon character whose blood could be seen draining from the body. After Troy's conviction, Daddy crumpled entirely.

"I would rather die than bury a child I love," Joseph said to Troy on what was his final visit, shortly before Troy was moved to death row. Joseph stopped eating and stopped taking his insulin. He went into diabetic shock, followed by a diabetic coma. In the hospital, Troy's was the only name Daddy responded to. Once he even opened his eyes and searched the room for Troy. The doctor wrote to the prison authorities asking that Troy be allowed to call the hospital and speak to Joseph. Perhaps hearing Troy's voice might pull him out of the coma. The warden refused.

When Joseph passed on February 3, 1992, after having been in a coma for over a month, the warden told Troy that he could talk to his family for as long as he wanted, but Troy ended the call after five minutes. The warden would not let him talk to Daddy when he was alive; Troy didn't want the warden to feel magnanimous about granting Troy any special favors now that Daddy was gone.

Martina was wracked with guilt after Daddy's death and replayed Troy's trial in her mind over and over. The family had sat together on a bench in the hallway, with Joseph standing apart from everyone else, staring wordlessly out a window. Martina kept thinking about how, when court was adjourned at the end of each day, she, Louie, Mama, and Kimberly went home with family members, but Daddy went home by himself, to silence.

Martina had dropped in on Joseph a few months after Troy's conviction. A few of his friends were over, drinking gin. Martina hadn't seen her father

drink in a long time. His friends knew he was diabetic and shouldn't have alcohol. She grabbed the bottle of gin and broke it, furious at him and at them.

"Y'all are not his friends if you're bringing him alcohol!"

But Martina hadn't been paying enough attention to Daddy to realize
how much he had been hurting. Perhaps if she had checked on him more,
she would have noticed that he wasn't taking his medicine. But it had been
such an awful time for the entire family. She had been more focused on her
mother's stress and trying to protect Ebony and Lester. And, of course, Troy
needed her.

Troy mourned alone, in his prison cell. It hurt, not being permitted to go
to the funeral and not having the chance to say goodbye. But he had to push
Daddy's death as far out of his mind as he possibly could. Blocking out the
loss was the only coping mechanism that would preserve his sanity.

✧

Troy was now represented by the Georgia Resource Center, an Atlanta-based
federally funded nonprofit whose mission was to assist Georgia's indigent
death row inmates in habeas corpus proceedings, otherwise known as the appeals process.

In 1995, just as Troy's case was entering the most critical stage of the state
habeas process, the US Congress voted to defund all the federally funded resource centers across the nation. The Georgia Resource Center's budget was
slashed by 70 percent. Out of eight staff attorneys and four full-time investigators, only two attorneys and one investigator remained to handle the crush
ing load of eighty death row cases in various stages of post-conviction review.

Martina tried not to be frustrated with the Resource Center. She knew
the two attorneys were making heroic efforts to perform triage, trying to avert
total disaster, but they were simply unable to provide any kind of effective
representation for Troy or any of their other clients. The situation was so grave
that one of Troy's fellow inmates, a low-functioning man named Exzavious
Gibson, had to appear at a state habeas corpus hearing with no lawyer at all—
forced to represent himself.

It was clear from the start: the fight was going to continue to be uphill all
the way.

✦ ✦ ✦

November 13, 2007

As De'Jaun's project about Troy's case made its way up the competition chain, Jay Ewart and the legal team from Arnold & Porter prepared for oral arguments in front of the Georgia Supreme Court.

Martina prayed silently that the court would grant Troy a retrial as she and her family slipped onto benches in the Atlanta courtroom, sitting opposite from the MacPhails.

Seven black-robed justices entered and took their seats on large leather chairs. Leah Ward Sears, the country's first African American female chief justice, sat in the middle. A marble wall rose behind them, with the carved Latin inscription: FIAT JUSTITIA RUAT CAELUM. Martina made a mental note to look up the meaning of the phrase.

Jay and David Lock, the chief assistant with the Chatham County DA's office, hashed out the now-familiar arguments. The magnitude of the new evidence makes this case stand out, Jay insisted. Although lower courts had determined that recantations do not count, the quantity and quality of the recantations related to Troy, combined with the new affidavits, were unprecedented and demonstrated credibility.

David Lock argued that Troy could not meet three of the six requirements in an extraordinary motion for a new trial, including the requirement of due diligence. The affidavits had not been obtained and brought to the courts in a sufficiently timely manner, Lock contended.

Martina's hair stood on end when DA Spencer Lawton stood to speak. It had been sixteen years since Troy's trial and Lawton still had that effect on her. But even Martina was unprepared for Lawton's quiet, controlled rant, made in his strong Southern drawl.

"For months, we've been subject to a drumbeat of one-sided ideology, masquerading as expertise in Georgia's law on evidence in criminal procedure. This not-so-helpful advocacy, I might even say pressure, has ranged all the way from the Vatican through Amnesty International and finally to the editorial board in the newsroom of the *Atlanta Journal-Constitution* . . ."

Martina thought she understood the subtext of Lawton's speech: Don't listen to those outside intruders, Lawton seemed to be telling the Georgia Supreme Court, furious that the world was watching and resentful at being held accountable to a broader audience. But it was a statement from David Lock that Martina found most illuminating. "The rules are established," Lock asserted. "You need finality in cases at some point."

The Chatham County chief assistant district attorney had just summarized the entire judicial system in a nutshell: Procedure took precedence over truth. Finality was more important than fairness.

The session lasted exactly forty-two minutes, with no indication of when the court would rule. Martina walked outside the Georgia Supreme Court to participate in a press conference that AIUSA had organized and caught sight of Governor Sonny Perdue outside the capitol building across the street. There had been a severe, months-long drought in Georgia and Governor Perdue, along with lawmakers and ministers, was leading a gathering of hundreds in a prayer for rain.

Late that night, Martina thought about the bizarre governor-led public prayer for rain as she searched online for the meaning of FIAT JUSTITIA RUAT CAELUM:

Let justice be done though the heavens fall.

✧

February 2008

De'Jaun stood next to his cardboard display, running through his talking points inside his head. Approximately one-third of Georgia's 159 counties were competing in the regional competition—De'Jaun would have to be sharp.

A team of judges approached the boy. "Tell us about your project," a white, male judge said, smiling warmly. De'Jaun took a deep breath, and began to explain the different aspects of how Troy Anthony Davis's case impacted Georgia. He tried to remember his mother's coaching: speak slowly and clearly and be sure to make eye contact. "Who is Troy Davis to you?" the judge asked when De'Jaun finished. Should he admit that Troy was his uncle? If he did, the judge might assume that De'Jaun's research was biased.

He avoided the question. The judge asked again, and again, De'Jaun tried to dodge.

"Are you related to Troy Davis?" the judge asked a third time.

An image of his uncle suddenly flashed through De'Jaun's mind. Troy was probably sitting in his cell, counting down the minutes before he could call home and hear how the competition went. As always, he would tell De'Jaun how proud he was of him and how much he loved him. De'Jaun looked the judge straight in the eye. "Yes, sir," he said. "Troy Davis is my uncle." De'Jaun held his breath for a moment, waiting for the response.

"In the future, you stand tall and proud and tell anyone who asks, yes, that's my uncle. Never be ashamed of that."

The judge, a law professor from Georgia Southern, said he had heard about Troy's case, but learned much more from De'Jaun's display. He had felt certain that Troy must be a relative, given the amount of time and attention that De'Jaun had so clearly devoted to his project. The judge shook De'Jaun's hand, complimenting him on his firm handshake.

Later that afternoon, De'Jaun and Martina stood in front of De'Jaun's display looking at the closed folder that contained his score and any ribbons he may have earned. If his project were to advance to the state level, it needed both a blue and a purple ribbon.

De'Jaun began to reach out to the folder and then withdrew his hand quickly.

"You open it," he told his mother. Martina opened the folder. De'Jaun saw the blue ribbon first, and then—a flash of purple!

De'Jaun pumped his fist in the air.

"Yes!"

How Does the Troy Anthony Davis Case Impact Georgia? would be competing in Georgia's statewide competition.

✧

March 22, 2008

On March 17, 2008, the Georgia Supreme Court denied Troy's extraordinary motion for a new trial in a 4–3 vote.

De'Jaun tried not to think about that latest rejection as he set up his display for the state competition in Clayton College's cavernous auditorium with hundreds of other students from all across Georgia. There were projects in that auditorium about subjects he had never even heard of. He was surrounded by a bunch of child geniuses.

Martina watched from the bleachers as De'Jaun presented in front of a team of three judges, noting with approval that his posture was straight and he was looking directly into the judges' eyes.

The winners were presented with awards at the end of the day. Martina sat stiffly on the edge of her seat next to De'Jaun, who was chewing his fingernail as the Class I prizewinning students heard their names and made their way down to the podium to accept their awards. She didn't want to be like one of those toddler-tiara beauty-pageant moms, but she knew how hard her son had worked and how much this meant to him. Class II, De'Jaun's group, was next. First, second, and third place winners in all three categories in Class II were read out—none of the names were his. Martina watched as the nervous anticipation slowly drained from her child's face, replaced by dejection.

"You made it to State, De'Jaun, you've done an exceptional job," Martina said briskly, patting his knee. "All those kids and their parents and the judges saw your project and learned about Troy's case. This has just been wonderful." She was so focused on comforting De'Jaun that she almost missed the announcement.

"Best in Class II: Antone De'Jaun Davis-Correia."

De'Jaun had won the top, overall prize for his entire age group in all of Georgia! Martina was on her feet whooping with pride and joy before she fully registered what had just happened. Teachers, students, and other attendees of every race and color instantly swarmed De'Jaun, patting him on the back as he walked down the bleachers to receive his glass plaque and gift certificate.

"This project is outstanding. We've been teaching our students about the case. Well done!"

"Keep fighting, young man!"

Martina was speechless. She had expected that De'Jaun would face animosity by focusing his project on Troy. Instead, they were surrounded by an outpouring of support, the likes of which she had never before experienced. These were not human rights activists or anti–death penalty advocates crowding around De'Jaun and Martina, congratulating them effusively—they were ordinary Georgians.

Martina was unusually quiet on the ride home, her mind unraveling the day's events and all that had led to it. De'Jaun's project almost had not made it out of Mercer Middle School. It mirrored Troy's situation: just when they reached a dead end, the case always twisted in an unexpected direction. The Georgia Supreme Court may have denied Troy a retrial, but this was not the end of the road. Her son went all the way despite the odds, and so would her brother.

She glanced over at De'Jaun, who was glowing in the seat next to her.

"What a great way to end your middle school career, right, De'Jaun?" De'Jaun nodded, and they fell silent again.

Just as Martina thought her child had nodded off, she heard him say, "I can't wait to tell Uncle Troy."

✦ ✦ ✦

July 24, 1994

Martina carried her brand-new baby boy, dressed in a little white onesie with matching hat and socks, into the prison. She wanted her little guy to look good when he met his uncle for the first time.

The guards greeted Martina warmly as she and Kimberly signed in and handed over their IDs.

"We haven't seen you in a long time!"

"I've been busy." She lifted the blanket-wrapped baby in her arms for them to see.

"Well, now, isn't he precious?" the guard poked De'Jaun's nose gently. The sleeping infant did not stir.

Martina and Kim walked through the tunnel and up the stairs, through yellow gates that clanged shut behind them before another set of yellow gates opened in front of them. Martina bounced her baby gently in her arms as they waited for the guards to bring Troy. Finally, Martina and Kim were able to pass through one more set of locked bars to access the narrow side room where death row inmates sat with their visitors, sequestered from the general prison population.

"Hey," Troy said, putting his arm around Martina in a half hug, not wanting to disturb the little bundle she had in her arms.

He leaned over the bundle, moving the blanket a bit so he could take in the tiny, brown, wrinkled, beautiful face.

"Hey," Troy repeated, much softer and a full octave higher. "How ya doin', little man?"

"You want to hold him?"

The baby was in his arms before he could answer. Troy froze in fear. What if he dropped him? What if he broke him? What if the pressure of his big hands somehow damaged the frail little body? He extended his arms toward Martina.

"He's so little! Take him, Tina! Come get him!"

"No. You get him. You hold him." Martina walked across the narrow room, leaned against the olive-green tiled wall and crossed her arms, grinning widely. She loved watching Troy's eyes widen with adoration as he gazed at his sleeping nephew. You'd have thought she had just given her brother a gold bar.

Several other guys from Troy's block, also in visitation, gathered around. "Who you got there, Davis?"

"This is my nephew, De'Jaun. Say hi to everyone, De'Jaun."

Troy carefully cupped De'Jaun's head in his hand and angled him up ever so slightly so the other inmates could feast their eyes.

"Well, take a look at him." Jo-Jo scratched his head and smiled.

"Nice to meet you, De'Jaun." Jack Potts lifted De'Jaun's little hand between his thumb and forefinger and gently pumped it up and down.

Troy looked down at the tiny, sleeping boy proudly. He had never felt quite this way about another human being before.

Martina, Kim, and Troy, still with De'Jaun in his arms, gathered themselves on chairs so Martina could finally tell Troy the full story of her pregnancy and De'Jaun's miraculously healthy arrival into the world.

Martina had begun dilating when she was not even three months pregnant. An incompetent cervix, the senior perinatologist told her at the hospital. They would have to induce labor, which would mean, essentially, a miscarriage.

"You're young," the doctor told her gently. "You can try again."

Martina lay in the hospital bed that night, highly medicated and distressed. She was going to lose her baby.

Suddenly, Martina heard the curtain around her hospital bed rustle. She sat up and looked through the crack in the not-fully-drawn curtain. The only one in the room with her was Kimberly, sound asleep on a cot. She lay back down and closed her eyes, when she felt the presence of someone sitting next to her on the bed. She opened her eyes again, but Kim was still sleeping on the cot. "Quit playing," Martina mumbled to Kimberly, and then drifted off to sleep.

Daddy appeared in her dream, reassuring her that everything would be all right. Martina was surprisingly calm when she woke in the morning. Though Joseph had passed two years earlier, she was certain that it was he who had rustled the curtain's chain and sat next to her on the bed.

A young OB/GYN resident came into her room after breakfast. "I want to try a cervical cerclage," he told Martina. They would stitch a band of strong thread around her cervix and pull it tight, he said. She would have to be on bed rest until her baby was born. The procedure was performed, and months of grueling bed rest began.

On June 21, Martina woke up drenched. Though only at six and a half months, she knew her water had broken. All 3.8 pounds of her son emerged at 5:12 the following morning, wailing at the top of his barely formed lungs. Martina stared at the creature nestled in her arms with amazement. Her little man-child had so much hair! She had already decided that his name would be Antone De'Jaun Davis-Correia. Future pregnancies would likely hold the same complications, the doctors told her. De'Jaun was to be her one, precious child.

The baby began to stir, making small hunger noises. Troy reluctantly handed De'Jaun back to Martina so she could feed him. By the time the baby had his fill, visiting hours were over. Troy cradled his nephew in his arms one final time, trying to commit to memory the feel of the infant in his arms so he could hold onto the sensation until next week's visit.

"Thanks for bringing him, Tina!" Jack Potts called out as Martina and Kimberly were about to walk back through the iron gates. "It ain't every day we get to see a baby on death row." Martina tucked the blanket securely around De'Jaun's neck and made sure it covered his tiny toes.

"Don't worry, Jack. You'll be seeing a lot more of this one."

✦ ✦ ✦

September 3, 2008

"How could an execution order be given?" Martina asked Troy, flabbergasted when he called her to report that a new execution date for September 23 had just been set. "You're still in the middle of an appeal!"

Jay and the legal team had appealed the Georgia Supreme Court's denial of Troy's extraordinary motion for a new trial to the US Supreme Court. Their argument was that the Eighth Amendment, which prohibits cruel and unusual punishment, gave the innocent the right not to be executed. The US Supreme Court, which was still in recess, had not yet determined whether or not they would hear his case. How could Georgia go ahead and set Troy's execution date without bothering to wait for the US Supreme Court's ruling?

Troy sounded stronger than he had when last year's date had been set, even philosophical. "Look, Tina, I don't want to be a martyr," he said. "But if I have to die for something I didn't do, at least I know that my life made a difference for somebody coming behind me."

Martina sat at the kitchen table, helping Troy once again draw up his final visitor list and make his burial arrangements. It wasn't until she had hung up and walked toward her bedroom that she saw fourteen-year-old De'Jaun sitting on the living room sofa. De'Jaun had heard the entire conversation.

✦ ✦ ✦

Troy got over his fear of breaking the baby and held De'Jaun proudly, strutting around the tiny visitation room every Saturday to show off his little nephew to the other guys on the death penalty block. The men all took turns holding De'Jaun, bouncing him up and down, trying to make him laugh. It was never difficult to coax a smile out of baby De'Jaun.

Troy grilled Martina about every detail of his nephew's development. De'Jaun's pediatrician had expressed concern that perhaps Martina was feeding De'Jaun too much; his cheeks had grown waxy and fat. Martina explained that Virginia was putting mashed potatoes with gravy on her finger and into De'Jaun's mouth. Once the baby got the taste of salt in his mouth, he had no use for baby food. The pediatrician told Martina that she needed to instruct Virginia to stop feeding De'Jaun.

"What did you say?" Troy wanted to know.

"I told him to tell Mama himself! That's a black woman who raised five kids!"

Troy roared with laughter, causing waxy-cheeked De'Jaun on his lap to laugh as well, just before trying to grab his Uncle Troy's nose.

Wrappers from the vending machine snacks were the only materials available for toys. Three-year-old De'Jaun watched in fascination as Troy fashioned a paper airplane by bending and folding the edges of a Reese's peanut butter cup container. Troy and De'Jaun threw the paper airplane back and forth until Troy beckoned his nephew to his side. "Throw it at Jo-Jo!" Troy whispered in De'Jaun's ear, pointing discreetly to the inmate talking to a visitor a few feet away from them. De'Jaun took careful aim and fired off the tiny brown paper projectile. Jo-Jo whirled around, wondering what had just struck the back of his head, when he caught sight of De'Jaun smiling and waving. Jo-Jo recovered the paper airplane under his chair, pretended to look angry, and flicked it back to De'Jaun, who fell down laughing.

Troy stood with his hands on his hips one Saturday, surveying his now four-year-old nephew.

"You know how to play football?"

"No."

Troy grabbed Ebony's plastic Coke bottle, now empty, and shook a few remaining chips from a crinkly bag into Lester's hands. He wrapped up the bottle in the bag. "Okay, stand over there," Troy instructed De'Jaun, teaching him how to pass and catch.

"Careful!" Martina warned them sharply. She wasn't sure that the concrete floor was the best place for her brother to teach her young son how to tackle. But Troy always made sure that De'Jaun landed on top of him during the tackling lessons, which usually ended in a tickling match.

The family ended each visit with the same ritual: standing in a circle, holding hands and praying. De'Jaun pulled his uncle by the arm toward the iron bars when the prayer was over.

"Come on, Troy, let's go! Come home with us!"

"He has to stay here," Martina told De'Jaun, gently. "Uncle Troy is in a special school."

"What kind of special school is this, Uncle Troy?"

It was Martina who answered. "It's a school where he can't come home yet. He'll come home with us one day soon." De'Jaun leapt into his uncle's outstretched arms, giving him a giant hug and quick kiss.

"See you later, Troy, have fun in school!"

Troy felt a brief, intense stabbing pain in his heart every time De'Jaun implored him to come home with the family. There was nothing on this earth that he wanted more.

✧

By first grade, De'Jaun started asking more questions.

"Mom, why is Troy behind those big yellow gates? Why does he wear that white uniform?"

Martina believed in being honest with children, but she also wanted to protect her son from what he was too young to cope with. "He's in a bad place right now but he'll come out soon," she told him when the questions persisted. De'Jaun began working on other family members. "Auntie Kim, can you look something up for me on the computer?"

"Sure, what do you need?"

He repeated the words he had overheard that he wanted her to investigate on his behalf.

"You're only six years old and you want to know the meaning of 'incarceration' and 'capital punishment?'"

"Can you just look it up?"

Auntie Kim told him to go and ask his mother—which lead to more vague answers.

Martina caught De'Jaun on her laptop one day.

"What are you doing on the computer?"

De'Jaun turned to face his mother. "I want to know where Troy is."

Martina saw the worry on her son's little face. Keeping information from him was not shielding him, she realized; it was making him more anxious. She sat down next to De'Jaun.

"Uncle Troy is in prison, sweetheart. He's there because they think that he did something bad. We're all working really hard to show that he didn't do it, so he can come home."

Martina did her best to answer De'Jaun's follow-up questions. Some were about the crime that Troy had been convicted of. Others were about the prison and what efforts were under way so his uncle could come home. She was surprised by the maturity of his inquiries. Where had he picked up all this?

When De'Jaun seemed satisfied that his questions were answered, he turned back to the computer, this time to play games. "If you have any more questions, you can come to Mommy," Martina told him. "I'll do my best to answer them." De'Jaun nodded, already immersed in his video game.

Martina had not mentioned anything about the death penalty during their talk. It was enough for her child to understand that his uncle was incarcerated and why. He didn't need to worry about the state of Georgia planning to kill him. It wasn't yet time to tell him the full truth.

Martina thought about Joseph as she tucked De'Jaun into bed that night. She distinctly remembered the first time Daddy had been confronted with educating his daughter about some of the world's harsher realities.

✦ ✦ ✦

1973

Six-year-old Martina loved accompanying Daddy to Kmart, especially when Joseph thought there might be a Blue Light Special. Martina could spend hours looking at the shiny earrings and bracelets at the jewelry counter. She imagined herself draped in the sparkly jewels or, better yet, bringing them home for Mama.

Martina stood on her toes so she could see the entire jewelry rack, rotating it slowly to appreciate the full selection. A similar-sized little girl came up to the rack as well, with blotchy pink-and-white skin, a T-shirt with a stain down the front, and straight blond hair pulled back into a ponytail. Martina spun the rack to get her attention. The little girl spun the rack back the other direction, as if to respond. Martina spun the rack another time, taking a small sideways step toward the little girl, and the blond girl did the same. Martina twirled the rack one more time. Her arm and the other little girl's arm brushed against each other.

Suddenly, the girl started screaming. "Daddy, daddy! That nigger touched me!" The little girl ran to a beefy man with a crew cut who was standing a few feet away inspecting a watch and, sniffling, buried her face in the leg of the man's jeans.

Martina looked around with alarm. What had her new friend been talking about? What nigger had touched her? Martina quickly jerked her hand away from the glittering earrings and necklaces. A nigger must be something nasty on the jewelry stand. She didn't want to touch it by mistake.

The girl's daddy towered over Martina in two giant strides, his arm draped around the blond child protectively. "How dare you touch my daughter?" he thundered. "If you ever get near my girl again . . ."

Before Martina could make sense of what the man was saying, Joseph materialized next to her, as if he had levitated there.

"What the hell is going on here?" Daddy demanded.

"You need to get your little nigger child away from my daughter!" the other father shouted.

Snatches of what Joseph hollered back burrowed into Martina's ears—things like *You better back off* and *Don't you ever try to threaten my child!*

She hated it when Daddy got upset like that, his voice shaking. She looked at the little girl, who remained buried in her father's pants leg, occasionally peeking at Martina and then burying her face again.

Daddy grabbed Martina's hand and stormed out of the store so quickly that Martina practically had to run to prevent herself from being dragged. He helped her climb into the passenger seat of his pickup truck and then went around to the driver's side, slamming the door shut. He started the engine ferociously, pulled out of the parking lot with a squeal of the tires, and drove without saying a word. Martina searched his face, as if clues to what had gone so terribly wrong could be found there. Anger slowly drained out of Daddy's face as he drove, replaced by pain.

Daddy parked the truck in the driveway. He turned off the ignition but sat there for a moment, playing with the key. Finally, he turned to Martina.

"That child had no business calling you a nigger, Tina. You know that, right?" Joseph anticipated her question before she had a chance to ask it. "A nigger is a person—of any color—who is ignorant and can't learn. That's what a nigger is. But here in Savannah . . . well, some white folks call black people 'nigger.' They mean it as an insult. But you're no nigger, no matter what anyone ever calls you, and don't you ever forget it."

Martina sat silently in the truck, trying to understand what Daddy was saying and what exactly about his daughter being called "nigger" caused that hurt in his eyes.

In bed that night, Martina overheard Daddy relay to Mama what had happened. "This girl looked like she stepped out of a damn trash bag and she thinks Tina is below her? Man, I wanted to punch that guy! If Tina wasn't right there, I might have done!"

Why would that girl have thought Martina was below her? Everyone was always telling her what a little smarty-pants she was. She lifted her arm out from under the sheet and poked it. She knew that her brown skin, compared to the blotchy pink-and-white skin of the little girl, had played a definitive role in what had happened when their arms touched. It had everything to do with the pain in Daddy's eyes. But it didn't make any sense.

Joseph started lining the kids up on the couch, once or twice a month. It was time they learned about life.

✧

Joseph nicknamed his eldest daughter "Motor Mouth," while Virginia cautioned Martina repeatedly that her mouth was going to get her in trouble one day. Martina shrugged off Mama's warnings. Knowing how to use her mouth, especially if something was not fair, had always been a point of pride.

Half-rubber, similar to stickball and played on the street, was the game of choice in Cloverdale. The name originated from a round rubber ball that had been sliced in half. The half-rubber ball was hit with a broom-sized stick. The further the ball was hit, the more points were scored.

On her first attempt, Martina could not connect the thin stick to the sliced ball.

"She can't get it!" Grover and Calvin, two neighborhood boys, taunted. Martina and Troy practiced every day, hitting the ball harder and further with each effort. Before long, they were the half-rubber rulers of the Cloverdale streets.

But Martina was not satisfied with half-rubber. Troy had been playing baseball with the PAL since he was five years old. If her brother was playing baseball for the PAL, ten-year-old Martina wanted to play baseball too.

"Girls can't play baseball," Grover scoffed when she revealed her ambition. "The ball comes too fast."

"If the ball hits you in the chest, your breasts won't grow!" Calvin teased her.

"That's just all kinds of craziness!" Martina snapped back.

But just to make sure, Martina asked Daddy that night if the part about the breasts was true. Joseph responded with a loud guffaw.

The following day, Joseph spoke to the PAL coach, convincing him to give her a chance. Daddy and Troy took Martina to a tryout the next day. The coach tried her at first base, third base, and center field, with Martina fielding everything that came her way.

"Well, young lady, you're not so bad. Not so bad at all," the coach said.

"You didn't try me in one position I'm really good at," Martina said.

"What's that?" he asked.

"Pitching."

"Girls can't pitch," the coach said firmly.

"I can strike out every boy y'all got there," Martina insisted.

She took the mound, pulled her oversized cap low over her eyes, and proceeded to do just that.

"You looked like a bean-pole out on the field," Troy teased her in the car on the way home. Martina arched her eyebrows at him majestically. "That's okay, little boy, go play on your little boys' team. I'm going to be on the JUNIOR team!"

The coach called that evening. Martina would be a starting player at the next day's game.

✧

Martina's compulsion to act when she saw something that was wrong or unfair grew with time. Mama always left the living room whenever Sally Struthers came on TV pleading with viewers to save a life for the price of a cup of coffee—Virginia could not tolerate the images of fly-swarmed children with swollen bellies in Ethiopia or Guatemala—but Martina could not tear her eyes away from the TV set. What kind of world was it where she and her family had a good home to live in and food to eat but kids her own age across the world were starving?

At dinner one night, thirteen-year-old Martina announced her intention to send seventy cents a day to feed a child. "The money you give to those organizations often doesn't actually get to the people that you're trying to help," Joseph responded. "Do some research first. Make sure you find an organization that's really doing something, making a difference, before you send your money."

Martina went to the library the next day and began looking up humanitarian and human rights organizations, applying her father's criteria to each program she found. Amnesty International was one of the first organizations she read about. From what she could ascertain, they were really doing something. They were making a difference. She decided to join.

✧

As Martina grew older, she became increasingly aware of injustice. She didn't have to look far—traces of Savannah's history of slavery were everywhere she looked. She occasionally passed the red-brick arched caverns, or barracoons, just behind touristy River Street. The barracoons used to be a part of slave trader Alexander Bryan's slave market; hundreds of slaves who had disembarked from ships and were waiting for auction would be packed within them. Martina could feel the presence of suffering humans whenever she stood in the arches, especially at night. City officials now parked their cars in the barracoons.

Laurel Grove cemetery, in midtown, was Savannah's original burial ground for whites; there was a companion burial ground for free blacks and slaves. Martina sometimes wandered among the unmarked graves of slave children, wondering if their parents had been permitted to shed tears at their graveside.

Friends from out of town always commented on Savannah's beauty, remarking particularly on the Spanish moss–draped oak trees lining the city's streets and squares. The majestic trees formed a canopy that shrouded Savannah's secrets. If those trees could talk, Martina knew, they would tell the story of a past far uglier than their grace and elegance conveyed and of a present still troubled by issues of class and race.

✧

It was not until Martina and Mama were chaperoning Ebony's Girl Scout troop to Savannah's Civil Rights Museum that Martina first learned that Virginia had been involved in the civil rights movement.

The docent was showing the girls a replica of the lunch counter from Levy's Department Store. "This is the first lunch counter that blacks integrated in all of Georgia," he said. He pointed out where the waitress would have been standing and how three students walked in, sat down, and asked for service, portraying the sit-ins as if they had been polite and smooth. "Excuse me," Virginia interrupted the guide. "You have it wrong. I was in those demonstrations and it wasn't all peaches and cream. There was nothing pretty about what happened. If you're gonna tell it, tell it like it really happened."

"You participated in the sit-ins?" the docent and Martina asked Virginia simultaneously.

"Yes sir, I was there, and if you like, I can tell the girls about how it happened and put the details in."

The guide invited her to do just that.

Coming up, Virginia had never understood the logic of why she was permitted to spend her money in the department store but had to eat at the lunch counter in the basement rather than at the nice one upstairs. She resented the Jim Crow water fountains at the Chatham County Courthouse. The fountain marked "Whites" spouted plentiful, cool water, while the one marked "Colored" offered a warm trickle into a basin that often contained the remnants of white people's spit. Why should she not be able to enter Forsyth Park, the largest park in downtown Savannah? Virginia paid the same textbook fees as white students, but her books were handed down from the white schools, with half the pages torn out and writing all over the margins.

On March 16, 1960, just six weeks after four black students first sat down at Woolworth's in Greensboro, North Carolina, three students from Savannah State College and Beach High School took seats at the lunch counter at Levy's Department Store in downtown Savannah. The threesome, Ernest Robinson, Joan Tyson, and Carolyn Quilloin, were arrested and jailed overnight.

The sit-ins continued, and Virginia knew she had to be a part of them. She signed up for a shift and went down to McCrory's with a group of five other students. The moment Virginia and her friends sat down on the metal-backed chairs, the waitresses roped off all the other seats, effectively closing the counter.

Virginia and the others sat silently and respectfully, holding their ground. One waitress rolled her eyes each time she walked past. Another taunted the group. "What are y'all doing here? We don't want you here and we're not going to serve you!" Angry white customers gathered, snarling threats. A gob of spit landed on the floor just below Virginia's feet. Another landed in the face of the young man sitting next to her.

"Get out of here, nigger dogs!"

Virginia clutched her purse stiffly, making sure that her posture was erect and that her face betrayed no emotion. The previous week, the sit-in had erupted into brawls, with the police doing nothing to protect the students. She hoped that would not happen today. Another hour passed, and then the police came.

"Y'all better get up and leave, or you'll be in violation of the anti-trespassing law and make no mistake, you will go to jail."

Virginia wanted to expose the ignorance inherent in segregation, but she had no interest in going to jail. She and two of her colleagues made their way through the still-taunting crowd and out of McCrory's, but not before watching the other two who had refused to budge be roughly dragged by the police right off the stools and into waiting police cars.

The next Saturday, Virginia signed up again. She would sit in at Kress's this time.

✧

Coming up as a smart black kid, Martina had been thought of as "uppity" by white classmates and black kids from the projects had accused her of trying to be white.

Subtle racism had been a part of all aspects of Martina's school life, often perpetrated by black teachers.

"Why isn't there information about black people in here?" Martina, holding up her thick US history textbook, had asked her tenth-grade history teacher, a black woman. The teacher had sent Martina to the principal's office. "Well, Martina," the principal had said, looking at her steadily from behind her desk.

"What do you want to know?"

"I want to know my history," Martina had answered. "I can't even find a book about black history in the school library except during Black History Month, and then it's just a few books on a display table about Martin Luther King Jr. and Harriet Tubman."

Martina's drill team coach, also black, used to tell Martina to stop talking ethnic. Martina had never realized that she "talked ethnic." All she knew was that she and the other dark-skinned black girls had to work twice as hard as the white or light-skinned girls to keep their spot on the drill team.

Martina had hoped that her son's experiences would be different from her own.

✦ ✦ ✦

De'Jaun left for school extra early on Read Across America Day, dressed in his pajamas and clutching his pillow under one arm and a children's book about African Americans during the colonial period tucked under the other. He couldn't wait to spend the day with the other second graders lounging on pillows in their jammies, reading.

Martina was surprised to see him return home that afternoon with a long face.

"What's wrong?" she asked him.

"Miss Kate said that it was a nice book, but that I need to bring it back in February."

"Your teacher didn't let you read your book?"

"No."

Martina confronted De'Jaun's teacher before school the following morning.

"Why isn't my son allowed to read his book until February?"

"I thought it would be more appropriate during that time," Miss Kate muttered.

"During what time? Tell me, what happens in February that doesn't happen in November?"

Finally, Miss Kate came out and said it: "Black History Month."

Miss Kate tried, unsuccessfully, to calm Martina down. Finally, Martina turned to storm out of the school. On her way out, she passed a bulletin board highlighting careers relating to math, technology, and design. Martina stopped and studied the photos of happy, productive computer technicians, doctors, and scientists. There wasn't one black or brown face. What did a board like this communicate to her child? How did it impact his sense of self-worth?

Martina had been unable to work since her cancer diagnosis and had time to volunteer in De'Jaun's school. She received permission to put up monthly displays in a large glass enclosure near the school's entrance. In February, the display focused on famous black people from Georgia, such as Matilda Beasley, Georgia's first black nun and dedicated humanitarian. In March, during Women's History Month, she created a display about black women who had struggled for social change. She organized special programs about Caribbean heritage and culture and coordinated a schoolwide festival focused on Africa. She posted trivia questions and distributed Pizza Hut coupons as a reward to students who got the answers right. She was prepared to do whatever it took for the kids to learn and for the African Americans to feel proud of who they were and where they came from.

✧

De'Jaun had a white friend named Benjamin, the son of one of Martina's colleagues. One morning after sleeping over, little Benjamin walked out of Martina's bathroom with his fire-red hair sticking up in every direction.

"What did you do to your hair?" Martina asked, suppressing a laugh.

"I put hair grease in it."

"How much hair grease did you use? The whole jar?"

"I wanted to be like De'Jaun." There was a slight quiver in Benjamin's voice.

"I want my hair soft, like Benjamin's," De'Jaun said.

Martina sat the boys down. "Benjamin and De'Jaun, you are like each other, because you are friends," she explained. "People look different, but they're not different on the inside. Do you understand what I'm saying?" The boys nodded, and then slid off the couch and scrambled into the backyard to chase each other.

Martina watched Benjamin and De'Jaun play, ruefully aware that rumors continued to circulate in Savannah that the Davis family hated white people. If only those circulating the rumors knew about her "brother," Fazio.

✧

Terry Fazio, a stout, white, muscular guy with a shaved head, had entered the pizza joint where sixteen-year-old Martina had her first after-school job. He was Italian and hailed from Detroit, he told Martina as she heated up his pepperoni slice.

Fazio returned day after day, and Martina began to get the notion that it wasn't the pizza that Fazio was interested in.

"Can I come to your house and meet your dad?" Fazio asked one day.

"No," Martina answered firmly.

A few days later, the doorbell rang. Martina opened the door to find Fazio standing on the doorstep with his bald, white head and a large grin. "What are you doing here?" she hissed.

"I just came to see how you're doing," he said.

"Who's at the door?" her father asked.

"Nobody!"

"Mr. Davis?" Fazio called out.

Joseph came to the door. "Yes?"

"Hi, I'm Terry Fazio, from Detroit."

"Can I help you?"

"I would like to date your daughter."

"Come on in," Joseph said in a tone of voice that made Martina want to crawl under the door seal and die. As Fazio entered, Joseph turned to his firstborn.

"Tina, you can go and step in the next room."

Martina slunk into the bedroom, as Joseph began to light into Fazio. "This is the South, son, not Motor City! Do you know how many problems it would cause if my daughter dated a white man?"

Martina paced the floor of the bedroom, unsure if she would survive to her seventeenth birthday. Was Fazio ripped to shreds yet? Then Martina heard laughter. She peeked into the living room. Daddy and Fazio were sitting on the couch watching TV together. Joseph immediately turned to Martina with reproach. "Why didn't you bring Fazio by before?" he scolded her. "How come I had to wait this long to meet him?"

Martina sat stiffly on a chair across the room as her father and her suitor continued to chum it up, bonding over serving in similar military units. Who did Fazio want to date anyway, Martina or Daddy? All the fun in the idea of a romance with Fazio evaporated. Where was the rebellion in it now? Fazio befriended the entire family and eventually became like a member of the family himself. It was nice, until Martina began to bring other dates home to find Fazio in the living room, introducing himself as the "brother."

✦ ✦ ✦

2008

Troy had friends of every race, religion, and nationality, some from countries that he had never heard of. His pen pals' descriptions of their homes, their postcards from their travels, the photographs of their families that they tucked inside the envelopes—these became Troy's windows to the outside world, which had suddenly grown much broader.

Troy tried to return each and every supporter's letter, even after Amnesty featured him in a holiday card action for Christmas 2007 and he received bags of letters each day. Martina printed postcards for him thanking people for their prayers and support so that he would need only to sign his name, but Troy insisted on writing a brief personal message on each postcard. As fast as he sent them out, responses poured in.

Troy always prioritized letters from kids. He treasured the children of his friends, whose hand-colored cards with drawings of the sun, rainbows, and smiley faces lit up his cell. "Educate yourself," he advised dozens of young people in his letters. "Surround yourself with people you can learn from."

Mama and Daddy had warned him about his no-good friends when he was a teenager, but he hadn't listened or taken opportunities for his education seriously. Troy wanted students to know that there were other ways to live in this world, there were places other than the hood, and they could develop self-respect and make positive decisions in their lives.

Friendships deepened as correspondences continued, and more and more people arranged visits with Troy in prison. Many of the new friends contacted Martina first, nervous about what to say when face to face with Troy. "Don't just go up there and talk about his case," Martina advised them. "Just talk to him. Let him know about your life."

Martina knew that Troy felt the need to explain himself repeatedly when people asked him about the case, stemming from years of nobody believing him, and this need to constantly prove himself was draining. "Troy, your friends already believe in your innocence," Martina tried to reassure him.

Martina did not want to monitor Troy's relationships, but she could see more quickly than he could that not everyone who claimed to be his friend truly was.

"Can you put me on Troy's visitation list?" a new supporter asked her before she had ever corresponded with Troy, as if Martina were Troy's gatekeeper and her brother was unable to make his own decisions.

"First of all, you need to write Troy a letter," Martina answered coolly. "You need to let him know who you are and why you want to visit him. If he agrees, then fine. He can either send you a visitation request form or tell me to send one."

"I just want to see what he's like," another woman said to her, as if her brother were a monkey in a cage to be gawked at.

Pen pals occasionally expressed surprise to Martina that Troy was so articulate in his letters and that his handwriting was so neat. Some cared about Troy only when they needed a favor from Martina, and others showed up whenever Troy was in the limelight but disappeared when the cameras turned off.

Yet the support that came from the genuine relationships was a deep blessing for Troy and his family and was appreciated more than Martina knew how to communicate. There were dear friends who had been visiting Troy years before his case had broken through the media, such as Rosanne Fabi from Rochester, New York, who met Martina years before at an anti–death penalty conference and began corresponding with Troy soon thereafter, and Ledra Sullivan-Russell, whose husband Walker and parents Larry and Lisa Sullivan also grew to know and love Troy. There was Randy Loney, a pastor from Glad River Congregation, and Mary Sinclair and Sara Totonchi from the Southern Center for Human Rights. There were those who learned about Troy's case once the execution dates began and quickly became devoted friends, such as American University professor Gemma Puglisi, whose students created a blog about Troy and sent him birthday messages, and Megan Thomas in Seattle, who spoke to Troy on a near-daily basis. There were Laura Tate Kagel from GFADP, Lynn Hopkins, Carolyn Bond, Sheila Strider, Gloria

Colonnello, Ellen Kubica, Lainey Shany, TK Kirkley, Gautam Narula, Sharonda Johnson, and many more, all of whom continued to stand by Troy and his family year after year.

Everyone who visited Troy exited the prison with renewed commitment, both to preventing Troy's execution and to ending the death penalty. It always gratified Martina to see the impact that Troy had on people from around the world, as if her brother had left his imprint on them. But it was beyond gratifying when Martina heard a testimonial about the imprint her brother had left on one young man many years before.

✧

September 2008

Martina was doing a radio interview in Atlanta with Laura Moye from AIUSA a few weeks before the execution date. Martina never knew what to expect from those who called in on those talk radio shows. Some wanted to express their support—others wanted to make it known that they considered Troy a cop killer who deserved to die.

The first caller was on the air.

"My name is Earl and I know Troy Davis from Cloverdale."

Martina's mind started to churn: Earl, Earl, who was Earl?

"I'd just like to say that from how I know Troy, there is no way he could have done this. We all knew he's innocent."

Earl! The little boy from Cloverdale whose daddy had drowned! Martina's memory clicked just moments before Earl told the whole story on live radio:

Troy had been almost sixteen when nine-year-old Earl moved to Cloverdale. Earl had looked up to Troy from the start—everyone in Cloverdale did. Troy made sure the neighborhood stayed at peace.

"Go get Rah!" someone would say if the small kids were fussing with each other on the basketball court or if the older guys were tussling. Troy would be there within minutes to straighten things out. It had helped that Troy was a big guy; no one wanted to fight him, so everyone listened to him.

Tragedy struck a year after Earl's family moved to Cloverdale. They were on vacation at the beach in South Carolina and Earl, his brother, and his cousins were walking out into the ocean. The further out they walked, the lower the water got, lapping playfully around their ankles. They didn't know anything about currents and riptides or that they were actually walking up an underwater cliff. Suddenly, the little boys dropped off the edge into a whirlpool. The other kids were able to swim back to safety, but Earl's six-year-old cousin got caught in the whirlpool and Earl's daddy went in after him. Somehow, he was able to pick up the child from the midst of the whirlpool and throw him to Earl and his brother, but he was unable to extricate himself. The whirlpool pulled him down, spit him out, and then snatched him back under again. Horrified, ten-year-old Earl and his family watched, unable to do anything. After several ago-nizing minutes, Earl's daddy stopped resurfacing. Twenty-four hours later, his body washed up on shore at the precise location where he had gone under.

After that, everyone in Cloverdale seemed to give Earl funny looks. The neighborhood guys drove by Earl and his little brother in their front yard and blew their horns and waved to show their support. But Troy was the one guy who always stopped and got out of his car to speak to the boys and ask how they were doing. He checked on their mother and cut their grass from time to time. Once or twice, Earl saw Troy slip his mom a ten-dollar bill.

"He seemed to understand what it meant for little boys to lose their daddy like that, how much tough it had to be," Earl said on the air. "It made a big difference for me and my brother. Troy didn't have to do that. He could have just not cared, like anybody else. But it hurt him to see us hurting. That's the kind of person Troy Davis is."

As soon as the show was over, Earl called the station to talk to Martina.

"Earl, how are you?" Martina said with a smile so big she was sure Earl could hear it on the other end of the phone.

"I couldn't believe it when I heard your voice on the radio," Earl said. "I was helping a lady at work adjust her antenna, and I thought, that voice sounds real familiar and I kept listening and then I realized—that's Tina!"

Earl, who was now a professional rapper and went by E.Red, told Martina that it was Troy who had first encouraged him to pursue his love of rapping. Troy had kept Earl in line in many ways. If Troy ever suspected the boy had been up to no good, he would get up in his face. Earl had liked it when Troy fussed at him. It made him feel as if Troy were his big brother.

"Let me know if there is anything I can do," E.Red said to Martina. "I want to be there for Troy, the same way Troy was there for me."

♦ ♦ ♦

September 13, 1997

Troy's latest appeal had been denied on September 9. The state habeas corpus court ruled that witnesses' claims of coercion by police officers should have been raised earlier in the appeals process. Martina knew the delays were because the financially gutted Georgia Resource Center could work on Troy's case only sporadically; yet, according to the courts, it wasn't the Georgia Resource Center that had neglected to raise the concerns in a timely fashion, it was Troy Anthony Davis. This recent rejection was now layered onto the entire maddening legal process.

At the start of the day's visit, Troy began, yet again, to analyze his case with his family. Martina's irritation grew with each new detail that Troy parsed—how could he have been convicted on such flimsy evidence?

"Did you talk to the lawyers yesterday?" Troy asked Martina.

"I called the Resource Center, but no one could speak."

"Didn't you call them back?"

Martina suppressed an urge to scream. She called the Resource Center all week, every week, trying to get someone to do work on her brother's behalf.

Next, Troy started bringing up events that had occurred when he was nineteen years old, as if 1988 were yesterday. It grated on Martina that in certain ways Troy was stuck as a teenager. She knew it was because his exposure to the outside world had been cut off at the age of twenty and that her brother had found remarkable ways to grow as a human being in that stifling, limiting environment. But on this particular day, she could not seem to control her impatience.

It all came to a boiling point as an argument began about the Father, the Son, and the Holy Ghost. Martina and Troy were going around and around about whether the Trinity was one entity or separate entities. When Troy began reciting the Bible to back up his point, adding passages from the Torah and the Qur'an for good measure, Martina erupted.

"I don't have to listen to this! Mama, Kim, I'm leaving!"

She stormed out of the visitation area, exited the prison, and sat fuming in the car. Mama, Ebony, and Kimberly came out an hour later.

"Troy kept going to the gate to look for you," Mama said. "He was hoping maybe you had just gone to the ladies' room and were coming right back."

Martina refused to be moved. She was not finished feeling irritated.

By the time they were halfway home, Martina had grudgingly admitted to herself that Troy had likely been correct about the theological point, and by the time they had reached Savannah she acknowledged to herself that the Bible verse was not what she had actually been angry about.

Soon after they got home, the phone rang.

"I'm sorry, Tina," Troy said on the other end of the crackling line, tumbling over his words. "I don't want us to be fighting. I don't want you to be mad at me."

Suddenly, Martina realized what she had done. She had been free to get up and leave, but Troy was trapped, powerless to go after her. By walking out on her brother, she had abused their power difference. And, frustrated as Martina was with Troy's case, she knew that Troy's sense of impotency ran far deeper. His ability to help himself was severely restricted, forcing him to rely on his family to advocate on his behalf. No one wanted to hear what he had to say, including his lawyers, who didn't have the money to defend him. The courts were denying him at every turn. And then, on top of it all, his older sister walked out on him and all he could do was peer through the locked yellow gate, hoping that she was coming back.

No wonder Troy called right away to apologize, even though she had been the one who had behaved badly. With everything else stacked against him, he couldn't stand the thought that his big sister was angry with him.

Martina hung up the phone and sobbed. She didn't care how difficult things might get, she would never walk out on Troy again. Not until he was free to come after her.

That night, Martina dreamt that she said goodbye to Troy at the end of visitation, and, on the way out, passed a glass window where she could give her brother a final wave. But Troy was still sitting, talking to a tall, slender African American woman. Who was that woman? Martina peered closer through the glass and realized that the woman talking to Troy was herself. *But wait*, she thought in confusion, *I already left the visitation room, I'm right here!*

Martina awoke, unsure if she was still with Troy on death row or not. Then the meaning of the dream hit her. She snatched a piece of paper and a pen from her bedside table and wrote down the words that were swimming in her brain: *I am Martina Correia and I'm on death row because that is where my brother lives.*

✧

1998–2004

In the early 2000s, the state of Georgia stepped in to provide additional fund ing to the gutted Georgia Resource Center, which also received grant funding. The nonprofit slowly reconstituted a strong team of attorneys and investiga- tors and, to Martina's relief, was finally able to dive into Troy's file. Yet Martina worried that it was too little, too late—a critical window in Troy's appellate process had already closed. New information backed by solid investigative work started to trickle in, but claims that had not already been raised and factually developed could no longer be brought up.

Martina was further discouraged when President Bill Clinton signed into law the Antiterrorism and Effective Death Penalty Act (AEDPA) in 1996 and made it ten years retroactive so that it could be used against the perpetrators of the 1993 World Trade Center bombing and 1995 Oklahoma City bombing. One AEDPA provision set a statute of limitations of one year for filing an appeal in a federal court and severely restricted the grounds on which a federal court could rule favorably on a petitioner's appeal. When a federal judge in May 2004 refused to grant Troy a hearing, he cited AEDPA statutes as one reason.

Despite these setbacks, Martina was eager to cooperate with John Hanusz, a young, white, six-foot, brown-haired, energetic lawyer with the Resource Center assigned to Troy's case in 2002. John visited the Davis home at the start of his first trip to Savannah.

"The trial transcript and initial police reports are filled with problems and inconsistencies," John told Martina. A previous investigator had obtained a significant recantation from eyewitness Dorothy Ferrell a few years earlier and the Resource Center had been abuzz about that. He was excited to roll up his sleeves and discover what other evidence was out there.

Every subsequent trip began and ended with John stopping by the Davis house to update the family and check in on whether they had any new information. Unlike John, Martina had her finger on the pulse of the community and knew how to find leads on the witnesses, most of whom had been living on the margins of society at the time of the crime and many of whom still were. John cautioned her not to talk to the witnesses herself but to relay whatever intelligence she had on how he could find them.

"People are really scared," John told Martina at the end of one trip as Virginia set an extra place for him at the dinner table. "They're dodging me." John told them about a witness who had failed to show up that morning at an agreed-upon time and place. The day before, John had distinctly spotted a woman peeking at him through barely cracked blinds as he knocked on her door without response.

D.D. Collins, who still lived in Cloverdale, was easiest to find but reluctant to talk. John tracked down Antione Williams through his mother-in-law, who lived in a housing project just north of Yamacraw. John had to drop by Larry Young's place half a dozen times, leaving business cards with his mother on each occasion, before finally catching Larry at home. After months of fruitless searching, he finally located Benjamin Gordon living on an island near Savannah. He had to chase down Jeffrey Sapp for a month.

Martina understood why folks were reticent. The murder, investigation, and trial had been a traumatic chapter in their lives and they did not want to revisit it.

"I get the impression that many of the witnesses feel substantial pressure to keep away from anything to do with the case," John remarked to Martina. They had nothing to gain by getting involved, yet potentially quite a bit to lose. Speaking up might result in harassment from law enforcement officials. They might be worried about trouble with Redd, who remained a feared individual—especially when he had been drinking—and was reputed to still be packing heat. "It can't help matters that I'm a white guy from Atlanta," John added with a grin.

Soon, John started coming with David Mack, an investigator from the Resource Center. Some of the witnesses felt more comfortable opening up to

David, who was black. David joined John in sitting down with Martina, Virginia, and Kimberly and updating the family as De'Jaun played nearby.

"When I show witness after witness what they testified to at trial, they say they were pressured to say that," John reported. "Then they tell me the real story of what happened that night." John and David often wrote up the witnesses' declarations on the spot, notarizing their affidavits then and there. They did not know if they'd be able to locate them again.

On a stormy day in October 2002 David tracked down Harriett Murray, Larry Young's former girlfriend, who had also been homeless at the time of the murder. She was living with her mother in a run-down part of Hilton Head, South Carolina. "Don't talk to them!" Harriett's mother shouted at her from the other room as David and John explained why they had come. "You're asking for trouble if you get yourself involved!"

Harriett, who was now overweight, disheveled, graying, and in poor health, agreed to talk for a limited period of time. In the early morning of August 19, 1989, Harriett told David and John, she had been sitting on a small wall at the edge of the Burger King parking lot. Her boyfriend Larry Young went to the Time Saver convenience store to buy some beer and a man started following Larry and fussing at him as he returned to the Burger King parking lot.

At trial, Harriett had identified Troy as the shooter. Now, however, she said it was the man following Larry, harassing him over a can of beer, who then pulled a gun out of his pants, slapped Larry in the face with it, and shot the police officer.

John was not entirely surprised to hear what Harriett had to say. Though Harriett had implicated Troy at trial, the version of the events she was now telling John and David was more consistent with the initial statement she had given the police the morning of the murder, before they had Troy's name. Harriett reviewed the affidavit as her mother screamed from the other room and rain beat down on the roof.

"We need you to sign this at a notary's office," David appealed to Harriett. John was a notary in Georgia, but not in South Carolina. "It won't take long,"

"I'm not going with you to a notary," Harriett said firmly. She was not feeling well, she said, and she had to go pick up her medication. "I'll sign it now and that's it. We're done."

Martina absorbed this new development as Virginia poured fresh cups of coffee. John and David did not have to explain the significance of Harriett's statement that the shooter was the same man who had been fussing at Larry. There was no dispute about who had picked the fight with Larry Young: that was, even by his own admission, Redd Coles. Yet, without notarization, would the affidavit hold legal water?

"I'm tracking down every member of the Air Force who was in the van at the Burger King drive-through," John updated Martina over another late-night cup of coffee. Daniel Kinsman, who had been in the van, told John that the lighting was too poor to be able to determine shapes and colors, and that the scene was too chaotic to make accurate identifications. But two things stood out to Kinsman. The shooter had been left-handed and the gun had had a shiny finish. Martina understood the relevance of both those details. First of all, Troy was right-handed. Secondly, Kinsman's description of the gun not only contradicted trial testimony that the murder weapon had been a black snub-nose with a brown handle, but it also matched the chrome .38 that Coles had been seen with a half hour before the murder.

John made multiple attempts to talk to Steve Sanders, who had also been in the Air Force van that night. The morning of the murder, Sanders had declared in his police statement, "I wouldn't recognize them again except for their clothes." Two weeks later, he had again indicated that he would not be able to identify the shooter. Then, two years later, Sanders confidently identified Troy at trial—after having seen his picture in the paper the day before.

John showed up on Sanders's doorstep in various cities as the latter moved from home to home. John left messages with Sanders's wife, but he never heard back from him. Jay later sent Sanders a letter via FedEx asking for an audience, but the letter was returned. Sanders had refused to sign for it.

David, John, and Jeff Walsh, another Resource Center investigator, also tried to make contact with Redd Coles numerous times, but each time Redd, who was living with his mother and working at a box-packaging company, cursed them out and threatened to call the cops. In fact, one time Redd did call the cops, who drove up just as David and Jeff were pulling away.

"There's very little we can do if a witness flat-out refuses to talk to us," John explained to Martina. They did not have subpoena power. The state could hold criminal charges or threats of incarceration over the heads of re-luctant witnesses. The Georgia Resource Center had no such leverage.

Martina was always uplifted whenever John and David came by. She knew the battle for Troy was a steep uphill climb, but at long last, there were attorneys to speak to who were actually responsive and real progress on Troy's case was being made. And she loved watching John and David interact with De'Jaun, who was quick to charm and impress any adult who came into the house. Mar tina was aware that De'Jaun was absorbing some of her conversations with the legal team, even when he appeared to be doing his homework or playing on the computer, but she had no way of knowing for certain just how much.

❖ ❖ ❖

"Do you go to school to be talking? You go to school to learn!" Troy fussed at De'Jaun when Martina informed him that De'Jaun's fourth-grade teacher had scolded him for socializing during class. De'Jaun hung his head. Nothing mattered more to her son than making his uncle proud. "Okay, come on," Troy said to the boy. "Come here and give me a hug." Troy opened his arms, and De'Jaun received a Santa Claus embrace and a kiss on his cheek. "I love you. That's why I'm telling you this."

Martina never considered herself a single mother, as De'Jaun lived not only with his mother but also with his grandmother and his Auntie Kim. He also saw his Auntie Ebony and his Uncle Lester on a near-daily basis. Though Martina had been divorced from De'Jaun's father since De'Jaun was a baby, his father was a steady, loving presence in the boy's life, and Martina's boyfriend Trevor had known De'Jaun since he was a toddler.

But it was Troy who filled the role of father figure to De'Jaun. "De'Jaun, come over here, I want to talk to you," Troy said to his nephew on the first visit after De'Jaun had turned thirteen. Uncle and nephew went to the corner of the narrow visitation room and began talking in low voices. Snatches of their conversation floated over to Martina: *Now, you know, your body's gonna be changing, there's gonna be hormones hitting your body*   Martina glanced at her son. De'Jaun was nodding, grinning from time to time. He didn't seem to be self-conscious or blushing. Troy's posture was relaxed and his tone of voice matter-of-fact. He was making it comfortable for De'Jaun.

"This is what happened to me as a young boy growing up. It happens to all young men. Women, they go through things, and us guys, we go through things."

It was Troy who taught De'Jaun about respect for women, reiterating to him frequently, "Remember to always say 'yes, ma'am' and 'no, ma'am' and be respectful at all times to your mother, grandmother, and aunties, you hear me? You're the man of the house—so it's your job to watch out for the ladies."

It was with Troy that De'Jaun discussed his life goals and evolving plans: at the age of nine, to be a doctor so he could cure his mother's cancer; a few years later, to be a robotics engineer—still focusing on a cure for cancer. De'Jaun went to Troy for advice about difficult situations at school, whether it was how to handle drug dealers who hung around the school perimeter or what to do about gangbangers or bullies.

Troy called De'Jaun one Wednesday evening. "How'd your math test go today?"

"How did you know I had a math test today?"

"Boy, I have a calendar here with all your test dates marked down on it. Now—how'd it go?"

Troy often spent hours on the phone helping his nephew struggle through laborious assignments of fractions and long division. When Troy's phone time was used up, De'Jaun sometimes received a call from Jo-Jo or another guy on the row, who would call at Troy's request to make sure his nephew was keeping up with his schoolwork.

"You know, you're a younger version of me," Troy commented to De'Jaun one Saturday.

De'Jaun was feeling sullen. "No, I'm not."

"Yeah, you really are. This is what you're going through right now." Troy laid out to De'Jaun exactly what had been on the boy's mind.

De'Jaun looked at his uncle suspiciously.

"How do you know? Did Mom say something?"

"No. I just know."

De'Jaun grew to like it when family members and close family friends referred to him as "Mini-Troy"; Martina was delighted to see her teenage son develop qualities so like her brother's. Troy was always concerned about other people, and De'Jaun consciously tried to emulate him.

"Troy's worrying more about everyone else than about himself," De'Jaun observed aloud to Martina in the lead-up to the second execution date.

✦ ✦ ✦

September 12, 2008

Martina, Lester, and Virginia made their way inside the Sloppy Floyd building in Atlanta for Troy's second clemency hearing, this one eleven days before the execution date, pausing to say a few words of gratitude to those who were gathered in a circle outside the building for a prayer vigil. The world was watching Georgia.

Martina was cautiously optimistic as she took her seat in front of a row of supporters. At last year's hearing, the board had stated that "members of the Georgia Board of Pardons and Paroles will not allow an execution to proceed in this State unless and until its members are convinced that there is no doubt as to the guilt of the accused." There was even more evidence of Troy's innocence this time around.

"The task before you is critical," Jay began the hearing, thanking the board for taking the case so seriously. "This board is the final failsafe in Georgia's legal system." The parole board could exercise far more discretion than could the Georgia Supreme Court, bound as the court was by legal precedent and procedure. "The system that reviewed Troy's case involved human beings and is therefore fallible," Jay said.

April Hester, who had been seventeen years old the night of the murder, testified first. April had cohosted the pool party at her cousin's house in Cloverdale, though she herself lived in Yamacraw. She had seen Redd Coles at the pool party, drunk and trying to start a fight, she told the board.

Martina understood how significant this information was. At trial, a ballistics expert had testified that the bullet recovered from the jaw of Michael Cooper and the bullet recovered from MacPhail's body were possibly shot from the same gun and that shell casings found near both crime scenes also matched each other. The prosecution had contended that this evidence linked the two shootings and that Troy was the only one who had been at both crime scenes, so therefore Troy must have been the perpetrator in both shootings. But April was now stating that Coles had also attended the Cloverdale pool party.

April hadn't known that Michael Cooper had been shot, she testified, but soon after the party was over, her friend Sherman Coleman was shot in the leg outside the house in a drive-by. April and her cousin immediately called an ambulance for Sherman and then called the police.

When the police arrived, April heard over their walkie-talkies that an officer was down, so after the police left, April and her cousin headed to the bus station to check out what had happened. Police officers were swarming and flashing lights were everywhere around the parking lot.

As she walked from the parking lot to her house in Yamacraw, April saw Tonya Johnson talking to Redd Coles, who was sweating profusely and fidgeting with his hands.

"Walk with me up to the Burger King so they won't think that I had nothing to do with it," Redd said to April.

April was scared of Redd, who lived across the street from her and had a reputation for toting a gun and was always drinking, acting crazy, starting fights, and beating up people. She did as he said until her mother saw her and called her over.

Before she departed, Redd shot April a glare that she understood to mean: *You better not tell anybody what I said.*

April did her best to keep away from Redd after that night, but she could not avoid bumping into him from time to time in Yamacraw. Whenever she did, he glared at her, and her fear kept her silent.

In 1995, April had given a partial statement to Troy's lawyers, informing them that she had seen Redd at the Cloverdale party. But it was only many years later that she told Troy's attorneys all that had transpired. At that point, she was no longer frightened of Redd hurting her.

Joseph "Papa" Blige testified next. In 1989, sixteen-year-old "Papa" also lived in Yamacraw, near Redd Coles, whom he knew as someone who frequently got drunk and became violent. Papa didn't know Troy at that time.

Papa had gone to the Cloverdale pool party with four friends: Michael Cooper, Mark Wilds, Ben Gordon, and Lamar Brown. Papa also saw Redd Coles at the party; every time Papa went to get a drink, Redd was there. There were nearly fifty people at the party.

When Papa and his friends were ready to leave the party, they got into their car and began to drive away. Suddenly, shots rang out, at least six. Papa heard more than one weapon being fired, but couldn't identify the shooter, or shooters. It wasn't a surprise to Papa that someone at the pool party had a weapon. Most of the guys he knew from Yamacraw carried at least one, if not multiple, guns.

Michael Cooper, who had been hanging out the window yelling something, took a bullet in his jaw. The boys immediately drove Michael to the hospital, where they spoke to police. A sergeant took a bullet from behind the paneling in the door of the car and examined the different-sized bullet holes in the car. The boys left the hospital and went directly to a stash house in Yamacraw, grabbing an assortment of weapons—9mm, shotguns, handguns, revolvers—including a .38 special. They returned to Cloverdale, slowing down as they passed the pool party, and fired their guns out of the car window in a random act of retaliation; Sherman Coleman was shot in the leg. Then Papa and his friends sped back to Yamacraw and parked on Fahm Street, very close to the Burger King parking lot. As Papa headed home, walking through the bank parking lot to Yamacraw, he ran into Redd Coles coming from a side street, but Redd didn't say much—he was out of breath.

The next morning, the projects were surrounded. Police dragged teenage Papa out of bed at dawn and down to the station. The dozen or so officers coming and going didn't ask him about either Cloverdale shooting during the four-hour interrogation; their focus was entirely on Officer MacPhail. First they accused Papa of shooting the officer, threatening to throw him in jail. Then they said it had been Ben Gordon, then Lamar, trying to get Papa to name anybody at all.

"You kill one of ours," one officer threatened, going so far as to pull out a gun, "we'll kill one of you." Papa was scared, but he had no information to give about the MacPhail shooting, and they never asked him anything about the shootings of Michael Cooper or Sherman Coleman. Papa did not testify at Troy's trial, but his name was invoked many times—as a passenger in the car with Michael Cooper and in the testimony of Redd Coles's sister, who stated that Papa had come by her house shortly after MacPhail was shot and exchanged angry words with Redd.

Joseph Blige left the stand as Jay and his colleague Danielle pulled together a few threads: at trial, a ballistics expert had testified that the bullets recovered from MacPhail and Cooper were possibly from the same gun, but in 2007 a new Georgia Bureau of Investigation report revealed that the bullets failed to reveal "sufficient characteristics" to determine that they "were fired from the same firearm."

Matching shell casings had been recovered close to the sites of the Cloverdale and MacPhail shootings, but as Papa had testified, there had been multiple people firing a number of weapons that night. It was impossible to know which gun the recovered shell casings had come from. Perhaps the shell recovered in the bank parking lot near the MacPhail shooting had been dropped by one of the teenagers who drove to that precise area after shooting Sherman Coleman in Cloverdale.

There was absolutely no evidence connecting Troy to the Michael Cooper shooting, Jay concluded. In fact, there was not a whole lot of evidence about who shot Michael Cooper at all. Yet it was known that Redd Coles had a .38 special revolver on him that night, and there were now multiple witnesses placing Redd at the Cloverdale pool party.

Martina watched the board members carefully to see if she could discern any reaction as Jay and Danielle next laid out the reasons why the photo lineup used during the police investigation had been so problematic. On the night of August 19, Redd Coles had walked into the police station and pointed the finger at Troy Davis. Based on Redd's implication, Detective Ramsey then created a five-photo lineup with Troy's photo as one of the five. Redd's photo, significantly, was not included in the lineup, nor were photos of anyone else who was known to be at the site of the murder. Witnesses may have picked Troy's photo as a process of elimination; out of those who had been in the parking lot that night, Troy's was the only photo presented. But the flaws in the lineup ran even deeper.

On August 21, the Savannah paper's headlines announced that police were pushing the hunt for the killer, displaying the same photo of Troy that Ramsey had included in the lineup. On August 22, wanted posters went up around town, again using the same photo.

On August 23, footage of Troy turning himself into the police was broadcast on every Savannah television station.

Witnesses were shown the photo lineup only after they had already seen Troy's image splashed across the newspaper, television, and wanted posters, tainting their memories. In addition, there was the problem of witness initials on the photos. Most witnesses had been asked to initial the back of the photograph of the man they identified as the shooter. Witnesses who flipped over Troy's photograph would have seen initials already scribbled on the back, offering them instant validation. This was not only leading but misleading. D.D. Collins and Redd Coles, the only eyewitnesses who had known Troy previously, had been asked to initial Troy's photograph as a means to merely certify that this photograph was, indeed, Troy Davis. Other witnesses may have seen D.D.'s and Redd's initials on the back and assumed that their initials were there because they had identified Troy as the shooter.

Martina breathed with relief as she saw Dorothy Ferrell make her way to the stand. Dorothy had agreed to testify at the 2007 clemency hearing but had not shown up at the airport for her flight from Savannah to Atlanta. This time Dorothy, a short, heavy-set woman who was respectably dressed, took the stand and, in a quiet voice, told her story to the parole board.

The night of the murder, Dorothy had been homeless. Grace House shelter was full, so they had given her a voucher to stay at the Thunderbird Inn across the street from the bus station. Dorothy's room was on the second floor. She heard a woman screaming when she was in her room, so she came out and began to walk down the stairs. She had heard the gunshots as she was coming down the stairwell, she told the parole board, and she had seen three guys running away from the parking lot, but she had not witnessed the actual shooting.

The police had taken Dorothy to the station to make a statement. At the time, she was pregnant and tired and it seemed as if they wanted her to say she saw the shooting, so that's what she said, thinking that would be the end of it. Then a police detective started coming by her mother's place looking for her. He told her mother that if Dorothy didn't get in touch with him, he would put a warrant out for her arrest. Dorothy, who had previously been locked up for shoplifting and had just gotten out on parole, called the detective, who met her the very next morning. The detective showed her Troy's picture and Troy's picture only. Other witnesses had already identified Troy Davis as the shooter, he told her, giving her the impression that she should follow the others and say that he was the shooter, so she did. Dorothy was afraid that if she did not cooperate, the officer would find a way to have her locked up again.

At the preliminary hearing in September 1989, Dorothy testified, she had waited in the conference room with the other witnesses, including Redd Coles. She told Spencer Lawton that she thought the man she saw running away from the Burger King parking lot might be Coles—the complexion of the man was closer to Redd's than to Troy's—but Lawton told her not to change up on him.

Before Troy's trial, Dorothy sought the advice of two attorneys who had represented her previously. The attorneys told her that if her in-court testimony differed from her sworn statements, she could serve up to ten years for perjury. Dorothy did not want to return to jail, so, when asked if she could identify the shooter in the courtroom, she reluctantly pointed to Troy.

The night following Dorothy's trial testimony, the wife of Bob Barker, one of Troy's attorneys, received a phone call from a woman identifying herself as Dorothy Ferrell. The caller said that someone from the DA's office had come to her the previous year and offered to help her with her legal problems if she assisted in the Davis case. The caller said further that everything she had testified to was a lie. Dorothy was called back into court and testified about the call, without the jury or Troy present in the courtroom. Dorothy denied making the call.

But now, in front of the parole board, Dorothy Ferrell shed more light on that phone call. Dorothy had told her friend that she had lied on the stand and was feeling badly about it because she may have identified the wrong person, and that she didn't know what to do. Unbeknownst to Dorothy then (though she would find out later), the friend, pretending to be Dorothy, had taken it upon herself to inform Troy's attorneys.

Jay and Danielle summarized. The police, under pressure to solve the crime, had developed tunnel vision on Troy from the moment Coles gave them his name. The five-day media blitz left the police with no choice but to stick with Troy as their suspect. They never conducted a search for Coles's .38. Neither Coles nor anyone else at the scene of the crime were included in the photo lineup. But now, the recantations and new affidavits eviscerated the state's case. Four of the jurors who had found Troy guilty at trial and sentenced him to death were now having serious doubts. Not only was innocent life at stake but also the credibility of Georgia's system of justice.

Martina could not help but notice how exhausted Jay looked as he packed up his papers to prepare to leave the hearing room, making way for the prosecution's team. She knew Jay had been up nearly all night preparing for the hearing. The strain of the day had drained her as well, yet Martina felt hopeful as she left the Sloppy Floyd building and returned to her room at the Georgian Terrace. Media coverage of the hearing played in the background as Martina ploughed through her emails, until one particular statement from a member of the MacPhail family made after the hearing caused her to sit up straight. The statement referred to DNA evidence. DNA evidence? There was no DNA evidence in Troy's case! Martina called Jay to ask what the MacPhail family member could possibly be talking about.

"I have no idea," Jay answered in a tight voice. No one from Troy's legal team or family had been able to sit in on the prosecution's half of the clemency hearing, and there would be no record—written or otherwise—of the proceedings. "But you can be sure that I'm going to find out."

✦ ✦ ✦

2004

Martina and Troy had been writing to law firm after law firm for years, asking if they would represent Troy pro bono. They appreciated the Georgia Resource Center attorneys and investigators, who had been energetically pursuing leads and uncovering exculpatory evidence ever since the nonprofit had been able to reconstitute itself, but there was no way to undo the damage from those critical years when the Resource Center had been gutted and almost nothing had been done on Troy's case.

The final straw had come during a conversation with one of Troy's attorneys. The attorney had said that he believed that Troy was innocent, but that Troy was a black man accused of killing a white police officer in Georgia. "In the South, any black man will do," the attorney had concluded. Martina knew the lawyer had been referring to the attitude of the state and not the attitude of the nonprofit, but she was horrified by the statement nonetheless. It was time to look for new representation.

One night, as Martina had been checking her email, Court TV was on in the background. Suddenly, she heard an attorney discussing her involvement in the Roger Coleman case. Martina snapped to attention. Coleman, a coal miner from Virginia, had been executed for killing his sister-in-law, despite controversy as to his guilt. The attorney, Kathleen Behan, was an associate at a DC corporate law firm and had taken on Coleman's case pro bono, working tirelessly to prevent his execution. Behan sounded knowledgeable, passionate, and committed. Martina jotted down the name of the firm: Arnold & Porter.

The next day, Martina tracked down Kathleen Behan's email address and wrote Behan a brief explanation of who she was and what she was asking. A few days later, Martina received a reply from Kitty Behan instructing her to write a letter, in one thousand words or less, as to why she should take Troy's case. Martina complied immediately and waited to hear back. A week later, Kitty got in touch. She was going to be in Georgia the following week. Could she go visit Troy?

Despite the short notice, Troy was able to get the visitation request approved, and Martina and Kitty agreed to meet at the prison. Martina arrived at the appointed time and waited in her car. An hour passed, and then two. Had Kitty decided not to come? Just as Martina was about to give up, a little Hugo driven by a slender blond woman pulled into the parking area. The woman got out and surveyed the guard tower and the barbed wire.

Martina got out of her car.

"Kitty Behan?"

"Yes, you must be Martina!" Kitty strode to Martina with an outstretched arm. "I'm so sorry to be late, I had a problem renting a car at the airport."

"Troy's waiting for you," Martina said. "I don't have permission to enter for attorney visits, but it should be all set for you to go on in and talk to Troy."

"I'll only be in with him half an hour or so," Kitty said, taking her ID and locking her purse in the car. "I'll talk to you afterwards."

"That's fine. I'll wait at the Wendy's at the truck stop across the street."

Martina waited at the truck stop for more than two hours before Kitty Behan joined her.

"I'm starving," was Kitty's only comment before placing an order at the counter for a hamburger and french fries.

She set her tray on the table and took a seat across from Martina, silently dipping fry after fry in ketchup and eating. *What's wrong with this chick?* Martina wondered, her impatience growing.

Finally, Kitty spoke. "He doesn't deserve to be there." She would go back to Arnold & Porter, she said, and strongly recommend that she take on his case pro bono. The next month, Martina received a letter from Arnold & Porter. From that point on, they would represent Troy. Maybe, just maybe, the tide was turning. Maybe God was going to answer their prayers.

Jay Ewart, a new associate fresh out of Emory Law School, had joined Kitty's team early on. When Kitty left Arnold & Porter, Jay became lead counsel for Troy. After the number of attorneys who had come and gone from his case, how could Troy truly trust that Jay Ewart intended to stick by him and his family? It didn't boost Troy's confidence that Jay was completely green. Yet Troy was grateful to Arnold & Porter for taking on his case and knew he had to give the young attorney a chance.

Jay had no experience dealing with capital litigation, but he was smart enough to turn for expertise to those who knew more than him; specifically, to the Georgia Resource Center, where executive director Tom Dunn and his colleagues continued to stay closely involved with Troy's case, guiding and advising Jay every step of the way.

Troy called Jay on a weekly basis, asking Jay about his family and relaying every detail of De'Jaun's achievements, adding Kiersten's antics to the updates once Ebony's baby girl was born, before turning their attention to the case. Whenever there were updates on his case, whether positive or negative, Jay got in contact with Troy immediately. It was Jay's job to get him out of there, Troy reminded him on each phone call, and to save his life. "You don't make it easy for a guy to kick off work early and go grab a beer," Jay would retort. One of the first things he would do when free, Troy would answer, would be to teach Jay, a white boy from rural Illinois, how to dance.

✦ ✦ ✦

Summer 2006

De'Jaun's dog Egypt did not run to the gate to greet Martina as usual, nor did she respond when Martina called her. Where was that dog?

They had gotten the boxer puppy six years ago, when De'Jaun was six, and he had chosen the name because he said her fur was the color of the sands of the Egyptian desert. That dog was De'Jaun's heart. Martina used to look out the window and watch Egypt and De'Jaun chasing each other back and forth in the yard; one minute, De'Jaun jumping on top of Egypt, the next moment Egypt jumping on top of De'Jaun.

Martina finally spotted Egypt's legs sticking out behind the hedges, and ran to her side. Egypt, covered in blood and dirt, turned her head to look at Martina, her warm brown eyes pleading for help.

"Oh, sweetheart, what on earth happened to you?"

Egypt struggled to her feet when she heard Martina's voice, limped a few steps dragging one leg behind her, and lay down again.

It looked like Egypt had been hit by a car, the vet told Martina and De'Jaun after examining X-rays. Her leg was broken in three places.

"She needs surgery," the vet said. "She'll need pins in her legs, and she'll need to undergo physical therapy. . . . I think we're talking about something upwards of $10,000. Otherwise, you'll have to put her to sleep."

Martina nearly choked. Where was she going to get $10,000?

"I can keep her comfortable for the night. Why don't you get back to me in the morning?" the vet said.

Martina and De'Jaun got in the car to drive home. How could she possibly come up with $10,000? Who had that kind of money lying around? She turned into her subdivision, mind still reeling, trying not to let De'Jaun see how upset she was.

De'Jaun, who had been silent the entire ride, finally spoke. "Mom, are you going to put my dog to sleep like they're trying to put Uncle Troy to sleep?"

Martina turned sharply to look at her son and found De'Jaun staring at her steadily, his eyes filled with tears that had not yet been released. She battled to hold back her own. All that agonizing about how and when to tell him, and De'-Jaun already knew. Not only was he aware that the state was trying to kill his uncle but he also understood about lethal injection—that the method Georgia planned to use to kill his uncle was the same method used to put down a dog.

"I promise you, De'Jaun. Egypt is going to be just fine."

Martina would pawn her car if she had to or take a second mortgage on her home, but she could not put Egypt to sleep. She was not going to further traumatize her child.

The next morning, Martina found a vet able to treat Egypt for a much more reasonable sum. The surgery went smoothly and, after a month of physical therapy, they were able to bring Egypt home. Soft fuzz grew over Egypt's long scar, soon replaced by thicker fur. Eventually, the scar could scarcely be seen. Martina was more worried about the invisible scars that her child might be carrying.

Martina and Troy decided together to talk openly to De'Jaun about what it meant that Troy was on death row. They wanted De'Jaun to feel free to express whatever anxiety he might be experiencing. But he didn't seem to exhibit much stress, at least not in ways that were apparent to Martina. Until the execution dates began.

✦ ✦ ✦

September 12, 2008

Martina was more numb than shocked as she read the parole board's statement: "After an exhaustive review of all available information regarding the Troy Davis case and after considering all possible reasons for granting clemency, the board has determined that clemency is not warranted."

What had happened behind those closed doors with the prosecution? Had the board held any real deliberation, or were they just trying to protect their system, as the courts did? Was this decision the result of a back-door deal with the prosecutor? And to what could the MacPhail family member's statement about DNA, made after the parole board hearing, possibly refer?

"This case illustrates the deep flaws in the application of the death penalty in this country," former US president Jimmy Carter wrote, calling on the board to reconsider its decision. "Executing Troy Davis without a real examination of potentially exonerating evidence risks taking the life of an innocent man and would be a grave miscarriage of justice." Amnesty issued an appeal for the board to reverse its decision and organized a demonstration in which three hundred people marched from Woodruff Park in downtown Atlanta to Ebenezer Baptist Church, where Martin Luther King Jr. once preached. But the board refused to reconsider and the Georgia Supreme Court would not grant a stay of execution.

Two days before the scheduled September 23 execution, Troy was moved, for the second time, to a holding cell in the death house, where two corrections officers monitored him around the clock. Martina's cellphone rang at 2 a.m. the following morning, pulling her from the anxiety-ridden sleep she had been drifting in and out of.

"Hello?" she answered groggily.

"I just want you to know that Troy is doing okay," the caller said in a hushed voice. "We're making sure he's warm and that he has food. We're taking turns praying with him."

The guard could not talk for long and would not reveal his identity.

Martina hung up and fell into her first real sleep since the parole board had announced its decision. Even on the inside of that horrible place, there were people looking out for Troy.

✧

September 23, 2008

Martina stared in disbelief as she drove past the officers with automatic weapons and police dogs stationed every hundred yards down the long driveway. She had never before seen the prison so militarized.

"God stopped the first execution, and if God can do that once, He can do it again," De'Jaun said to Martina with confidence as they took their IDs and locked everything else in the car. She knew that De'Jaun was resolved to be strong because Troy had told him to be strong—De'Jaun would never want to let his uncle down.

Motivational posters lined the tunnel that connected the entrance of the prison to the visitation area. Martina bitterly noted the irony of seeing images of rock climbers, an eagle soaring over clouds, an array of hands of all pigmentation on a basketball, each with an inspirational one-word message—*LEADERSHIP, OPPORTUNITY, ACHIEVEMENT, FOCUS, TEAMWORK*—as she walked through the tunnel to reach her brother in order to say goodbye before the state killed him.

The visitation room was crowded with the family and friends whom Troy had put on his list of those to visit and say goodbye. Looking at the sorrow in everyone's faces, Martina knew that she needed to focus on something concrete or she would break down. She stationed herself by the door of the small visitation room, where eight visitors were permitted with Troy at one time, and shepherded people in and out, making sure that everyone got equal time.

As Martina took charge of the logistics, Troy took on the role of caretaker.

"How you doing?" he greeted each new group of family and friends that Martina sent in for their rotation. "You all right?" Troy tried to reassure friends who were upset or uncomfortable. "It's going to work out," he said. "And even if it doesn't work out, I'm going to a better place. I don't want you to cry. I need you all to be strong for me, and I'll be strong for you."

Troy cracked jokes to make everyone, especially De'Jaun, laugh. He talked about the first foods he would eat when he could enjoy Mama's cooking once more.

There was other, unsavory business that Martina had to tend to. Troy had to give the warden the names of the five people he wanted to be with him during the execution. Martina wanted to be one of them, so that Troy would feel her love and support during those final moments, but the Georgia Department of Corrections would not permit a prisoner's family to witness his execution. Instead, Martina consulted back and forth with Troy and his friends in the waiting area. Jay, Troy's lawyer, would be one witness. Filmmaker Terry Benedict, who was making a documentary about Troy, would be another. Sue Gunawardena-Vaughn, AIUSA's death penalty abolition campaign director, would be a third, and Wende Gozan Brown would be her alternate. Troy had asked Reverend Al Sharpton, as his spiritual advisor, to be there as well.

Just when Martina thought that was settled, word came from a prison official that the warden would not confirm whether Troy's witnesses were approved or whether Troy would be permitted to have anyone with him at all—it seemed the warden wanted more seats for the press and the MacPhail family. It was unclear if even Jay would be granted approval.

A hot flash of anger and frustration rose within Martina. Troy might not be allowed anyone with whom he could make eye contact or who could provide him with any sort of comfort in the execution chamber? This was just too much to bear. Martina exited the visitation room quickly so that she would be out of Troy's sight before tears erupted violently.

Wende and Gemma Puglisi, the family's dear friend, were at Martina's heels as she pushed her way into the ladies' room.

"Can we get you anything?" Gemma asked helplessly.

"Why are they doing this to my brother?" Martina sobbed.

Gemma put her arms around Martina, but Martina could not afford to accept comfort or she risked collapsing entirely. She grabbed a paper towel, wiped her eyes, and walked briskly back into the waiting room. She was done with her crying.

Prison staff walked through the waiting room. Martina wondered which guard had called her in the middle of the night to reassure her that Troy was okay. Perhaps it was the one staring mournfully at Mama, who was fervently praying in the waiting room.

A nurse strode crisply across the waiting room. Would she be preparing the execution IV? The nurse disappeared behind the second sets of yellow gates into the guts of the prison.

Martina tried to keep watch on De'Jaun without his knowing. She was grateful that there were so many people to distract and care for him.

"You ever see the quarter trick on *Happy Days?*" Wende asked De'Jaun and Valerie's son, Elijah, holding up a quarter.

De'Jaun and Elijah shook their heads no—they hadn't even heard of *Happy Days*. Wende balanced a stack of quarters on the top of her bent elbow and then snapped her arm straight, catching the quarters in her hand.

"Cool! I wanna try!"

Martina smiled as De'Jaun and Elijah chased bouncing quarters all over the waiting room. Trust Wende to turn vending machine quarters into a source of entertainment for the kids.

At 2:00 p.m., the mood turned somber. In another hour, visitation would be over. Martina set her jaw tightly and organized the final rotation, making sure everyone got a turn to pray with Troy. Troy held hands in a circle with each small group and led the prayers.

"Are you okay? Do you need anything?" friends asked Martina as they left the visitation room, many of them in tears. What Martina needed was for the state of Georgia not to kill her brother.

Troy spent the final minutes alone with his family, taking each family member to the side of the small room one by one for a private moment. Troy faced De'Jaun, both sitting in plastic chairs, looking so much like they had when Troy had explained the birds and bees to De'Jaun not long ago.

"I still have faith that it's going to work out, but if it doesn't, you and Lester will be the men of the family. Take care of the family. Do what you've got to do for your mom, and make sure you respect your grandmother and your aunties. I want you to continue to do good in school, and pick the right friends. Choose a profession that you love. You have to be my legacy, De'Jaun. You tell my story, so people know about this injustice. You do that and my life will not be in vain."

Troy told Mama and Aunt Mattie to continue to be the foundation for all the family and to keep praying. He handed Virginia a package containing his personal items: letters, photos, his list of contacts.

"I'll see you again. Don't cry, Mama. Hold your head up."

Virginia held her son's face tightly. "God will never leave you alone."

Martina had only a few moments alone with Troy.

"I've found peace with God," he said, hands on her shoulders and looking straight into her eyes. "Maybe they can take my physical form. But that's all they can take, because they can't take my spirit and they can't take my faithfulness. I know that my case has impacted people around the world. No matter what happens, Tina, I want you to continue to fight."

"Time is up," a guard announced.

The guards herded everyone toward the exit.

"Oh, Jesus. Oh, Jesus," Virginia repeated softly, Gemma holding onto her arm to keep her steady as she walked through the double yellow gates.

Just as they reached the top of the stairs, Mama crumpled under Gemma's hand and collapsed onto the floor.

Ebony and Lester helped Mama get back to her feet, as the guards returned Troy to the death house. Troy had had to prepare himself for the executions of twenty-nine of his fellow inmates over the past seventeen years. Now the prison would "prepare him" for his own, less than four hours away.

✦ ✦ ✦

December 1993

Troy had never intended to make friends on death row, but there was something disarming about Chris Burger. Chris was tall, trim, strong, and gave off a tough demeanor, but he showed warmth and affection to his friends. He sketched beautifully with colored pencils, often sending his drawings to his mother, to whom he was devoted. He was older than Troy by more than ten years, but there was something vulnerable and childlike about him, perhaps stemming from his history of severe childhood abuse. Chris had been only seventeen years old when he had participated in the murder of Roger Honeycutt. When his execution date was set for December 7, 1993, he confessed to Troy how frightened he was.

Troy saw the guards parading Chris sadistically in front of the other death row inmates on the evening of December 7 before leading him to the execution chamber to strap him into the electric chair. Troy sat in his cell, hunched over on his bed, waiting for the horrifying moment when the lights would flicker, indicating that a high-voltage current of electricity was coursing through Chris's body.

Every man on the row twitched in silent agony when the flickering began at 9:50 p.m. Troy knelt on the hard floor, gripping the steel frame of his bed tightly, and prayed for his friend. Only later did he learn that Chris Burger's last words had been an apology to everyone he had ever hurt and a plea for forgiveness. One of the guards who had paraded Chris leaned against the bars of Troy's cell. "Hey, Davis!" Troy heard the guard say.

Troy looked up.

"Yeah?"

"How'd you like some fries to go with your Burger?"

Troy resolved never to become quite so close to anyone else on death row again.

✧

Martina never saw monsters or murderers when she met Troy's fellow inmates. Martina saw individuals who had been addicted to drugs or who were uneducated—more than half of Georgia's death row inmates never finished high school and several had IQs that indicated mild retardation or borderline intellectual functioning. She saw men who came from extremely damaged families; who got in with the wrong crowd; who were very, very poor. She saw some who had repented and were now trying to do the right thing. She saw human beings who had never been given a fair shot at life, much less in the legal system. Troy was not the only one facing injustice.

Martina knew that she only saw the lucky ones when she visited Troy—those out of the one hundred–odd prisoners on Georgia's death row who received visitors. Prisoners without connection to family or friends never made it to the visitation room.

De'Jaun was greeted by a chorus of high-fives and pats on the head from an extended family of uncles every time he walked through the double set of yellow gates into Georgia's Diagnostic and Classification Prison.

"Hey, De'Jaun, how you doing, buddy?"

"What's up man?"

"How you doing, Jo-Jo?" De'Jaun would reply, basking in the attention. "What's up, Speedy?"

One inmate helped De'Jaun with his karate stance. Another taught him a few words of Spanish. "De'Jaun is getting so big!" they'd all say to Martina, shaking their heads at how fast time was passing. If Martina ever dared to show up without her beloved child, she'd be chastised by inmates and guards alike the entire visit.

"Where's De'Jaun?"

"Why didn't you bring your son?"

Jack Potts in particular was very taken with De'Jaun. "How you doing in school?" he asked the boy every Saturday. "You still making good grades?"

Jack had hepatitis and cancer of the nose. A piece of Jack's nose was missing and the bones of his cheeks protruded sharply. As a small child De'Jaun had liked to touch Jack's face, his fingers exploring the dents and crevices. Jack got a kick out of it.

De'Jaun sent his report card to Troy every term, and Troy would reward every A with a small monetary gift.

"Send me a copy of your report card, too," Jack told De'Jaun when he was in third grade. "I'll give you $100 for each A."

"You don't know what you're getting into, Jack," Troy warned him jocularly. "My nephew makes straight As—he's been cheating me out of my money for years! I never would have made my deal with him if I knew how smart he was!"

"I get a military pension, I can afford it," was Jack's response.

The week after sending Troy and Jack his report card, eight-year-old De'Jaun received a money order in the mail for $500.

That Saturday, Martina took Jack aside. "You can't send him $100 for every A or you'll be broke!"

The next report card, Jack sent De'Jaun $25 for each A.

Much to De'Jaun's disappointment, Martina asked Jack to stop sending her son money. It was one thing for Troy to challenge De'Jaun like that. She didn't want other inmates to use their scarce resources to reward her son.

"So, have you received any letters or phone calls from nuns in Sussex, England?" Jack asked Martina on one of her first visits with Troy after her cancer diagnosis. She had, in fact. The nuns had told her they were praying for her for thirty days and thirty nights, though she had had no idea who they were or how they knew she was gravely ill. Jack's grin cleared up the mystery. He had been in contact with the nuns for years and had asked them to pray on Martina's behalf.

As Jack's cancer spread, dementia set in.

"Hey, Jack, how you doing?" Martina would ask him each Saturday.

"Hey," Jack would reply vaguely, leaving Martina uncertain if he knew who she was. But when Jack saw De'Jaun, his face lit up and his eyes showed clear signs of recognition. "De'Jaun! Buddy! How's school going?"

Martina had never known Jack as the healthy young man with strawberry-blond hair who gazed back at her from the photograph the *Atlanta Journal-Constitution* ran on September 8, 2005, the day after he passed away. Martina lingered for a few moments on the photo before reading the headline: "Convicted Murderer Jack H. Potts Escaped the Death Penalty by Dying of Natural Causes." Martina tossed the paper aside in disgust. The man had been on death row since 1976 and the media had the temerity to suggest that Jack had escaped punishment by dying of cancer before the state had been able to kill him.

✧

Once or twice, Martina made the mistake of taking De'Jaun to visit Troy the weekend before someone faced an execution date. There the condemned prisoner would be, perhaps an individual her son was attached to, joking around with the boy in visitation. Three or four days later, the man would be dead.

Martina no longer took De'Jaun to vigils on execution nights either.

"Mom, it's seven o'clock," he would tug at her arm during the vigil. "Does that mean Curtis is dead now?"

It was horrible for De'Jaun. It was awful for Martina as well.

Jose Martinez High's execution was scheduled for Tuesday, November 6, 2001, making him the second prisoner in Georgia to be executed by lethal injection. Martina saw Jose the previous Saturday when visiting Troy. What could she say to him? That she was praying for him? That she hoped they didn't execute him? What words could she possibly utter to Jose?

A card awaited Martina in her P. O. box on Thursday, November 8. It was from Jose, postmarked the day of his execution. *Be strong,* Jose had written, *and take care of your health. Keep up the fight.* He wanted to thank her for the work she was doing. He wanted her to know that it was not in vain. *When you fight for Troy, you fight for all of us on the row,* the card said.

A photo fell out of the envelope and Martina bent down to pick it up. She examined the image of a good-looking youth in a prison uniform with light brown skin, playful smile, and wide-set eyes. The kid looked a lot like Jose—had he a son who was also in jail? Martina flipped the photo over and saw Jose High written on the back. The photo must have been taken years ago, just after Jose's incarceration. Death row, Jose had scratched underneath his name. 22 years, 11 months, 5 days, 7 hours. The date and scheduled time of his execution was penciled just below.

Martina stared at the back of Jose's photo, unable to move.

✦ ✦ ✦

September 23, 2008, 3:30 p.m.

Martina stood rooted to the ground, trying to grasp what she saw as the family got into their cars to leave the prison grounds. Was that actually a hearse, waiting to carry her brother? She thought about those advocating for Troy's execution. Could they not understand how hurtful this was?

It was too early to stand vigil in the prison yard. The family went to wait at New Hope House, founded by a group of ecumenical churches to provide support for families of those on Georgia's death row. New Hope House was only minutes from the prison, but it felt a world away. The wood-framed house was surrounded by fifteen acres of woods on an unpaved, rutted rural road. Martina breathed in the comforting, farm-like scent of bare wood, old furniture, and open kitchen as the family gathered on folding chairs on the screened-in porch.

Martina's cell phone rang. It was Laura Moye, calling to update her about actions that had taken place that day in Atlanta. At 2 p.m., a dozen protestors wearing white T-shirts on which they had written, "Don't Murder in My Name. Save Troy!" had silently approached the entrance of the Sloppy Floyd building and dropped to the ground in a dramatic "die-in." There they had stayed, sprawled out in front of the sliding doors, until police, who seemed stunned by their action and did not know how to respond, asked them to leave. Media captured the action as well. The effect, they decided, had been powerful. Spontaneously, the activists went to die in in front of the capitol as well.

GFADP, SCHR, and the Georgia State Conference of the NAACP had appealed to all those involved in carrying out the execution—from the prison staff who would escort Troy into the execution chamber to the nurses who would prepare the IV lines—not to come to work. They focused especially on Dr. Carlo Musso, president of Rainbow Medical Associates, the organization contracted by the Georgia Department of Corrections to oversee executions for an estimated $18,000 per execution. "Remember your humanity! Your oath is to facilitate healing, not killing," the coalition had announced in its press release. A handful of activists had ratcheted up the action even further, holding protests outside Dr. Musso's home that morning. Now, folks were getting ready for a large demonstration on the capitol steps in Atlanta. "No one is prepared to stand back and let the system roll forward as usual," Laura told Martina. "Everyone knows that this is a righteous cause."

At 4:15 p.m., Martina and Mama began to head to the truck stop across the street from the prison. They were supposed to meet Reverend Al Sharpton from the National Action Network (NAN) there. The Department of Corrections had still not informed them of who from Troy's list would be permitted to witness the execution. The rest of the family would join them on the prison grounds shortly before the scheduled execution time—if things got that far. Martina looked around for De'Jaun before getting into the car with Wende. Friends were keeping him occupied. He would be okay.

Terry Benedict, Sue Gunawardena-Vaughn, pastor Randy Loney, photojournalist Scott Langley, and Jay were already at the truck stop when Wende, Martina, and Virginia arrived. The execution was scheduled to proceed in two and a half hours. "Any word from the US Supreme Court?" Martina asked Jay, who was checking his cell phone obsessively. Their last hope was that the court, which was not scheduled to consider the appeal on Troy's motion for a retrial until it went back in session, would order a stay of the execution, knowing that Georgia had jumped the gun. Jay shook his head mutely.

5 p.m. It was time to go to the prison grounds. Jay and Terry, who had finally learned that they were the only ones granted permission to witness, made their way inside the prison to await the execution while Martina, Virginia, Wende, and Scott got into the Reverend Sharpton's Suburban to drive across the street, passing the low brick wall that marked the entrance to Prison Boulevard. Martina counted more than a dozen olive-uniformed armed guards and watched policemen with fierce-looking German shepherds patrolling the perimeter. They were determined to show their force, it seemed to her, but in looking at them, Martina saw their fear.

Martina, Mama, Wende, and the Reverend Sharpton presented their IDs to guards who tied green ribbons around their wrists to identify them as protestors as Scott got out of the car to register with the media table just a few feet away. The young African American guard overseeing the journalists had a kind, somber face. He mumbled something inaudibly to Scott.

"What did you say?" Scott asked.

"I hope the truth comes out," Scott heard the guard repeat, averting his eyes.

After receiving their wristbands, they drove slowly over dirt and tree roots down a small incline, parking the SUV under trees outside the protest pen, on the very edge of the prison grounds.

Approximately fifty supporters were already in the pen, wearing cobalt-blue "I Am Troy Davis" T-shirts and carrying signs, some slickly printed, others handwritten in marker on posterboard: Free Troy Davis. No Evidence, No Execution. Troy Davis Is Innocent.

The chanting grew louder as Martina walked into the pen delineated with thick yellow rope.

"What do we want?" a young man called from the center of the pen.

"Justice!" the protestors responded in unison.

"When do we want it?"

"Now!"

Martina tried to suppress her bitterness at being roped off in a pen, surrounded by armed guards and police dogs. Instead, she surveyed those who had come to stand with her family in solidarity and protest. It was not so long ago that she had been a voice in the wilderness, hoping that someone, anyone, would start paying attention. Now there were six times the number of people who usually came out to protest an execution. Faces of every color were in the crowd: men and women; young and elderly; dear friends of Troy's and theirs; those who had never met Troy but believed in his innocence; those who believed that every execution was wrong and must be demonstrated against. The faces around her were proud but pained—or was Martina seeing a reflection of her own pain?

The chanting continued.

"No justice!" a NAN activist shouted.

"No peace!" the crowd shouted back.

Journalists and cameras thronged the opposite side of the yellow rope in their designated area as Wende "worked the rope" separating the media from those standing vigil in order to give quotes and updates to reporters. Another roped-off area lay beyond the media—this reserved for those supporting the execution. It was too far away and difficult to see, but Martina was almost certain she recognized some members of Georgia's Fraternal Order of Police.

There was only an hour and a half to go. Martina glanced toward the prison, far out of sight down the long driveway. The guards would be offering Troy a sedative right about now, which he would refuse. Martina had tried to remain prayerful throughout, but anxiety began to dig deeper. Was Troy actually going to be killed tonight? Whatever happened at 7 p.m., she would hold onto Troy's message to her from that afternoon: His life had had an impact on the world.

Suddenly, Wende materialized next to her, pulling on her elbow.

"Martina!" Martina turned to face her. Wende was glowing as she reached up to whisper in Martina's ear.

"We got a stay of execution!"

"What?" Martina was not sure she had heard right.

"From the Supreme Court. Danielle just told me. It's only for a week, but we got a stay!"

Martina grabbed Wende in a fierce hug. "Praise God!"

Reverend Sharpton notified the press that Amnesty International had something to say.

"I'm Wende Gozan from Amnesty International," Wende said to the ex pectant media. "We just got some news and I want to let Martina Correia make the announcement."

Martina worked to keep her voice calm and steady. "I would like to make the announcement that we just found out that my brother was granted a stay, at least for one week, until the court can review his case . . ."

Shouts and cheers from supporters erupted before Martina could finish the sentence. Arms were raised in jubilance.

"Hallelujah!" someone in the back of the crowd shouted in a voice choked with tears.

Reverend Sharpton wrapped Mama in a hug while an unknown woman in red embraced Martina. Another woman began to sob.

Virginia and Reverend Sharpton linked their inner arms, stretching their outside arms up and out in prayer.

"God is great! God takes care of everything!" Virginia was radiating relief.

Wende hugged Mama. Reverend Sharpton hugged Martina. The entire crowd continued hugging, clapping, and shouting out praise to God.

"Let us pray! Let us pray!" Reverend Sharpton called out.

Martina, Mama, Wende, and Reverend Sharpton gathered in a circle with Troy's supporters.

"Let us pray, dear God, we thank you . . ." Reverend Sharpton began.

"Thank you, Lord!" someone from the crowd interjected.

"Even at the brink of our worst fears, you told us if we would but trust you . . ."

"Yes, Lord!"

" . . . that you would make a way out of no way."

"Thank you!"

"All the way until even the last two hours, this mother and sister never doubted you and never turned back!"

"Yes!" Virginia nodded her head in strong confirmation. She had not doubted God.

"We ask you to bless them for their strength, we ask you to keep holding them up, and give comfort to the family of the policeman . . ."

"Yes Lord!"

"We feel their pain."

"Yes!"

"Let them know we're not here in any way to belittle their loss . . ."

"No, Lord!"

"We just don't want two wrongs to deal with the rights that was lost by their loved one."

Martina shook her head back and forth, absorbing Reverend Sharpton's prayer. Virginia swayed to the reverend's words, eyes closed, deep joy spread over her face.

An older black gentleman bowed low at the waist, his arm thrust upward as if in the Black Power salute, but with his hand open instead of fisted, palm up, in gratitude.

"How are you feeling?" a reporter asked Mama as the prayer concluded.

"I'm feeling good because I was praying to God, and I knew God wasn't going to leave him alone . . . God stepped up and showed up!" Virginia leaned forward with emphasis and shone with confidence.

"A one-week stay doesn't seem like a long time," Reverend Sharpton addressed the media and the crowd. "But if you have two hours to live, then one week . . ."

Mama finished his sentence: " . . . is a lifetime."

Danielle, tears in her eyes, pushed her cell phone into Martina's hand. "It's Troy—he hasn't heard yet."

"Troy!" Martina almost shouted into Danielle's phone. "The Supreme Court gave you a stay!"

There was a moment of silence while the information registered. Then, softly, "Thank God. Thank God."

Martina held the phone up so that Troy could hear the ebullient chanting.

"I Am!"

"Troy Davis!"

"You are!"

"Troy Davis!"

"We are!"

"Troy Davis!!!"

"You want to say anything to all these people?" Martina asked Troy, pressing the cellphone into her ear so she could hear his response.

"Yeah, I do." Troy paused after each sentence so Martina could shout out his words. "Have people pray for the MacPhail family. Tell them to keep working to dismantle this unjust system. Tell them I would not be fighting this hard for my life if I was guilty."

Jay strode triumphantly down the driveway into the prison yard, his jacket over his shoulder, an unlit cigarette in his hand, and hugged Virginia.

Martina, Mama, Wende, Reverend Sharpton, Jay, Danielle, Scott, and the protestors exited the prison grounds, walking tall and proud across the street to the truck stop. The friends and family who had been at the New Hope House met them there and the shouts of elation and praying began all over again. De'Jaun ran around giddily, laughing and hugging everyone. Strangers pulled into the truck stop to fill up on gas, heard what the celebration was about, and joined the prayer.

De'Jaun put his arm around Martina's shoulders and squeezed. "I promised Uncle Troy that I would look after you, take care of the family, and be the man of the house," he said to Martina. "And even though Troy made it, I'm still going to keep that promise."

The relief was overpowering—yet Martina knew that tomorrow she would be back on the roller coaster. The US Supreme Court had given them one week before possibly having to face this all over again.

Virginia and Martina pray fervently in the prison yard with supporters on September 23, 2008, Troy's second execution date. Courtesy of Scott Langley, deathpenaltyphoto.org.

September 23, 2008: Virginia and Martina celebrate the news that the US Supreme Court halted the execution.
Courtesy of Scott Langley, deathpenaltyphoto.org.

September 23, 2008:
Virginia hugs Jay Ewart,
Troy's attorney, who had
been in the death house
preparing to witness
Troy's execution.
Martina, in the back-
ground, wipes away
tears of relief. Courtesy
of Scott Langley.
deathpenaltyphoto.org.

De'Jaun sitting on Martina's lap.
Courtesy of the Davis family.

Part Three

October 9, 2008

Troy's fortieth birthday came and went without an answer from the US Supreme Court. One answer that did arrive, however, was an explanation of the MacPhail family member's comment about DNA to the press after the parole board hearing.

Jay had filed a Georgia Freedom of Information Act request to everyone he could think of, including the Georgia Bureau of Investigation (GBI). As a result, he obtained an email that Spencer Lawton had written to the Board of Pardons and Parole mentioning "bloody shorts." Martina knew this was a reference to the pair of black shorts that had been removed by the Savannah Police Department (SPD) from Mama's washing machine on the night of August 19, 1989, when they had barged into her house to look for Troy. Because the shorts had been seized without a search warrant, they had been inadmissible as evidence at trial. But since the hearing in front of the Georgia Board of Pardons and Parole was a political proceeding rather than a judicial one, there were no evidentiary standards.

Jay discovered that the GBI had done testing on the shorts ahead of the 2008 parole board hearing and obtained a copy of the test results immediately. He studied the results carefully, consulting with forensic and serological experts, and relayed their conclusion to Martina: It was not possible to determine that there was blood on the shorts. The swab used in the test had tested positive for blood throughout the shorts, including under the waistband, yet no bloodstains were visible anywhere. "Either the shorts were soaked in invisible blood—or the test yielded a false positive," Jay said to Martina.

A number of factors could have caused the false positive, including bleach—a significant detail, as the shorts had been seized from a washing machine. Even if blood were on the shorts (which was unlikely as there were no bloodstains) there was no evidence that the blood was Officer MacPhail's. Might not blood on the shorts have been Larry Young's, who had been viciously pistol-whipped and had bled profusely near Troy? DNA was found on the shorts, but the amount was so miniscule that it was not testable. There was no way to know what—or whom—the DNA was from.

Martina had a strong hunch about how the state had spun the test results to the parole board at Troy's clemency hearing. The shorts tested positive for blood, she imagined they argued, and DNA evidence was not necessary to determine that the blood must be Officer MacPhail's.

It was too late to refute anything that the state may have claimed about bloody shorts and DNA to the parole board. But if the state ever introduced the GBI report in a future innocence hearing, Troy's legal team would be ready. Martina and Troy continued to wait for the US Supreme Court to decide if such a hearing would be granted.

✧

October 2008

"Let's go, Davis," the warden said, unlocking Troy's cell.

The warden and two guards led Troy through an outdoor part of the prison he had never seen before. He knew that Reverend Sharpton and Congressional representatives John Lewis and Hank Johnson, who had both gotten involved in his case, were supposed to come for a visit, but he didn't know that the warden had organized a special room for the meeting.

Troy walked slowly, not wanting to make any sudden moves, until he saw grass growing along the sidewalk. Grass. Troy had not stepped in grass in eighteen years.

"Could we please stop for a second?" he asked the warden.

"What?" the warden said.

"I want to put my feet in the grass."

The warden agreed, and Troy removed his shoes and socks.

Occasionally, a stray blade of glass would manage to push its way up through cracks in the courtyard paving stone, and Troy would pluck it, trying to keep it alive in a small can of water in his cell. Once, years ago, a bird had flown into the small window of his cell, and Troy had quickly thrown his bedsheet over the window to try to keep this flapping life with him, even if only for a few minutes. But trapping nature in his cell, whether a blade of glass in a can or a confused bird searching its way back to freedom, was not the same as feeling the plush carpet of blades under his bare feet.

✧

On October 15, the US Supreme Court declined to review the Georgia Supreme Court's denial on Troy's petition for a new trial, with no explanation offered. On October 20, the DA asked for a new death warrant. The execution date was set for October 27.

For the third time, Troy made his list of final visitors, preparing himself to be put on death watch as Martina prepared her family to say goodbye to her brother. Mama would have to stand in the prison yard again, surrounded by police dogs and CERT officers.

Virginia had been loving her children through one difficult time to the next.

March 2001

Martina had been going to see various doctors for her gastrointestinal symptoms for over a year, but no one could figure out why she constantly felt sick. She was voraciously hungry, but could only eat small amounts without intense pain. Though she had always been in tip-top physical form, she now got winded immediately whenever she tried to exercise.

"Gulf War syndrome," her gastroenterologist (GI) told her, upon learning that Martina had specialized in the military in nuclear, biological, chemical warfare and medicine and was a veteran of Operation Desert Shield.

"Cervical polyps," Dr. Cobb, her OB/GYN and in whose practice Martina worked, said.

The physician's assistant thought the problem was acid reflux. Then, the GI grew certain it was irritable bowel gastritis. All the tests came back negative. Her internal medicine doctor sat her down. "Martina, I think you are experiencing psychological pain," he told her. Martina knew herself and knew her body. Whatever was going on, it did not stem from psychological pain.

Martina chewed up Tums as if they were Skittles, yet her symptoms intensified. She made an appointment with a new GI doctor for April 1, less than a week away, obtaining her records from her internist. Martina sat on her bed that night, examining her medical file. Could she be seeing right? Her liver enzymes were over five hundred when they should be under forty-two. How had her doctor overlooked that?

"Hey, can you help me do an ultrasound?" Martina asked her colleague Angie at work the next day. Martina and Angie stared at Martina's interior on the screen. Her stomach was squished up in one corner. That must be why she was experiencing so much pain when she tried to eat. Her right lung was also scrunched up in the corner. That explained why she had been having so many problems when she tried to run. The reason, she saw, was because her liver had expanded to the size of a football and was covered with liver spots.

"Take a lot of pictures," Martina told Angie. "The GI doctor will want to see that."

Martina got dressed and went to the lab to continue her workday. Dr. Cobb entered the lab shortly afterwards, and, taking Martina's hand, asked her to follow her to her office. Perplexed, Martina did.

"I thought you told me that the doctors said you had irritable bowel gastritis."

"Yeah, that's what they said."

Dr. Cobb sat Martina down.

"Is there hepatitis in your family?"

"No."

"Is there cancer in your family?"

"No."

"We're going to schedule you for a liver biopsy tomorrow," Dr. Cobb said. "For now, go on home."

"But I have patients," Martina protested.

"Don't worry about the patients. I'll take care of the patients."

Mama drove Martina to the hospital early on the morning of March 28 for the biopsy. Dr. Cobb came into the pathology lab as they were getting ready to perform the procedure.

"I don't want her to be uncomfortable," Dr. Cobb instructed the radiologist. She kissed Martina's face. "I don't want you to feel any pain."

The pathologists and histology tech, all friends of Martina's, refused to look her in the eye. The sedative took over before Martina could ask anyone why all of them were acting so strangely, and she drifted off to sleep.

Martina awoke surrounded by doctors—the new GI doctor, the internist who had told her she had psychological pain, her former GI doctor, and Dr. Cobb. They were all shouting at each other.

"How did you not see this?"

"What were you thinking?"

The sedative made it hard to speak, but she managed to push out a soft moan to let them know she was conscious. The room grew immediately silent. Just then, another doctor Martina had never seen before entered the room. He pushed his way between the two GI doctors and stood right by Martina's bed.

"Martina, my name is Brian Kim," he said. "I'm an oncologist. Do you know what that means?"

She pushed through her sedated brain to answer.

"Yeah, you're a cancer doctor."

"I think you might have breast cancer."

Martina blinked, trying to absorb his words.

"I can't have breast cancer, I don't have a breast lump."

"Women can have breast cancer without lumps," he said. "The cells we found in your liver are breast cells. Can I examine your breasts?"

"Sure." Martina glanced at the team of doctors. How could all of them have missed this?

✧

"We don't fully know what's going on yet," Martina said to member after member of her family as they piled into her hospital room one by one, reminding Martina of clowns squeezing into a Volkswagen Bug. "They're testing me from the rooter to the tooter."

When Dr. Kim entered, Mama and Kimberly were sitting on chairs on either side of Martina's bed, Ebony was perched on the windowsill, Lester was leaning against the wall, cousin Valerie was arranging flowers on the nightstand, and Aunt Mattie was supervising six-year-old De'Jaun, who was playing with a car toy on the floor.

"Sweetie, why don't you play out here?" a nurse said, coaxing De'Jaun out into the hallway.

Martina heard the words coming from Dr. Kim's mouth—*breast cancer, metastasized to liver, tumors too numerous to count*—but the words sounded like they were being spoken from deep underwater. Virginia found her voice first.

"How bad is it?"

"Amazingly, the tumors have not entered the blood stream, so the cancer has not spread anywhere else. Even so . . ." Dr. Kim's voice grew somber. "You're HER2-positive, Martina, which makes your cancer extremely aggressive. Most oncologists would tell you that your prognosis is six months or less. But I'm a man of God. Only God knows when somebody's time is up."

Six months. A thought broke through a wall of shock and disbelief, crashing over Martina like a tidal wave: Who would take care of De'Jaun? She tried to fight off the panic as another thought crashed down on its heels: Who would fight for Troy?

Then Martina's eyes fell on Mama. Virginia had already endured Kim's paralysis, Troy's being on death row, the divorce from Joseph and then his untimely death, and Martina's prolonged hospitalization during her pregnancy with De'Jaun. How much more could Mama take? Who would support and care for her? What would happen to Ebony, Lester, and Kimberly? Martina had never been so lost.

Dr. Cobb came to see her shortly after her family took De'Jaun home.

"I made sure Dr. Kim was the oncologist to take care of you," Dr. Cobb assured Martina, holding her hand. Some of the other doctors in the practice didn't think there was any sense in treating her, Dr. Cobb said. But Dr. Kim had insisted on doing whatever could be done. She's young, Dr. Kim had argued with the doctors who thought her case was too far gone: "She has a small child."

He was going to start her on a very aggressive course of chemotherapy, beginning the next day.

Martina lay in the hospital bed, head whirling. Why did this happen to her? She had always tried to live healthily. She didn't drink or smoke, she had given birth before the age of thirty and had nursed her baby, she wasn't obese—all this should have reduced her risk of breast cancer. Was it due to radiation exposure from her time serving in the Gulf War? Was there anything she could have done to prevent it?

Martina suppressed those thoughts quickly—self-pity would not be helpful. She lifted the Bible from her bedside table and began flipping through it, searching for her favorite verses, proverbs, and psalms. Her eyes fell on a roll of medical tape that had been left on the windowsill.

Shortly afterward, a nurse walked into the room to find Martina kneeling on the bed, fastening proverbs and psalms onto the wall with medical tape, the Bible laying open on her bed, jagged edges where missing pages had once been.

"What are you doing?" the nurse asked.

Martina was too focused on her task to answer. She ripped another page out of the Bible and taped it on the wall next to her bed. The nurse rushed out of the room and returned a few minutes later with Dr. Kim.

"Martina? What's going on?"

Martina turned to meet Dr. Kim's worried gaze.

"I'm arming myself with the word of God," Martina said.

She might have cancer, but cancer did not have her. She was going to fight as hard as she possibly could to see her child grow up and her brother walk free. Martina saw a flicker of recognition in Dr. Kim's eyes and permitted herself a small, steely smile as she ripped out another psalm and taped it directly above her head. "Sorry about tearing up your Bible," she added.

✦ ✦ ✦

October 24, 2008

Martina was packing to head to Atlanta for the final two days to say goodbye to Troy. It was the third time her brother had entered death watch in sixteen months. Activists had been rallying all week. Yesterday, Amnesty had held a day of global action with twenty-five events worldwide.

"Praise God!" she heard Mama call out as she was closing her suitcase. Martina rushed into the living room just as Virginia was hanging up the phone. "That was Jay," Mama said, in a voice somewhere between joy and tears. "The execution was stopped."

Martina called back Jay immediately to get the full details. On October 21, Troy's lawyers had requested permission from the 11th Circuit Court of Appeals to file a new federal habeas petition, and, wanting more information before determining whether or not to grant permission, the court had halted the execution.

That evening, Martina logged into her email to find dozens of messages of congratulations and solidarity. Reading through them, she stopped short at one email calling her a "nigger bitch." The following day she received an email that pledged that, should her brother get out of prison, he would be killed before he made it back to Savannah.

"Our prayers are with Troy's mother," wrote Randy Robertson, the first vice president of Georgia's Fraternal Order of Police. "But justice must be served. God Bless You." One FOP officer expressed compassion about Martina's breast cancer. His sister had died of breast cancer, he wrote, so he knew what Martina was going through. If Martina would only back off, he implored, then everybody else would back off and it would all be over. Troy would be executed and both families could move on.

There were black SPD officers who had been on the force at the time of Officer MacPhail's murder who let slip to Martina that they knew information about the problematic investigation, but, whether due to a code of police loyalty or fear of consequences, it seemed to Martina that the black officers would not cross the blue line.

Martina knew that Troy's case was not the only problematic investigtion in which the SPD was implicated. Gary Nelson had been charged with the 1978 rape and murder of a six-year-old girl and was convicted and sentenced to death in 1980. In 1991, the Georgia Supreme Court vacated Nelson's conviction, due in part to suppression of evidence on the part of the DA's office. The SPD had been complicit in this suppression of evidence, withholding information that two women who worked for the *Savannah Evening Press* had told SPD detectives that they had received calls from a man (not Nelson) who had confessed to the crime. Investigators from the force had also committed perjury on the stand during Nelson's trial, testifying that the murdered little girl's playmate had "readily identified" Nelson in a photo lineup. Only during post-conviction investigation were tapes of the police questioning the young witness revealed, tapes that revealed that the playmate had actually said that the photograph of Nelson looked "something like" the man she'd seen. Not only that, but Roger Parian, the same forensics expert from the state crime lab who testified at Troy's trial about the matching bullets recovered from Michael Cooper and Officer MacPhail (a conclusion that was later discredited by a 2007 GBI report), had committed perjury in Nelson's trial when testifying about a hair found on the victim's arm.

Martina was well aware that problems with the SPD and Chatham County's DA office ran far deeper than Troy's case.

✧

December 9, 2008

Martina might have enjoyed the grandeur and stateliness of the 11th Circuit Appeals Court building's vaulted lobby ceiling and marble window and door frames, had so much not been at stake. If the judges ruled in Troy's favor, he would be able to petition the US District Court for an evidentiary hearing. If the justices ruled against Troy, a new execution date might be set within days.

Martina and her family, along with supporters from AIUSA, NAACP, GFADP, and other friends of Troy, sat on the oak benches on one side of the courtroom aisle, while the MacPhail family, surrounded by members of the Fraternal Order of Police, sat on the other.

Jay had warned Troy and the family not to be overly optimistic—they had an enormously high legal standard to clear. But Martina could not help but feel hopeful as Justices Stanley Marcus, Joel Dubina, and Rosemary Barkett, clad in black robes, entered, took their seats behind the bench and the oral arguments began. After all, it was highly unusual for a death penalty case to proceed this far. Plus, this was the same court that had stayed the last execution in order to hear these very arguments.

The hearing lasted over an hour, with the judges questioning the attorneys:

Was the new evidence sufficiently clear and convincing that no reasonable juror would have found Troy guilty? Furthermore, was the new evidence presented with "due diligence" at the earliest possible legal opportunity? And if the exonerating evidence was determined to be clear and convincing, yet it hadn't been presented with "due diligence"—could Troy still be executed?

Executing Troy, an innocent man, Jay and Danielle argued, would violate not only the Eighth Amendment of the Constitution's prohibition on cruel and unusual punishment but also the Fourteenth Amendment, with its due process clause.

Susan Boleyn, Georgia's assistant attorney general, argued that the affidavits did not adhere to due diligence and that, regardless, Troy had presented no credible evidence of actual innocence. The Georgia Supreme Court, the Georgia Board of Pardons and Paroles, and this same Court of Appeals had all previously ruled against Troy, Boleyn concluded. "You can't just keep getting bites of the same apple."

Martina watched the judges closely, trying to gauge where they stood. Justice Dubina seemed to be against Troy's receiving an evidentiary hearing, but Justice Barkett seemed to be in favor of bringing Troy's innocence claims into a courtroom. Martina could not read Justice Marcus. Whatever the outcome, it looked as if this would be yet another closely divided ruling.

At the hearing's end, Martina approached the MacPhail family. She had tried unsuccessfully to reach out to them in the past, but it was time to try again. From the *Atlanta Journal-Constitution*, she knew that Officer Mark MacPhail's sister had burst into tears when the third execution was halted and that his mother had said that her nerves were completely frayed.

"Excuse me, Ms. MacPhail . . ." It was difficult to speak with the FOP officers blocking her. "This is not our family against your family, as people portray it. I've never wanted it to be like that. We do this fight to find the truth about what happened to your son and your brother just as much as we do it for Troy." Martina was addressing their backs. She took a deep breath and continued. "I know you can hear me. We have no ill will against your family. I have a mother, too." Nothing. "I wish that you all would at least respond."

Finally, one of the FOP officers intervened. "Officer MacPhail's sister is deaf."

"All of them are not deaf."

"I'll give them the message."

What more could Martina do? She knew the MacPhails were hurting deeply. They would be mourning Mark and the void his absence had created for the rest of their lives. The MacPhails deserved every bit of the support and consolation they received. But wasn't Mama's pain as real as the pain of Officer MacPhail's mother?

The system pitted two innocent, victimized families against one another. Martina's family had a lot more in common with the MacPhail family than what kept them sitting on different sides of the courtroom aisle. Martina wished they could see it as well.

✧

January 2009

There were not enough hours in the day for Martina to accomplish all that she was trying to do. She would routinely go to a conference on a Monday, return home that Thursday, repack, and fly out again Friday. Anti–death penalty organizations wanted her input on strategy or needed a statement from her. Well-intentioned supporters called to ask if she had tried this tactic or that idea. She spent half her chemotherapy sessions sitting in the infusion center with her cell phone pressed against her ear, participating in conference-call meetings. As quickly as she churned out emails, responses flew back into her inbox, at one point so numerous that they crashed her system.

The coalition working on Troy's case continued to grow: the American Civil Liberties Union was on board, the National Coalition to Abolish the Death Penalty, the Campaign to End the Death Penalty, the FTP Movement. GFADP and the SCHR had been supporting Troy and the family in various ways long before anyone knew the name Troy Davis, and their involvement was growing. In fact, SCHR was honoring Martina with their prestigious Frederick Douglass Human Rights Award and GFADP was awarding her with the MaryRuth Weir Human Rights Award. Bob Barr, former federal prosecutor and former Republican congressman, had come out in 2007 against executing Troy given the level of doubt in his case, as had the conservative former FBI director William Sessions. Larry Platt, a sixty-two-year-old civil rights activist, wore a Troy Davis button during the famous *American Idol* audition in which he sang "Pants on the Ground." In 2007 filmmaker Terry Benedict had begun a documentary about Troy's case. Musician Chad Stokes of State Radio wrote a song about Troy called "State of Georgia." E.Red, the rapper whom Troy had supported as a little boy when his father drowned and who now visited Troy regularly and was family, wrote a hip-hop song about Troy entitled "Life," which got national exposure. AIUSA printed up boxes of "I Am Troy Davis" T-shirts to keep up with the demand and Amnesty UK made its own version of the shirt. Troy started to receive letters from pen pals in Ireland and Switzerland with photos of actions on his behalf. He stared at the photos, in disbelief and overwhelmed with gratitude at the idea that strangers were wearing T-shirts and buttons with his name on them.

Very few in Savannah had been willing to stand publicly with the Davis family in the early years. Among most white folks, showing support to the Davis family was equated with being against law enforcement. Black folks had felt it was wiser to "stay in one's place," shunning the Davis family if necessary rather than paying the price for rocking the boat.

Martina was reminded of how little progress had been made in Savannah when she was canvassing for Troy in a predominantly black neighborhood alongside Savannah activists Solana Plaines, DeNise Chaney, and Sister Jackie Griffith, SSJ.

"I know who you are, you're Troy Davis's sister, I saw you on TV!" a diminutive, elderly African American woman said with excitement upon answering her door. She reached up and patted Martina on her cheek.

"You're so pretty!"

"Thank you!" Martina answered. She held out the petition on which she was gathering signatures and asked the woman if she would sign it.

The woman shook her head gravely.

"I believe in what you're doing for your brother, and I'm praying for him, but I can't sign your paper 'cause then they might take my Social Security."

"Nobody's going take your Social Security for signing a petition!" Martina protested, but the woman was firmly convinced otherwise.

Three houses later, another older man expressed trepidation that he would be fired from his job if he signed.

Martina understood their fear. These folks had come up at a time when white bosses could fire their black workers at will. But that fear was the very reason that the black community in Savannah needed to mobilize. That elderly woman's grandson, the gentleman's nephew—any of them, in the wrong place at the wrong time, could just as easily have been in Troy's situation. The slogan *I Am Troy Davis* said it all: Troy could be any black mother's son. Frightened as many in Savannah's black community remained, people worldwide continued to learn about Troy's case and get behind the effort to prevent his execution.

One day, Martina walked toward her gate at the airport in DC, heading home from a speaking engagement, her laptop bag with a Troy Davis button on it slung over her shoulder.

"You know about the Troy Davis case?" she heard a woman behind her ask. Martina turned around. "Oh!" the woman said, startled. "The sister!"

It used to be that people who asked if she was Troy's sister did so in a whisper, as if they thought it must be a shameful secret that Martina was guarding. But now, when people identified her as Troy's sister, it was as if they were star-struck. One of these days, Martina told herself, she would get herself a T-shirt that said: I Am the Sister.

✧

Martina longed for some normal brother/sister time during visits with Troy, but there was always something pressing related to his case to discuss. Visit after visit, Troy laid out his ideas of who to reach out to and what to ask of them.

"I've already contacted them, Troy, and they work on the policy level, they don't do work for a particular case . . ."

Troy would bring up his next idea, and Martina would have to bite her tongue to avoid expressing frustration. She had already been down every avenue. She was doing as much as she possibly could.

Next Troy would fuss about Martina's travel schedule.

"You're in a plane every couple of days, Tina! You need to slow down."

Martina wanted to laugh at the mixed messages, but she knew that Troy worried constantly about how much she had sacrificed on his behalf, blaming himself in the early morning hours for Daddy's untimely death, for the pain that Mama carried, and for Martina's illness. Yet what choice did Troy have but to lean on Martina?

✧

April 16, 2009

Martina skimmed through the forty-seven-page 11th Circuit decision, but Jay had already given her a heads-up on the final two words: Application Denied. Understanding the rest of the 2–1 decision was merely a matter of deciphering procedural gobbedy-goop.

"Claims of actual innocence based on newly discovered evidence have never been held to state a ground for federal habeas relief absent an independent constitutional violation occurring in the underlying state criminal proceeding."

Absent an independent constitutional violation? Wouldn't executing an innocent man be a constitutional violation?

"What matters is whether [Davis] with the exercise of due diligence, could have discovered [the facts he now presents to us] at the time he filed his first federal habeas petition."

With the exception of a 2008 affidavit from Benjamin Gordon, the justices determined, the other recantations did not satisfy the due diligence requirement.

New evidence, the justices continued, must "be sufficient to establish by clear and convincing evidence that, but for constitutional error, no reasonable fact-finder would have found the applicant guilty of the underlying offense." The post-trial affidavits, they asserted, were tortured and difficult, at best. Regardless, most of the affidavits were disqualified due to the first procedural bar and Gordon's affidavit, standing alone, could not negate the rest of the state's evidence at trial.

Martina silently fumed at the judges' own admission of what a high standard this was, calling it "actual innocence plus." Shouldn't the *possibility* of innocence be enough for the court to order an evidentiary hearing?

The ruling was peppered with other callous terminology, such as the court's responsibility to "gatekeeping requirements." Apparently being an effective gatekeeper was more important than her brother's life.

The one bright spot was Judge Rosemary Barkett's nine-page dissent, in which she wrote, "To execute Davis, in the face of a significant amount of proffered evidence that may establish his actual innocence, is unconscionable and unconstitutional."

Scrolling through the decision, Martina's eyes were drawn to a statement about the court's inherent suspicion of recantations. Recantation testimony was not only unreliable, the ruling stated, but also upset society's interest in the finality of convictions.

It came down to the same thing, time and again: finality over fairness. It was heartbreaking. It was disgusting. But this was no time for despair. The 11th Circuit extended Troy's stay of execution for another thirty days so he could appeal to the US Supreme Court.

The fight was still on.

March 31, 2001

Troy entered the visitation room and found only Kimberly and Aunt Mattie waiting for him. They hugged and exchanged their regular greetings.

"Where's Mama?" Troy asked them. "Where's Tina and De'Jaun?" Kim and Aunt Mattie made quick and silent eye contact.

"What's wrong?"

"Tina's in the hospital," Kim finally said. "It's breast cancer."

"When was she diagnosed?" He had talked to Martina last week, and she hadn't said a word about cancer.

"Just a few days ago."

Troy felt for the edge of the plastic chair and lowered himself onto it slowly. He didn't trust himself to stand right then.

"How bad is it?" It had to be pretty bad, he knew, if Mama, who never missed a visit, hadn't come.

"She's already had surgery and Mama and Lester and Ebony are in the hospital with her."

"She gonna be okay?"

"Yes," Kim said.

Kimberly had never lied to Troy. Troy desperately wanted to believe her, but her face didn't look like the yes she had uttered.

"God's going to watch over her because she's got a lot of work to do on God's behalf," Troy said with as much resolve as he could muster, forcing the gathering tears to retreat and dry up. He knew that if he started crying, he might never stop.

Lester patched Troy through to Martina's hospital room that night. Martina's voice was groggy and her throat sounded sore, causing Troy's emotions to pitch high again. He and Martina had been almost like one person since they were born, always there when the other was in need. How could his sister, his rock, be lying in a hospital bed, wracked with cancer, barely able to speak?

"I'm going to be okay," Martina pushed the words out thickly. "I just need to get some rest."

Martina dropped to sleep as Mama took the phone back.

"She'll be fine," Virginia reassured him, but even over the phone, Mama could not hide her fear from Troy. "God will heal her."

"How's De'Jaun handling this?"

"Seeing his mother hooked up to all those tubes scared him," Mama said, as a recorded voice notified them that there was one minute left on the call. "Tina called him over to her bedside, but he was afraid to approach her. It broke my heart."

The call was disconnected.

Troy returned to his cell and dropped immediately to his knees. *Please God, heal Tina, keep her strong. Take her cancer from her and guide her to doctors who will know how to help her.* He prayed silently on the concrete floor until exhaustion overcame him. Then he pulled himself onto the bed and continued to pray.

✧

April 15, 2001

Martina didn't want De'Jaun coming to the hospital and seeing her in the state she was in, but every day they spoke by phone.

"Where are you, Mom?" her son would ask each evening, his voice quivering.

"I'm in the hospital, sweetheart."

"Why are you there?"

"I'm getting treatment for cancer."

"I don't know what that is."

"It's a disease, De'Jaun, a sickness. It's pretty bad, but I'm trying real hard to get well soon." Martina had been too weak and drugged up to say much more.

Today, Martina did not care how weak she was. Come hell or high water, she was determined to be there when De'Jaun gave the Easter speech at church, his first time speaking in public.

The nurses had informed Martina that her blood counts were much too low for such an outing to be permissible, but Dr. Kim told her that if the counts came up enough, he would discharge her for the day. Martina had been focusing all her energy on raising her blood counts.

"Go to church," Dr. Kim told her Easter morning. "See your little boy give the Easter speech. But don't you dare sit near anyone who is coughing or sneezing!"

Trevor, her boyfriend of four years, brought her something to wear and drove her to church, helping her get in and out of the car. She felt woozy and wobbly and the mirror of the church bathroom revealed an ashy, gray complexion.

But she glowed with pride when De'Jaun got up in front of the congregation, wearing his beige suit and little pillbox hat. As he finished his speech, ending with "Happy Easter" and a smart salute, a burst of energy flooded Martina. She had to hold herself back from whooping and clapping in church.

The newfound energy drained quickly. Trevor helped her leave the sanctuary, and she had to lean on him to avoid falling down as the family took photographs outside.

Trevor slept on the cot in her hospital room that night, crawling into bed with her when the nurses and doctors finished coming in for the night, as he had several times during these past two weeks.

"You're on my IV! Get off my IV!" she had had to scold him more than once.

As Trevor slept next to her, she thought about the look she had seen on the faces of her fellow churchgoers and the tone in their voices as they greeted her, as if she already had one foot in the grave.

Suddenly, Martina pulled the sheet off Trevor's head.

"You need something?" he mumbled, disoriented.

"What I need," said Martina, "is for you to get dressed, put your shoes on, and when you leave, don't come back. Find yourself a healthy woman who can give you children."

"Are you finished talking?" Trevor asked.

She wasn't. Martina told him how serious her cancer was, how sick she truly was, how expensive the treatment would be, and how the outcome was not likely to be positive. It wasn't fair to cause him all this pain, she said, when he might end up having to bury her.

Trevor waited until she stopped talking, and then waited a moment more.

"Anything else you want to say? Anything to add?"

"No—I'm done."

"Then good night," he said, rolling over and pulling the sheet back over his head. "I'm not going anywhere."

✧

May 2001

De'Jaun got over his fear of the tubes and ran to hug his mother when Virginia brought him to the hospital after school. Martina moved over so he could climb up onto the bed next to her.

"Do you have any homework today?"

He did, a spelling test.

"Let me study with you."

De'Jaun pulled out his vocabulary sheet and handed it to his mother while Virginia went down to the cafeteria to get him a snack.

"Friend," Martina read the first word on the list.

"F . . . r . . ." De'Jaun hesitated, trying to remember whether i or e came next. Before he made his choice, Martina had begun to drift asleep.

"Mom!" De'Jaun tugged at her nightgown sleeve. "Come on, let's do my homework!"

Martina shook herself awake and tried to read him the next word, but the strong pain meds had taken over. She struggled with her eyelids, but she was defeated.

De'Jaun slipped off the bed and curled up on the chair, crying. Why did his mom keep falling asleep on him? Why wasn't she listening to him and helping him with his vocabulary? A passing doctor saw the weeping boy and took him out to the hallway.

"You shouldn't be crying like that," the doctor said. De'Jaun wiped his eyes, trying to stop. "You know your mom may only have a few months left to live. You need to spend time with her without crying. You need to be a big boy."

Martina woke up, bleary and unfocused, and found her son standing at the foot of her bed, staring at her with watery eyes and a scrunched-up little face.

"What's wrong?" Martina asked him.

"The doctor said you were going to die."

"What?"

"The doctor said you were going to die in a few months."

"Don't listen to that doctor. I'm gonna be fine. Come on, let's finish studying for your test."

That Saturday, the family was in their normal routine of laughing and joking during visitation with Troy. But De'Jaun faced the counter with his head in his arms.

Troy pulled the boy aside. "De'Jaun, do you believe in God?" De'Jaun nodded silently. "When you pray, you've got to believe what you pray for. You've got to believe that God's going to heal your mother."

"Yessir."

"Write me a letter if you need to talk to me. And I'll call as much as I can. Don't be afraid to express yourself. You don't have to hold your feelings inside."

De'Jaun had held back tears since the day the doctor had told him to stop crying, but now he started sobbing uncontrollably.

"I wish you were my dad," De'Jaun choked out.

Troy held his nephew tightly in his arms.

"If I had a son, I'd want him to be just like you. And I will always be here for you no matter what."

That night, Troy called Martina in the hospital and reported back to her the conversation he had had with De'Jaun. Martina told him what the doctor had said to De'Jaun a few days prior. Troy was furious.

"The doctor had no business saying that to a little boy!"

"I know . . . but the truth is, I don't know how much time I have left with my son. I want our time together to be quality time—and I can't do that if I'm high as a kite all the time."

Martina told Troy the decision she had just made: She was going to stop taking the barbiturates, cold turkey. The withdrawal would be intense and the pain would be severe, but more important to her than managing the pain was being present for her child.

✧

It was a sunny, shining Sunday morning, but De'Jaun was suspicious as the family left for the hospital. Something was going on. He tried to calculate the passage of time inside his head. Had it been a few months? Was this the day the doctor said that his mother was going to die? De'Jaun planted his heels in the hospital's lobby. He didn't want to take another step.

"What's wrong with you, child?" Ebony practically had to drag De'Jaun to the elevator. They arrived at Martina's room. She was sitting up in the chair, dressed, with a packed bag next to her.

"Mommy! You're alive!" De'Jaun ran to her and buried his face in her lap. Martina stood up slowly and took her child's hand.

"Come on, sweetheart. Let's go home."

✦ ✦ ✦

May 19, 2009

Martina was elated at the turnout in Atlanta for Troy's day of global action, cosponsored by AIUSA, the NAACP, and GFADP. Atlanta's event was only one of the rallies being held across forty-five states and twenty-eight countries.

Earlier that day, Jay had filed Troy's habeas petition directly with the US Supreme Court, petitioning the court to order the case back to a federal judge for an evidentiary hearing on innocence claims. "It's something of a Hail Mary pass," Jay had warned Martina. "Cases usually make their way up to the US Supreme Court from a lower court through appeals. The Supreme Court has not taken a case filed directly to its docket in over fifty years."

But seeing nearly a thousand supporters gathered on the capital steps gave Martina confidence that anything was possible. The now-familiar chants filled the warm evening air:

"What do you want?"

"Justice!"

"When do you want it?"

"Now!"

E.Red pumped the crowd up with the song he had written about Troy, his long dreadlocks pulled back from his narrow face.

First I heard the news, then I saw it with my eyes, E.Red rapped. *And when I read the story, I knew it was all lies. The man that they're talking about ain't the man that I know . . . they trying to take my homeboy's life!*

Juan Melendez, who had spent seventeen years on Florida's death row before being exonerated in 2002, spoke fiercely from the podium, his brown eyes blazing. "You can always release an innocent man from prison, but you can never release an innocent man from the grave!"

"If you were to write a Hollywood script on Troy Davis, no one would believe it," Dr. Reverend Warnock, the pastor at Ebenezer Baptist Church, said from the podium. "Somebody ought to hit pause, rewind, and say 'let's see the evidence.'" The crowd cheered their agreement.

As the evening light turned golden, Martina took the podium, as she always did at rallies for Troy. Though coaxing Mama to talk at Troy's rallies had always been like pulling teeth, Martina had decided that tonight would be different.

"Today is my Mama's sixty-fourth birthday," Martina said. "And I'd like to invite her up on the stage to say something about Troy."

Before Virginia could object, Edward DuBose, the robust, energetic president of the Georgia Conference of the NAACP, led the crowd in a rousing rendition of "Happy Birthday" to Virginia. By the time the song was finished, Mama was standing behind the podium, a "Justice for Troy Davis" banner behind her.

Martina stood to the side and watched Virginia grip the sides of the podium with fingers that were slightly twisted from her rheumatoid arthritis, lift her head high, and begin talking.

"I am Troy Davis! I AM Troy Davis! I speak for Troy Davis! It is so wonderful and so beautiful to see all of you supporters out here, all the people who love him and believe in him and are fighting for him. It makes my heart full with joy. Troy, I was talking to him a few minutes ago, and I was just telling him, from the babies in the cradle on up to my age, I said thank God for each and every one of you all. For twenty years I've been fighting for my son. I have not stopped. I have shed a few tears, but I asked God to wipe those tears away from my eyes. And He gave me the strength to go on to fight, and I will fight until the end!"

Martina almost pinched herself—was this her meek mother on the podium? Martina felt as if she were witnessing the birth of a new child: Virginia Davis, the activist.

"We have fought a long battle but the battle is not over yet. The battle will not be over until we bring these walls of injustice down!" Mama was on fire. "And we're going to bring them down like the walls of Jericho came down! We're gonna BRING IT DOWN!"

The crowd caught on fire too, with shouts of "Yeah!" clapping, and cheering. Mama had held so much inside all these years. Now that she was wound up, Martina worried that she might not ever stop!

"I'm gonna march and march and march until I can't march anymore. We're marching on up to justice! Because in 1960 and '61, in Savannah, Georgia, I was in the civil rights movement and I marched for justice then . . . and you know what? I'm still marching! I became sixty-four years old today, and I'm gonna still march!"

"Give it up for Miz Virginia Davis!" Ed DuBose roared out to thunderous applause.

Martina had always viewed herself as a feisty firebrand like Joseph had been, but tonight she realized for the first time that her core of inner strength came from Mama. It was Virginia who absorbed the full impact of each new blow that was delivered to the family. Perhaps Mama wobbled from time to time, but she never fell.

Martina had been taking the lead for a long time. Tonight, Mama proved that it was time for other members of the family to start speaking out.

✧

July 15, 2009

Martina glowed with pride as she watched her fifteen-year-old son behind the podium. She knew that De'Jaun was praying that the thousands of people gathered in front of him for the NAACP centennial could not hear the pounding of his heart.

The NAACP had been collaborating with Amnesty International on a local level for some time, under the supportive leadership of Ed DuBose. But in the last year, with Benjamin Todd Jealous now at the helm of the NAACP, the organization had taken on Troy's case at the national level. Martina had met Ben years ago at a death penalty abolition conference, and, long before he became the president and CEO of the NAACP, she had appreciated the work he did on many prison-related issues, including campaigning to end the death penalty for minors.

Ben had asked De'Jaun to introduce him, as well as to deliver the keynote address for the parallel youth conference. De'Jaun had written the speech himself and practiced it over and over. But as well-intentioned folks crowded around him as he waited to deliver his speech, advising him on how to speak and what lines to change, Martina saw him begin to get flustered. She took her son aside.

"The NAACP asked you to give the speech, not them," she told him. "It's your speech. You've been waiting a long time to do this. You do it your way."

Martina watched De'Jaun spread his notes on the podium nervously, but as he began to speak, she could tell that his anxiety was evaporating. She watched her son gain strength and confidence as he described his experiences growing up as a high-achieving young black male in Savannah and the subtle racism he faced daily: "When people hear that I am in the honors program at my school, that I did a summer course at American University, that I plan to study robotics in order to develop medical technology, they tell me that I'm an exception. No, I tell them back. I'm not an exception!"

She noticed that De'Jaun no longer needed to rely on his notes as he spoke about the justice system and the injustices that it perpetuated. Martina saw tears in people's eyes as her son talked about his Uncle Troy.

✦ ✦ ✦

June 2001

It was wonderful to be home, but Lord, chemotherapy was rough. Martina's body felt like it had been turned inside out. Every bit of energy had been wrung from her body. She could barely dress herself. Mama fed her, bathed her, helped her get dressed, and took her to the doctor. If Virginia was not able to be there, Trevor filled in. Martina met women in chemotherapy whose husbands had left them due to the strain of the illness, but Trevor was always ready to be by her side.

There was little else to pass the time, aside from watching television. And there were developments in the news that impacted Troy. The Georgia Supreme Court was in the midst of debating whether or not use of the electric chair constituted cruel and unusual punishment. According to the news that Martina was watching, Georgia seemed poised to join the growing number of states that now executed its prisoners via lethal injection instead of electrocution.

The pain always spiked between two and five in the morning. No matter what position she lay in during those pre-dawn hours, she could not get comfortable. Turmoil roiled inside her stomach. She wasn't sure at which end it would find its release. She made her way to the bathroom quietly, not wanting to wake anyone, but no sooner had she switched on the bathroom light than Mama was by her side.

"You OK?" Virginia asked.

"I'm fine. Go back to bed, Mama."

Martina waited until she heard her mother's bedroom door close, and then carefully lifted the toilet seat, vomiting as noiselessly as she could.

Mama was back at her side before Martina finished wiping her mouth. "Are you sure you're all right? You need anything?"

"I'm OK, Mama."

Mama would stay by her side all night if Martina did not insist that she return to bed. There was not much sense in Martina trying to make it back to bed; even if she could get there, she would just have to turn around again and come back to the bathroom. Best to just curl up right here, between the toilet and the tub.

How long would the chemotherapy poison her like this? She thought about Georgia's likely switch to lethal injection in the near future. What unbelievable irony. Here she was, injecting toxins in her system in order to live, while the Georgia Supreme Court was on the verge of deciding that toxins would be injected into Troy in order to kill him.

Martina lay there for hours with the cool porcelain pressed against her cheek. When new light began to streak the sky pink, Mama came in, helped her stand up, moistened a washcloth to wipe her face, and got her back into bed.

✧

Martina held De'Jaun's Little League baseball team photograph. She had been coaching the team before her diagnosis and had managed to drag herself out of bed for the team picture. Now, staring at herself in the photograph, she could see how ill she really was. Her skin, offset by a bright red shirt, was a terrible, sickly, charcoal gray. Dark circles sunk under her eyes and her hair was falling out in clumps.

"I need to ask you something," she said to Troy from the privacy of her bedroom when he called that night. "If you get out, and something happens to me, I want you to raise De'Jaun."

There was silence for a moment. Then, Troy answered, with a slight crack in his voice. "You and I are going to raise De'Jaun together."

"Promise me," Martina persisted. "If I die, you will raise De'Jaun. Wherever you're at, De'Jaun will stay with you."

Troy, who sounded as if he suddenly had a cold, finally agreed.

Martina hung up the phone and made her way into the living room, where De'Jaun was watching TV with Mama, Kim, and Ebony. She stared at her child for a long time.

Please God, she prayed silently. Protect my baby and have mercy on Mama. If you take me, God, please, spare Troy.

✧

It was another bad night of vomiting, retching, and diarrhea. Martina stayed curled up in bed in the morning, listening to the sounds of Mama getting De'Jaun ready and then everyone leaving the house.

In another few weeks, her son would be seven years old. In another few months, her brother would have spent ten years on death row. Martina scratched her head, coming away with a clump of hair. She stared at the fistful of hair for a long moment before pushing back the blanket, slowly sitting up in bed, and pushing her feet into her slippers. She had a child to raise and a brother to get off of death row.

It was time to get up.

Martina opened the front door. Aside from the baseball-team photo session, she had left the house only to go to chemotherapy. She took one shuffling step and then another, making it as far as the mailbox, against which she leaned for support, feeling the warm Georgia sun beat down on her face. She knew she wasn't supposed to be exposed to the sun while she was getting chemo, but it felt so good. She could feel herself soaking up energy as she closed her eyes and turned her face directly into the rays.

"Tina, you all right?" It was her neighbor from across the street.

She didn't open her eyes or turn away from the sun.

"I'm all right."

She let the sun warm her for a few more minutes. She might be dying, but she wasn't dying today.

She made her way back into the house and, without fully realizing what she was doing, found herself in the bathroom rubbing a generous amount of Nair onto her head.

When De'Jaun came home that afternoon, Martina was waiting for him on the couch, wearing her favorite dress and her head fully wrapped in a colorful scarf with an African motif. As he approached to give her a hug, she pulled off the scarf, unveiling a shiny, bald head.

De'Jaun jumped back for a moment. Then he wrapped his arms around her and squeezed tightly. "It doesn't look bad, Mom. You look really pretty today!"

She got up the next day and walked a few steps further.

"Come on, let's walk down the street," her neighbor suggested the day after that. Martina took her hand and they slowly made their way to the corner and back. When Trevor picked her up to take her to chemo, Martina was fully made up, wearing jewelry and loud Caribbean colors.

"I might have cancer," she told him when he looked at her quizzically. "But cancer doesn't have me."

Martina's strength slowly returned, and as her renewed strength lasted, she decided that not only was she not dying today, she also wasn't dying tomorrow. She likely wasn't dying next week, or even next month. She could take a deep breath, relax, and live her life, without worrying that every moment might be her last. Perhaps her illness was her Creator's way of telling her: I need your attention. There's more that you need to do and I need you to do it more abundantly.

She took De'Jaun on mother-son trips, even riding with him on a roller coaster, though she hated roller coasters. And now that she could no longer work, she threw herself fully into human rights and death penalty abolition work.

If she wasn't dying today, then she was going to live today.

✦ ✦ ✦

August 17, 2009

Martina already knew the news from Jay, but she liked hearing Amy Goodman, who had covered Troy's case from the start, announce it on *Democracy Now!*

"The Supreme Court has taken the rare step of ordering a new hearing for Georgia death row prisoner Troy Anthony Davis. The nation's highest court ordered a federal district court in Georgia to 'receive testimony and make findings of fact as to whether evidence that could not have been obtained at the time of trial clearly establishes his innocence.'"

The only dissenting opinions were Justices Antonin Scalia and Clarence Thomas. Martina was shocked by Scalia's dissent: "This Court has never held that the Constitution forbids the execution of a convicted defendant who has had a full and fair trial but is later able to convince a habeas court that he is 'actually' innocent."

Thankfully, the majority opinion, written by Justice John Paul Stevens, stated that the substantial risk of putting an innocent man to death clearly provided adequate justification for holding an evidentiary hearing.

The federal judge was also to determine whether or not the Eighth Amendment of the Constitution prohibited the execution of a man who was convicted in a fair trial but whose innocence was later proven.

This will not be a retrial, Jay warned Martina when he called her that morning. In a retrial, the state would have to convince a new jury that Troy was guilty beyond a reasonable doubt. In the evidentiary hearing, however, it would be Troy's burden to prove innocence, an extremely high and arduous standard. Martina knew that the deck was still stacked against Troy, but she was elated nonetheless. This was the opportunity they had been waiting for.

Martina was mindful that the decision came just days before the twenty-year anniversary of the murder of Officer Mark MacPhail. She knew the MacPhails were as exhausted as her family by the appeals continuing one after another and wanted everything to come to a close. Her family also wanted it all to end. But the two families were praying for very different outcomes.

✧

November 23, 2009

Martina sat next to De'Jaun on a plane headed to London, each scratching notes on a piece of paper, trying to determine what words of theirs would be included in Aunt Mattie's funeral program. Martina had gotten the call from her cousin Valerie as she and De'Jaun were packing. Aunt Mattie, Mama's sister and Valerie's mother, had just passed at sixty-eight years of age. She had recently had bypass surgery and, due to an alarmingly high heart rate, had gone back in the ICU, where she died.

"I'll cancel the trip," Martina had said immediately, but Valerie had insisted that Martina and De'Jaun go to London.

"You can't do anything for my mother now—she's gone—but you can continue fighting for Troy," Valerie had said resolutely. "That's what Aunt Mattie would want."

Martina glanced over at De'Jaun's notes, smiling when she saw that her fifteen-year-old son had written "Aunt Mabbie" rather than "Aunt Mattie." As a little boy, De'Jaun hadn't been able to pronounce his Ts, so her aunt had been Aunt Mabbie to him—and Aunt Mabbie she always remained.

Martina's own memories about growing up with Aunt Mattie cascaded over her. "Come over here and scratch my hair!" Aunt Mattie had often been heard commanding her children, nieces, and nephews. Scalp massages relaxed Aunt Mattie like nothing else; she would already be asleep by the time Martina had parted her hair to scratch the different sections. But Aunt Mattie would be wide awake the moment Martina took the comb out of her hair.

"You finish already, child?"

Troy, Aunt Mattie's pet, would scratch Aunt Mattie's hair all day if she wanted him to.

Troy received permission to call Mama's cell phone during the funeral. Virginia would put the phone up to the microphone so that Troy could address the mourners. Which stories about Aunt Mattie would Troy tell, Martina wondered? Would he mention how Mama and Aunt Mattie used to talk about soap opera characters as if they were gossiping about neighbors? Or would he talk about Aunt Mattie and the Pink Champale?

Champale was a type of malt liquor popular in the late seventies and early eighties that came in miniature champagne bottles and tasted like sparkling wine. If you lived in the projects and were drinking Champale, you knew you had arrived. Aunt Mattie, who lived in Yamacraw, used to send Martina, Troy, Valerie, and her brother Vernon to the corner liquor store on Fahm and Olgethorpe to get her a four-pack of Pink Champale for three dollars. (Ironically, this was the same liquor store where Larry Young had bought beer the night Officer MacPhail was murdered.) On the way back to Aunt Mattie's the kids would crack the seal, sip a tiny bit out, fill it back up with water, and replace the seal.

"Bring me my Champale!" Aunt Mattie would regally command the kids when they returned to the house.

"Oh, let me open it for you!" Troy offered, winking to his sister and cousins.

They would pretend to crack open the seal, give the Champale to Aunt Mattie, and slip into the other room, trying not to crack up.

The trip to London was De'Jaun's first time outside the United States, and it was wonderful. The trip had been organized by Kim Manning-Cooper, Amnesty UK's death penalty abolition campaign manager, and had grown out of a visit Kim had made to Georgia with Member of Parliament (MP) Alistair Carmichael and Richard Hughes, the drummer from the band Keane. Martina had taken Kim, Alistair, Richard, and Laura Moye to meet Troy and, as Martina had seen happen time and again, Troy and his visitors talked and laughed like they were old friends.

"What did you think?" Martina had asked as they left the prison.

Kim had struggled to find words. "He's so positive . . . and warm . . . and humble. No trace of anger or bitterness."

Laura had been able to find words more readily. "It felt like I've known him for years . . . he's so clearly a Davis."

The British delegation had returned with Martina to Savannah for meetings and media interviews after visiting Washington, DC, to meet with the British Embassy and other EU governments to enlist their support in Troy's case.

"We have to get you and De'Jaun over to London," Kim Manning-Cooper told Martina, after watching De'Jaun speak to a group of African American students at Savannah State University. Kim had acted quickly, and now, just a few months later, Martina and De'Jaun were speaking in Amnesty UK's auditorium, moving the British audience to tears and receiving a standing ovation. They also gave a talk for Members of Parliament inside the House of Commons.

Though capital punishment was now abolished throughout Europe, Alistair reminded De'Jaun of what a grizzly part of their history it was, showing him where the famous Scottish patriot William Wallace had been jailed and tried, before being taken into the streets of London to be hung and then drawn and quartered.

Though hobnobbing in Parliament was exciting, it was while her son conducted a presentation at a London high school that Martina knew she had made the right decision in coming. The talk had been arranged by a teacher named Roger Silverman, whose father, MP Sydney Silverman, had been instrumental in bringing about the abolition of capital punishment in the United Kingdom. Students swarmed around De'Jaun after the presentation. They wanted more information; they wanted to know how they could get involved.

"It's so hard to hold these kids' attention," Roger commented to Martina as she glowed from the back of the auditorium. "But look at your son, he has them transfixed!"

Martina loved watching De'Jaun with folks from Amnesty and NAACP. Their staff members had become a second family to him. Wende had been "Auntie Wende" for some time and now, Kim Manning-Cooper was "Auntie Kim." Amnesty and NAACP also provided De'Jaun with a social outlet with youth who cared about human rights. It was good for him to be amongst other teenagers struggling against inequality and injustice. De'Jaun's Amnesty and NAACP friends didn't treat him as a kid whose uncle was on death row. To them, De'Jaun was a fellow activist—and through them, he was gaining access to a larger world.

✦ ✦ ✦

August 2001

Troy wrapped Martina in his arms as if he never intended to let go. Then he held her at arm's length, looking her up and down. Martina's counts had not been high enough since her diagnosis for her to risk a prison visit until now, and Troy had not seen his sister for four months. Troy had lain in bed on sleepless nights, praying to God to heal his sister. He had jotted down addresses of hospitals and doctors whenever he saw something about cancer on television, and had carefully torn out and sent to Martina every relevant article he could find about cancer in the newspaper. But it never felt like enough.

Now, at least, he could see her and touch her.

"How you doing, Tina? You all right?"

Troy knew that Martina had been playing down the extent of her pain when they spoke so that he wouldn't worry, but his brown eyes went liquid-soft as he took in how much weight she had lost and how gray her skin had become.

"Do you want to see my bald head?" Martina asked Troy, pulling off her colorful scarf before he could respond. "We look more alike now—except you only wished you looked this good." Martina poked his belly and, on cue, Troy reared back and laughed like the Pillsbury Doughboy.

It was sweet how Troy doted on her, leaning over her every five minutes to ask her if she was in pain or if she needed anything. Every time she dozed off, she opened her eyes to find Troy or another inmate leaning over her with concern. "How you feeling, Tina?"

Three o'clock approached and the family formed a circle, held hands, and said a prayer. Then they all, aside from Troy, left.

Troy calculated the moment his family would walk in the door at home so he could call right then, to check that Martina was okay after the long ride back to Savannah. He stared at a photo of Martina as he waited.

When I get out of this place, he pledged to the photograph, I'm going to accompany you to each chemotherapy treatment. I'll take you to every medical appointment and question your doctors about your progress and what I can be doing to help you get better and stronger. I'm going to make sure you're taking your medicine and getting plenty of sleep.

It was going to be his time to take care of his big sister. In the meantime, Troy waited for the next visitation day, when he would be able to hug Martina again.

◆ ◆ ◆

January 2010

Troy stood on one side of a black iron grille that had been installed in the death row visitation room. His family stood on the other.

"How was New Year's?" he asked De'Jaun, leaning toward the grille and then pressing his ear against the metal to hear De'Jaun's response.

Georgia's death row was on lockdown. Previously, Troy and his fellow inmates had been able to move throughout the cell block a few hours a day. Now the men were locked for twenty-three hours a day in an eight-and-a-half by six-and-a-half-foot cell whose walls Troy could practically touch with his outstretched arms. He still had yard call twice a week, but the amount of time outdoors was reduced. Each time Troy or his fellow inmates left their cell block, they had extra "escorts" and were forced to endure a cavity check. And, harshest of all for Troy—contact visits were revoked.

"They're saying they found pipe bomb materials in the yard," Troy told Martina. "The warden's claiming the materials were passed to an inmate during visitation."

Martina scoffed in disbelief. All visitors were searched thoroughly before entering the prison and could bring nothing in with them, save a plastic baggie of quarters for the vending machines. If explosive material had been found in the yard, it must have gotten into the prison the way all contraband did— through a guard.

Over the years that Troy had been on the row, Martina had seen the inmates' rights and privileges steadily erode, and this lockdown was one more form of collective punishment. The knitting and crocheting program had been a wonderful source of creativity for Troy and other prisoners. Mama's house, as well as the homes of many of Troy's friends, was filled with beautiful gifts that Troy had crocheted: angels of all sizes and colors; a colorful church that fit snugly over a tissue box; a thick, beautiful sweater; coasters and doilies. Troy had even crocheted a baby outfit for newborn De'Jaun. According to prison officials, the program had been terminated due to an escape attempt. Colored pencils had been prohibited at the same time with the justification that they could be used to create dyes, which could then be used to alter the color of clothing in an escape attempt. Anything that offered the men dignity, a sense of purpose, and a way to stay occupied was eventually rescinded. It almost seemed to Martina as if the authorities wanted the men on the row to act out, so that they would have an excuse to punish them further.

Troy was determined that visitation be as "normal" as possible, but it wasn't easy given the physical barrier separating him from his family. Lester already hated visiting Troy on death row—he couldn't stand hearing the gate slam—and when he did visit he would sit quiet and withdrawn until Troy pulled him aside to talk. How could Troy pull Lester aside under these conditions?

And what about Kiersten? Tiny Kiersten—Ebony's funny, charming, little two-year-old girl, who was way too smart for her own good—was the apple of Troy's eye. How could Troy develop the same close relationship with her that he had with De'Jaun if he couldn't hold her, hug her, tickle her, play with her? Kiersten objected to the changes as well, banging on the iron screen throughout the visit and calling out "Unca Toy! Unca Toy!"

Visitation was over before anyone could adjust to the new circumstance, but Troy was not going to let the steel and bars prevent his family from maintaining the circle of prayer that had concluded every visit for over eighteen years. Troy pressed his hands flat against the black iron grille. Martina, Lester, Kimberly, Ebony, and Kiersten held hands in a semi-circle, with Virginia and De'Jaun on either end. Mama pressed her hand firmly on the opposite side of the grate as Troy's right palm, and De'Jaun did the same on the left. They closed their eyes and bowed their heads as Troy thanked God for the blessings they had received and asked for the strength to continue their struggle.

✦ ✦ ✦

2002

Martina took seriously the commitment she made to human rights work once her strength started to return and attended the annual conference of the National Coalition to Abolish the Death Penalty in Chicago. For the first time, she found herself in a room full of people of all backgrounds, all of whom were against capital punishment. Some were against the death penalty as a matter of human rights, others came from a faith perspective. There were relatives of murder victims and family members of those on death row.

On the first day of the conference, Martina observed a disturbing dynamic: death row family members seemed to cower in the back of the room, as if they had committed the crimes for which their loved ones had been convicted. Even here, in the death penalty abolitionist community, they were still inhibited by the shame and isolation that they had internalized.

Martina stood up the next morning during the question-and-answer period of the very first session and reiterated the statement she had scribbled down after her dream so many years ago. "I am Martina Correia and I am on Georgia's death row because that's where my brother, Troy Davis, lives. I love my brother and I am going to stand up for him."

Martina took her seat, glancing over at the other death row family members. Some of them seemed to be sitting a little more erect than they had been the previous day. From now on, Martina resolved, she would not stop talking. She would speak up whenever and wherever she had the opportunity, for her brother's sake, the sake of other death row family members, and for the condemned prisoners whom they loved. She would be relentless.

Martina began to travel from one conference to the next, telling Troy's story and studying additional facts, statistics, and information. She was horrified to discover that the United States was one of the world's leading executioners, sharing this unholy accomplishment with China, Iran, and Vietnam. As she learned details of other cases, she realized that her brother was far from the only person on death row with a strong innocence claim. And the more she learned about the death penalty, the more she realized how arbitrary, racist, and economically biased its implementation was. In fact, David Baldus had conducted landmark studies that demonstrated racial bias in death penalty sentences on none other than Georgia's death row in 1980 and 1982, revealing a strong pattern of discriminatory conviction when the murder victim was white compared to when the victim was black.

Martina began to speak about Troy's situation within the broader context of the death penalty itself. The problem was not merely that an injustice had been committed in Troy's case. The death penalty system itself was fundamentally flawed. As her proficiency on the issue expanded, her skills in speaking effectively did as well. Martina began to develop an international reputation as a fierce advocate, both for her brother and for the abolition of the death penalty.

Troy's attorneys cautioned Martina about speaking to the media. It could hurt his case, they said. The DA could get upset and set an execution date prematurely. But as the years dragged on, Martina used whatever platform she could to speak out and to state her brother's innocence.

One day, a stranger in the supermarket approached her. "I wish I had a sister like you," he said. Martina had no idea who the man was or what he had been through, but the comment gave her pause: what do people on death row endure when they don't have anyone to stand up for them?

❖ ❖ ❖

Beverly, one of Martina's favorite chemo nurses, pulled up a chair next to Martina as chemotherapy dripped from an IV into her veins. "We have a new patient, just diagnosed with lymphoma."

Helen was twenty-six years old, a new mother, and terrified, Beverly said. Beverly and several other nurses had tried to reach out to Helen without success. "You and Helen are scheduled for chemo the same day next week," Beverly told Martina. "Maybe you can try."

Martina liked the cheerful room at the infusion center at St. Joseph's/Candler Hospital, with its large, open windows, and staff who treated her as a person rather than merely a patient. It made coming for treatment much easier.

Martina had first come to Candler because her insurance had dropped her seven months into her chemotherapy, but when her insurance kicked back in, Martina told Dr. Kim that she intended to stay there. Martina could not get out the door after treatment without cracking jokes with all the nurses and collecting four or five hugs.

It hadn't taken Martina long to see that there were plenty of human rights violations right there in the chemotherapy room. Each time she came for treatment, she saw people who had to choose between whether to eat or to pay for their medicine. She saw people who were so tired of being sick and fighting the medical system that they were ready to just let go.

Martina began going to advocacy workshops for breast cancer. She started talking to state lawmakers about doing more for women with breast cancer, challenging the foundation of the health care system, and making sure that cancer treatment in Georgia got the necessary funds. Before she knew it, Martina was being invited to talk to members of Congress in DC about breast cancer issues and was leading educational workshops for other women with breast cancer. Martina and Beverly co-chaired Relay For Life and worked together on the Pink & Black Ball. Soon, Martina's smiling face was adorning the side of Candler's mobile mammogram van.

Whenever a new patient was having a difficult time, Beverly and the other nurses turned to Martina for help. Martina saw Helen sitting in her chair the next week, her scarf-covered head bowed down, an IV in her arm. Martina picked up Helen's blond wig, lying on the floor next to her chair. "Whose rag is this?" Martina called out. When Helen peeked out from under her scarf, Martina saw a little pink head and frightened, large blue eyes. Martina sat in the empty chair next to Helen. "Do you want to see a picture of my baby? He's gorgeous." Without waiting for an answer, Martina took a photograph of De'Jaun out of her wallet and passed it to Helen.

"He's beautiful," Helen said. "Do you want to see a picture of mine?" She dug a small album out of the purse and showed Martina her eight-month-old. Before the session was over, Martina and Helen were laughing and joking, with the nurses joining in. Helen changed her regular treatment day to Martina's.

Martina had first been introduced to Wanda Jones at the Cancer Center in Savannah eight months after her diagnosis. Wanda's job was to help newly diagnosed patients navigate the health care system, but before long it was Wanda who was contacting Martina for help. One young woman was living in her car with her kids when she was diagnosed. Wanda connected her to

Martina, who helped her find a place to live, got her on food assistance, found clothing for her kids, and got her into treatment. Another woman with a large, infected cancerous growth on her breast was absolutely terrified of hospitals. Wanda enlisted Martina's help and, by the following day, the woman had agreed to undergo surgery to remove the cancerous growth and to receive both wound therapy and chemotherapy, with Martina by her side for the surgery and the initial treatments.

Martina's own form of cancer was so aggressive that she had to treat it as a chronic disease. Though in remission, she needed to continue chemotherapy as a maintenance drug or her tumor markers would rise.

Martina heard different versions of the question "How are you still here?" from medical workers and breast-cancer survivors alike. Part of her was furious at the thinly veiled query of how it could be, given the nature of her cancer and its late detection, that she was not yet dead. But she also fully realized that she was blessed to still be alive, and with that blessing came the responsibility to do all she could.

"Martina, your feet are swollen," Wanda admonished her when she heard that Martina would be leading a breast cancer workshop that afternoon and speaking about Troy at a church that night. "And I just heard you say you were extremely tired."

"Well, I'll get a nap in between."

No one ever promised that she would live until ninety. It was what she did while she was here that counted.

✦ ✦ ✦

June 22, 2010

Martina stood on the pulpit the night before Troy's evidentiary hearing.

"We've come a long way, but we've got a long way to go," she said vigorously. "Because Troy is not the only person in this situation!"

Troy's supporters, from places as close as Atlanta and as far as Seattle, called out their agreement from the church's pews. Kim Manning-Cooper and Nick Krameyer, from Amnesty UK and France, respectively, addressed the gathering, as did AIUSA executive director Larry Cox.

Though Martina's energy was high as she spoke to the mass meeting, the years of chronic chemotherapy were taking their toll. Dr. Negrea, her oncologist, was constantly tinkering with her cocktail, aiming for maximum potency with minimum harm, but she had been experiencing new, painful side effects: neuropathy, thrush, stomach ulcers. Her ankles and feet were constantly swollen, her counts were low, and she was exhausted. She continued to do as much as she could, but she had to say no more and more, stop wearing herself down, and concentrate on her health. Her body just wasn't bouncing back like it used to.

Late that night, Martina read former Georgia Supreme Court Chief Justice Norman Fletcher's op-ed in the *Atlanta Journal-Constitution*. "I served on the Georgia Supreme Court when the Davis case came up on direct appeal in 1993," the former chief justice had written. "We upheld the conviction. But that was before most of the witnesses had recanted their trial testimony. I was no longer a member of the court when it rejected, by a 4–3 vote, Davis' extraordinary motion for a new trial in March 2008. The court did not order an evidentiary hearing. If I had been on that court, the vote might have been 4–3 the other way. It is by such razor-thin margins that we determine who lives and who dies." She hoped that Judge William Moore, the Georgia federal judge assigned to the hearing, had read it as well.

The following morning, Martina and her family walked through Wright Square, the second oldest of Savannah's lush squares, toward the US District Court for the first day of Troy's evidentiary hearing. The early morning sun filtered through the Spanish moss dripping from the oak trees as the youth activists from NAACP and AIUSA set up information tables and inserted signs that read "I Am Troy—Justice Matters" along every inch of the black iron railings that lined the square's brick pathways.

The Davis family walked up the white marble courthouse steps, passing dozens of people who had been lining the sidewalk outside the courthouse since before dawn in order to be ensured a seat at the hearing.

The MacPhail family was already seated with several members of the Fraternal Order of Police on the left side of the gallery, behind Susan Boleyn and Beth Burton from Georgia's attorney general's office. Dozens of friends and supporters filled the courtroom, offering smiles, subtle nods, and thumbs-ups to Martina and her family as they slipped into the bench reserved for them on the right, a few rows behind Troy's attorneys. In addition to Jay Ewart and Danielle Garten, the enhanced Arnold & Porter team now included Philip Horton and Stephen Marsh, who had been an assistant US attorney in the Southern District of Georgia. Attorneys and investigators from the Georgia Resource Center, which had continued to provide critical support to Troy's case in multiple ways, were there as well.

Martina was grateful to see such a strong display of support. At the very least, all those who had traveled to the hearing would have a chance to see firsthand the system that Troy had been up against. They would listen to the state's case and to Troy's. They would be able to gauge for themselves the credibility and the sincerity of the witnesses.

Some of the witnesses had been furious when they were served subpoenas to testify, John Hanusz had reported to Martina, and others had responded with a sense of deep fatigue. Each time they had been asked to give a sworn statement or to testify, the witnesses had been assured that this would be the last time. And each time, there had been a new twist or turn in the case, and they were called on yet again.

Judge William Moore entered and took his seat. Martina carefully studied the silver-haired, pink-cheeked seventy-year-old man who would unilaterally determine whether Troy would prove his innocence. The bar of clearly establishing innocence was extremely high, Jay had continued to remind Martina. In addition, events the day before the evidentiary hearing had taken a grim turn. "Bloodied Shorts among Davis Hearing Evidence," blared the headline of the *Savannah Morning News*.

Martina had been waiting for that shoe to fall, but hadn't expected to be ambushed like that. She and Jay had anticipated seeing the GBI reports about the black shorts a month ago, when all the evidence to be presented at the hearing was submitted, but there had been no mention of the reports on the state's evidence list. Then, just two days ago, the state had submitted a public motion seeking leave to add the GBI reports to the evidentiary record, alluding to the idea that there was blood and DNA on the shorts linking Troy to the murder. It didn't matter that Jay could prove that this was patently false; every media outlet had been on alert for any late-breaking developments.

Real damage had already been done. Just before the hearing, Larry Young and Dorothy Ferrell were suddenly acting skittish and nervous, as if they were second-guessing themselves. Jay assumed they must have seen the "bloody shorts" headline and gotten frightened and confused. Dorothy Ferrell had other concerns as well. There was a warrant out for her arrest and she was nervous that if she recanted on the stand, the prosecution might make sure that a marshal would be waiting for her afterward.

Martina knew that it would undermine the strength of Troy's case if Dorothy and Larry, two of the key recanting eyewitnesses, did not testify at the hearing. But having them testify in their current muddled, agitated state might do even more damage.

Judge Moore called the courtroom to order and four CERT officers led Troy to his bench, sitting directly behind him. Troy looked straight ahead, wearing a white Department of Corrections uniform and concealing his eyes behind thick-rimmed dark sunglasses. Martina knew that Troy was wearing the sunglasses in order to control his instinct to make eye contact with his friends and family—he understood that every move he made would be scrutinized by the media and possibly twisted to his detriment. A smile to a friend could show up in the *Savannah Morning News* as the smirk he was accused of wearing when he was first arrested.

Martina saw Troy lean forward slightly, which he always did when he was concentrating intensely, as Antione Williams, wearing dark jeans and a red shirt, took the stand. For the first time since his trial, Troy was in the same room with many of the individuals who had admitted to lying about him, forever changing the course of his life. It was frustrating having her brother just two rows in front of her, without being able to talk to him, touch him, or offer him comfort of any kind.

Antione reiterated what he had testified to in the 2007 parole board hearing: He had been in his car, behind heavily tinted windows in the middle of the night, when he had witnessed the police officer get shot. Terrified, he had immediately ducked down. He hadn't known at the time, and he still did not know, what the shooter looked like. He had pointed to Troy at trial because the prosecution had instructed him to.

Kevin McQueen explained again that he had invented a confession from Troy while incarcerated at Chatham County Jail.

"No matter how many times you come at me, the man did not tell me anything about shooting anyone. Period."

Kevin stood firm as the state tried to poke holes in his testimony and discredit him by dragging out a list of his prior convictions.

"Do you expect to gain anything from your testimony today, sir?" Philip Horton asked him.

"No," Kevin answered, looking straight at Troy. "Peace of mind, I guess."

Jeffrey Sapp answered the lawyers' questions diligently. RAH was short for Rahim and then had come to stand for Rough As Hell, which referred to Troy's car. Yes, Jeffrey had a prior conviction for possession of cocaine. Yes, he had made the statements about Troy confessing, but no, those statements were not true. He described how scared he had been when making those statements.

"Ma'am, you had to be there in 1989 to see the chaos and how angry them people were," he said to Beth Burton during cross-examination.

In the end, he had just repeated what the police had told him. At trial, he said, Spencer Lawton had instructed him to stick to his statement, so he had.

"You've known Troy Davis all your life, practically?" Beth Burton asked Jeffrey.

"Basically."

"Grew up with him?"

"Yes, ma'am."

"You don't want to see him get sentenced in this case, do you?"

"Sentenced to what?"

"Death is his sentence. You know that."

"No, ma'am, I wasn't going see nobody die, you know? The Bible say that."

"You don't want to see a convicted murderer die?"

Jeffrey stared at Burton and did not flinch.

"No, ma'am, if he's innocent."

Watching the testimonies, Martina realized what John Hanusz had meant by witness fatigue. Three years ago, when Jeffrey and Antione had spoken in front of the parole board, their testimonies had been gripping and compelling. Now they seemed somehow stale.

D.D. Collins took the stand next, sunglasses stuck in the front of his black T-shirt and wearing an earring. It was D.D.'s first time testifying since trial.

On August 18, 1989, D.D. had been with Troy at the pool party in Cloverdale. He had not known who fired the shot that hit Michael Cooper. Later, D.D., Troy, and Eric had headed down to Charlie Brown's pool hall in Eric's car. D.D. had seen Redd pull a gun from his waistband and lay it on the front seat of Eric's car. D.D. had told Redd that the gun couldn't be there, removed it from the car, and laid it by the side of the building in some bushes, then went inside the pool hall.

Not long after, he saw Redd arguing with a stranger over alcohol outside the pool hall. D.D. read from his 2002 affidavit that Redd had said, "You better give me a beer, motherfucker" and "You don't know me, I'll fucking smoke you, nigger." The other man was scared and tried to get away, with Redd following him, continuing to make heated threats. D.D. and Troy, being nosy, followed them. D.D. hadn't noticed if Redd's gun was still by the building or not.

D.D. had taken off when he saw a policeman come around the building and had not seen Larry Young being struck. That's when he had heard the gunshots. He had run back to the pool hall, got in the car with Eric, and got out of there.

The next night, more than ten policemen had come to his house, guns drawn. They had questioned sixteen-year-old D.D. for twenty minutes or so and took him to the barracks. His parents had been with him initially, but they had left after he signed a statement, assuming that the interrogation was done. But the interrogation had continued, with loud yelling, no parents, and no lawyer.

"I did not see Troy hit the man," D.D. had protested more than once, but the police didn't care—D.D. testified that they told him that Troy had hit the man. They told him, repeatedly, that Troy had shot the officer. They told him that they knew D.D. had seen Troy shoot Michael Cooper in Cloverdale as well.

"They were telling me I was an accessory to murder and that I would pay like Troy was going to pay if I didn't tell them what they wanted to hear. They told me that I would go to jail for a long time and I would be lucky if I ever got out, especially because a police officer got killed," D.D. read aloud from his 2002 affidavit, affirming on the stand that it was accurate.

He had tried to explain to them that it had been Redd messing with the man—but they hadn't wanted to hear that.

"Fine, have it your way," D.D. remembered the police threatening him, "Kiss your life goodbye, because you're going to jail for a long time."

D.D. had wanted to get out of the police barracks, so he told them what they had wanted him to say, even though it was not the truth. Whatever details the police had included, he had agreed to. They gave him a new statement, which he signed without reading. He never knew what had happened to the first statement he had signed with his mother and father present.

At trial, he had recanted about witnessing Troy commit the shooting in Cloverdale, but still had testified, falsely, that he had seen Troy hit the man in the Burger King parking lot. He had still been frightened, and that seemed to be what the police cared most about.

April Hester Hutchinson took the stand after D.D. and repeated what she had told the parole board in 2008: She had seen Redd at the party in Cloverdale, altercating and fussing at someone until he was asked to leave. She had also seen Redd down near the Burger King parking lot. She testified again about Redd asking her to walk with him so that it would seem like he hadn't done anything and about the look Redd had given her, communicating: *You better not say anything.*

"These events obviously took place quite a long time ago," Danielle said to April during the examination. "How do you remember the details of that evening?"

"It's hard to forget it," April answered.

"Explain what you mean by that," Danielle said.

"It's like it's plastered in my brain."

"And why is it that you've chosen to tell the full story in 2002 and here today?"

"Because I am older and I have kids and if I want them to do the right thing, then I have to do the right thing."

Anthony Hargrove testified in his Chatham County Jail jumpsuit. Anthony and Redd used to sell weed together and had been sitting on the front porch at a house party one night, smoking weed.

"While we were sitting there, he told me . . ." Anthony began.

"Your Honor, I'm going to object to anything that Redd Coles told him as hearsay," Beth Burton interjected.

Martina listened in dismay as Stephen Marsh and Beth Burton went back and forth about whether or not Anthony's testimony about Coles's confession should be accepted without Coles himself testifying.

Judge Moore ruled that Anthony could testify. "But I'll tell you now," Judge Moore warned Troy's attorneys. "This hearsay testimony is looked at with suspicion and great caution. And even though I'm going to allow this witness to testify, I may very well give this testimony no credence or no consideration whatsoever when I make my ruling in this case. My suggestion to you is that if you want it to have more weight than that with the court, that you should get Mr. Coles in here and we should do it the right way."

Martina tried not to show her surprise. Jay had told her that Judge Moore had ruled in a pretrial order that the hearsay rules were not applicable to innocence hearings and cases, deeming it unnecessary to call Coles—why was he changing the rules on them now?

"Okay, Mr. Hargrove, when you had that conversation with Mr. Coles, what did he tell you?" Steve Marsh continued questioning the witness.

Anthony continued describing the conversation that had taken place on the porch. Redd told him that a person he knew, Troy, had taken the fall for him.

"For what?" Anthony had responded

"I shot a cop over there at Burger King," Redd had continued.

"Nah, man, I didn't know that. For real?"

"Yeah, Troy took the fall."

Anthony had kept quiet and continued passing the joint with Redd. He didn't tell anybody about the conversation for years. He had had, as he described it, "legal problems," including eight or nine convictions and an arrest warrant in the state of Florida. If he had gone to the police, they would run his name. Finally, he had decided he was going to tell straight forward and break what he knew. He wrote to Troy in Jackson and Troy's attorneys had contacted him not long afterwards.

"So for twelve years you just never said anything?" Beth Burton asked Anthony during cross-examination.

"It's called self-preservation. I'm going to look after me first."

"So you're a pretty much admitted career criminal?"

"I'm not a career . . . I'm a guy that just gets caught."

Martina could swear that Anthony was grinning. She appreciated that he was telling the truth, but her brother's life was on the line. Couldn't he take this a bit more seriously?

Benjamin Gordon, an African American man with close-clopped hair wearing a prison jumpsuit, made his way to the witness stand next. Martina knew some of what Ben would testify from his February 2003 affidavit: that he had no idea who shot Michael Cooper in Cloverdale, though he had been in the car with Michael. His police statement describing Michael's shooter as wearing a white Batman T-shirt and dark jeans had been made under duress, Ben testified now. Police had been everywhere that night. They had run up to the porch where he was sitting and yelled at him to get down, rushing him as he complied. Two of them had hit him on the side of the head with their flashlights and a third had thrust a nightstick against his neck, threatening to kill him if he moved. They had dragged him into the paddy wagon and taken him to the police barracks. There they had cursed at him and accused him both of killing the officer and of having fired the shots in Cloverdale. If he didn't tell them what happened, they had yelled in his face, he would go to the electric chair. Sixteen years old, traumatized by the Cloverdale shooting, and scared as hell, Ben had signed whatever they had told him to sign without reading it.

Martina knew that Ben had revealed even more in a second 2008 affidavit and was expecting that part of his testimony as well. Redd was related to Ben through marriage and Ben considered Redd part of his family. Redd had always been a drinker and had a mean temper when drinking. Ben recalled Redd once shooting up a house party in Yamacraw. Redd loved guns and had more than could be counted, but his favorite was his .38 revolver. Redd had one on him almost every time Ben saw him.

Six years or so after the murder, Ben and Redd had been kicking back at Redd's sister's house, drinking. Out of nowhere, they had started talking about MacPhail's murder.

"I shouldn't have did that shit," Redd had confessed to Ben. "That shit was fucked up."

"You need to straighten it out," Ben had told Redd. "Because they got someone else locked up for the murder."

Redd had looked at Ben and started crying.

Martina was not expecting, however, to hear what Benjamin Gordon revealed on the stand in front of the packed courtroom. Nobody outside of

Troy's legal team was expecting it, and even they were not certain of how much Ben would actually say.

Martina learned the full story only later: A few months before the evidentiary hearing, Georgia Resource Center investigator Jeff Walsh had gone to the prison where Ben was incarcerated to inform him about the upcoming evidentiary hearing. Ben had listened quietly and seemed guarded as Jeff had explained that they would need Ben to testify about the contents of his 2003 and 2008 affidavits.

"There's more I have to say, but I don't know what to do," Ben had said once Jeff finished going over logistics with him.

Jeff had waited for a moment, but Ben did not continue. "All right. Just talk to me. Let me know what you know," Jeff had finally said, careful not to come on too strong.

"This is really hard. It's not something I want to do, but I have to." Ben hesitated, took a deep breath, and continued. "I saw the whole thing."

"Tell me what you saw."

Ben described it, slowly and deliberately, his body revealing anguish with every word he spoke. Jeff paused for a long moment after Ben, breathing heavily, had finished.

"This is obviously pretty important, Ben. We'll need you to testify to this at the hearing."

Ben's panic was immediate and overwhelming. He had needed to confess what he had witnessed to somebody, Ben said, but he didn't think he could do it in court. His testimony could put his wife and kids in danger. It could get Ben labeled as a snitch, which would make him vulnerable in prison. His family might cut him off entirely. Ben, who was normally low key and measured, was overcome with emotion.

Jeff continued to emphasize how crucial it was for Ben to come clean at the hearing.

"Man, you don't understand the risk I'm taking, what I'm putting out there!" Ben threw his arms up, pain and distress in every fiber of his being. "My wife, my kids." Tears brightened his eyes. "I have to think about it. I have to talk to my family."

When Jeff returned to the prison a week later, Ben had regained his composure. He had talked to trusted family members, he told Jeff, and they had given him their blessings to do what his conscience told him. His own sons had become teenagers while he had been in prison. He hadn't been there to guide them or help them make positive choices. He wanted to turn his own life around and to be there for his kids. Coming forward now would be a step in the right direction. It would signal a transition from criminal youth to a solid adult who wanted to do right by others. He couldn't promise what would come out of his mouth when he was actually on the stand, but he would try to tell the truth.

In twenty-two years of capital post-conviction investigations, Jeff Walsh had never met a witness who was more sincere, honest, or tormented than Benjamin Gordon.

"Okay, explain what you saw when you saw the second shot," Phil Horton asked Ben Gordon, as he sat on the witness stand.

"I saw an individual walk up to the individual laying on the ground and fire the shot," Ben answered. There was dead silence in the courtroom.

"Did you recognize the person who fired the shot?" Phil asked.

"Yes, I did," Ben replied. Martina clenched her fists, waiting to hear what Ben would answer. She peered at the judge—were Judge Moore's eyes actually closed?

"Who was it?"

"Sylvester Coles."

A ripple of electricity passed through the courtroom.

Ben was fully composed as he looked the attorney in the eye. "I have really had this burden on me for a long time. I was carrying this with me for a very, very long time. And even though this places me in direct danger with being in prison and my family out on the outside, I still made a decision to come in today and just let the truth be known."

Martina was still reviewing Ben Gordon's surprise testimony in her mind when the state's case began. Officer after officer from Savannah's 1989 police force took the stand.

"I was in no rush just to pick the first person that we could get our hands on and say, this is the suspect," Detective Ramsey testified. Redd Coles had not been considered a suspect because his description did not match the description witnesses gave of the shooter, Ramsey stated. Not one of them, the police officers all testified, had suggested answers, threatened, cajoled, intimidated, or coerced their witnesses in the investigation. Not a word had been put into witnesses' mouths. They all testified to having had precisely followed protocol in questioning witnesses. Martina was not surprised. Policemen were professional witnesses, and as far as Martina could tell, they were all following, yet again, the blue code of loyalty.

When Spencer Lawton took the stand, he could not seem to remember much about the case. "Two decades have transpired," he said. "I don't consider myself currently familiar with the details." Martina bit her tongue. Lawton had certainly seemed familiar with the details when he had penned an op-ed for the *Atlanta Journal-Constitution* on October 6, 2008.

Quiana Glover, a large African American woman wearing a denim skirt and a black-and-turquoise turtleneck, walked slowly toward the stand during the first day of testimony, coughing. It was an effort for her to be audible— her throat was sore and her voice almost gone. Judge Moore lost patience with her almost immediately and told her to come back the next day.

Martina knew that Quiana had recently been at a sports bar in Savannah when she had seen two local activists, Alicia Blakely and Hollis Mitchell, wearing "I Am Troy Davis" T-shirts and collecting petition signatures. Quiana had signed the petition and then, hesitating, had told the activists that she knew something about the case. Shortly afterward, someone from Troy's legal team had contacted her and she had signed an affidavit swearing to what she knew.

Quiana returned the next day, still sick, but her voice slightly more audible. She did not know Troy Davis, she testified, and had never met his family. She had been only five years old back in 1989 and did not learn about the shooting of Officer MacPhail until years later. Last June, she had been at a party and saw Redd there.

"During this gathering, was there a discussion about the shooting of Officer MacPhail?" Phil Horton asked Quiana.

"Yes."

"Did Mr. Coles take part in the discussion?"

"Yes, sir."

"Can you recall the first thing he said when the subject came up?"

"Excuse me, counsel," Susan Boleyn inserted. "Your Honor, we're going to renew our objection to this witness's testimony for the same reasons that we objected to those who attempted to relate conversations they allegedly had with Mr. Coles . . ."

A discussion about legal precedent ensued, but this time, Judge Moore lit into Troy's legal team. "Mr. Coles should have been called by you, and examined by you, and cross-examined by the state. . . . Davis has not done that, even though Coles is available to testify. And there's obvious reason for that!"

Why are you ignoring your own pre-trial order saying that hearsay would be admissible? Martina refrained from shouting out.

"Well, Your Honor, we certainly think it would be an exercise in futility because I don't think anyone expects Mr. Coles to come in here . . ." Phil Horton stammered.

"Whether you think it's an exercise in futility or not, the courts don't think that!" Judge Moore interrupted.

"Just if I may, Your Honor, I just wanted to let you know, in view of your statements yesterday, we did attempt to subpoena Mr. Coles to come. We were not able to serve him," Phil answered.

Martina leaned forward. Was Phil going to get the full story into the record? She knew that John Hanusz and Jeff Walsh had spent hours that morning trying to stake out Coles to serve him a subpoena—first in front of his apartment and then at his place of employment. Coles's boss had threatened them to get off his property or he would call the police. Was Phil going to report that John and Jeff had been physically prohibited from serving Coles? But Phil did not go into any of that detail.

"That's at the twelfth hour!" Judge Moore shot back. "Mr. Coles is a member of this community, lives in this community, and there are numerous opportunities for counsel to subpoena Mr. Coles!" Judge Moore sustained the state's objection. Quiana could not testify.

"I would simply like to proffer that . . ." Phil began.

"I know what your proffer is!" Judge Moore snapped. "Your proffer is going to be that she heard—I'm assuming that she heard or says somebody else heard that Mr. Coles said he was the shooter."

"So the record is clear, she would have testified that Mr. Coles himself said that he shot the officer in her presence," Phil managed to finish weakly.

Judge Moore then put the next question to Troy's attorneys. "Many of the witnesses that you say you have now recanted, you have not called in this case . . .

Why have you not called these witnesses and put these witnesses on the stand?"

Martina's heart quickened as Steve Marsh mumbled a response about calling the witnesses with the most meaningful recantations. What else could he say? Martina knew he could not explain Larry's and Dorothy's uneasy reactions to the provocative "bloody shorts" headlines. But Judge Moore was clearly furious at Steve's answer. The affidavits of the witnesses that Troy's legal team had not called would not be admitted, aside from Harriett Murray, who was now deceased and therefore unable to testify. Yet Harriett's affidavit had never been notarized, diminishing its probative value.

Jay tried to wrap the threads together one more time in his concluding argument. Any meaningful physical evidence—matching ballistics, bloody shorts—had been thoroughly discredited. There was no remaining evidence whatsoever connecting Troy to the Cloverdale shooting. The only remaining eyewitness who had not recanted regarding the MacPhail shooting, aside from Coles himself, was Steve Sanders, who had been in the Air Force van—and he was not credible.

The police had had tunnel vision on Troy to the exclusion of all other suspects, including Redd Coles. The photo lineup used in the investigation had been tainted. There were recanting witnesses and new witnesses. At this very hearing, the state was trying to discredit the very same witnesses that they had used in 1991 to convict Troy and sentence him to death. Taken altogether, Jay concluded as powerfully as he was able, a reasonable jury would find reasonable doubt.

The state kept their closing comments brief. The recantations were unreliable and to be looked upon with great skepticism, Burton said. The burden of proof was on Troy. This had been their chance. Davis had not met any standards of proving innocence, especially not the high standards of this hearing. Martina studied Judge Moore, trying to read him as best she could. Based on his countenance, not to mention the attitude he had exhibited throughout the past two days, the hearing had clearly been disastrous for Troy.

The CERT officers led Troy out of the back of the courtroom in order to return him to Jackson. He continued to look straight ahead of him.

Martina saw John Hanusz as she made her way out of the courtroom.

"I'm so sorry, Martina," John managed to push out, scarcely able to speak or maintain eye contact with her. "We tried."

"I know you did."

Martina had always known this hearing was going to be an uphill battle—fighting the entire system had always been an uphill battle. At the very least, everyone sitting in that courtroom had gotten a glimpse of how easy it was for an innocent person to get trapped in an unjust system.

John opened his mouth to try to say something else, but closed it without a sound.

Martina waited for Mama, Kimberly, Lester, Ebony, and De'Jaun to gather around her and then, holding their heads high, the Davis family walked out of the courthouse and down the white marble steps to Wright Square, where the television cameras awaited them.

June 23, 2010: Virginia and Martina walk into the United States District Court in Savannah for Troy's evidentiary hearing. Behind them, left to right: Larry Cox from AIUSA, Reverend Dr. Warnock from Ebenezer Baptist Church, and Benjamin Jealous from NAACP. Courtesy of Scott Langley, deathpenaltyphoto.org.

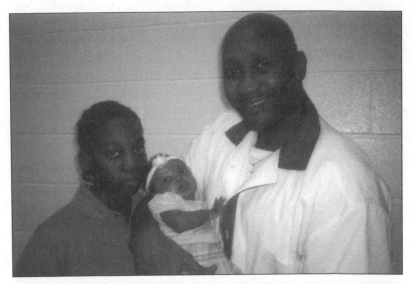

March 15, 2008: De'Jaun, two-month-old Kiersten, and Troy.
Courtesy of the Davis family.

De'Jaun and Virginia at an NAACP conference. Courtesy of the Davis family.

De'Jaun grows into an activist in his own right and an advocate for his uncle's case. Courtesy of the Davis family.

Martina rallies with Troy Davis supporters outside the Georgia Supreme Court in Atlanta. Courtesy of the Davis family.

Protestors chant in the prison yard and across the street as the scheduled execution time grows near. Courtesy of Scott Langley, deathpenaltyphoto.org.

Part Four

August 24, 2010

Martina did her best to read Judge Moore's 174-page ruling.

> Ultimately, while Mr. Davis's new evidence casts some additional, minimal doubt on his conviction, it is largely smoke and mirrors. The vast majority of the evidence at trial remains intact, and the new evidence is largely not credible or lacking in probative value. After careful consideration, the Court finds that Mr. Davis has failed to make a showing of actual innocence that would entitle him to habeas relief in federal court. Accordingly, the Petition for a Writ of Habeas Corpus is denied.

According to Judge Moore, witness after witness who had testified to intimidation and coercion from the Savannah police were less credible than the police officers who had testified that no such inappropriate questioning had taken place. The only meaningful, credible recantation, he wrote, came from Kevin McQueen—he determined the other recantations to be not credible, or not true recantations. Regarding Benjamin Gordon's testimony, Judge

Moore wrote, "The only explanation for Mr. Gordon's ever-evolving testimony is that it changes to reflect whatever details he believes are necessary to secure Mr. Davis's release. Therefore, his testimony is not credible." The hearsay evidence of Coles's confessions were all but dismissed. The ruling eviscerated Troy for not calling Dorothy Ferrell or Larry Young to the stand and for not subpoenaing Coles.

Judge Moore did conclude that executing an innocent person would violate the Eighth Amendment of the US Constitution. "However, Mr. Davis is not innocent," he wrote, though he acknowledged that the case against Troy "may not be ironclad."

"We're appealing," Jay told Martina. "Starting with the 11th Circuit and to the US Supreme Court from there." But Martina detected little optimism in his voice.

✧

September 22, 2010

It had been years since Martina had heard Troy sound as distraught as he did when he called home that day.

Brandon Rhode, a fellow inmate on the row who had been convicted in 2000 of a triple murder, had been scheduled for execution the prior evening. Hours beforehand, lying on his bed under a blanket while on death watch, monitored by two guards, Brandon had managed to slash himself with a razor blade, carving deep, gaping wounds into his arms and neck. By the time the guards discovered what had happened, Brandon had already been unconscious for an undetermined amount of time and had possibly sustained severe brain damage from oxygen deprivation. Prison staff rushed Brandon to a nearby hospital where he was revived and his wounds sutured, then returned him to the prison and restrained him in a chair to await a new execution date.

Martina felt nauseous when she hung up the phone. There had been thirty-three executions in Georgia since Troy had been placed on the row; thirty-three human beings Martina had witnessed make that journey and not return. With every execution, Martina relived the trauma of saying goodbye to her brother over and over. But Brandon Rhode's situation was beyond the pale. Had the prison staff really brought this man back from the brink of death in order to kill him? Was the state of Georgia truly preparing to strap Brandon's slashed and stitched-up body to a gurney?

On Monday, September 27, less than a week after his suicide attempt, the state of Georgia killed Brandon Rhode.

✧

November 17, 2010
Hello sweetie,
I wanted you to know that I feel blessed to have you in my life. Tina, you are more than a sister, you are a part of me, and my dearest friend, my twin soul. Whenever I think about the sacrifices you made on my behalf, it touches my heart. I just pray all day God heals you completely and lets us travel the world to continue His work. You make me so proud of you. God bless you, Martina, I love you, big sis.

Martina was experiencing intense pain and had to put down the letter from Troy in order to sit still and assess. Was the pain radiating from her stomach or her liver? Did she need to call her doctor or should she wait and see if the stabbing ache worsened?

Martina was drained from treatment, fed up with going to doctors. There were moments when she was tempted to stop fighting altogether. But whenever the thought of giving up crossed her mind, she would receive a letter like this from Troy.

Unable to sleep because of the pain, Martina roamed around the house, pausing outside sixteen-year-old De'Jaun's door as he slept. If she stopped getting chemotherapy and succumbed to the battle her body was in for survival, she would let down both her son and her brother. She had to keep going so she could see Troy walk free, De'Jaun graduate from high school, and Mama relax and enjoy her senior years. Martina did not want Mama to go to her grave with her son on death row and her daughter fighting cancer.

Martina was not the only one who saw that her mother's hair was graying and that the wrinkles in her skin had grown deeper and more numerous. She wasn't alone in realizing that Mama was snapping at small things that had never bothered her in the past. Troy noticed it all and, much as he tried, he could not hide the concern in his eyes.

Lately, Troy had also been looking at Martina with worry on visitation days, no matter how often she told him that her weakness was just a matter of not bouncing back from the chemo the way she used to. Troy regaled Kimberly and Ebony with questions about Martina's health, convinced that Martina was hiding her true condition from him in order to protect him.

"I'm being honest about what the doctors are telling me, Troy!" Martina kept insisting, though she didn't report to Troy every little pain she had. Why worry him to the point that he would not be able to sleep? There was already enough despair on death row. And though he didn't articulate it often, Martina knew that Troy continued to feel responsible for the family's financial problems—which began with Virginia taking a second mortgage on their home years ago to pay for Troy's legal fees during trial—and for Martina's deteriorating health.

"You're not a burden, Troy," she reminded him repeatedly. "You didn't give me cancer. You can't blame yourself."

Martina had been trying to slow down, but it was impossible to sit back and do nothing. She was still signed up to lead several breast-cancer workshops and she was determined to fulfill her commitment. And how could Martina rest when Troy's case was in such a vulnerable place?

Jay's petition to the 11th Circuit had been denied on November 5. The last slim legal thread was to petition the US Supreme Court. If the Supreme Court rejected this final appeal, it would pave the way for Georgia to set a new execution date. Troy continued to remain optimistic and each time she spoke to him, visited, or received a letter like the one in her hand, she felt hopeful and reinvigorated. If Troy wasn't giving up, neither could she.

✧

March 2011

Martina sat on the couch, recuperating from another week in the hospital. She had been in and out over the past several months—this time, it was due to a large stomach ulcer that was preventing her from eating. Dr. Hunter, her

GI doctor, wanted her off the chemo until the ulcer healed, but Dr. Negrea, her oncologist, was afraid that any extended period off chemo would cause her tumors to grow again. Tests on her liver were showing ammonia levels that were higher than they should be.

De'Jaun leaned over the back of the couch, bending over the side of her neck. "Mom, are you okay?" Martina looked at the child she had brought into this world. How could she protect De'Jaun from his anxiety? The night before, Martina had gone out to run some errands and returned home later than she had expected to find De'Jaun waiting up in bed. "What took you so long, Mom? I was worried," he had said.

As De'Jaun's mother, it was her job to teach and nurture him, to make sure that he got what he needed and was able to stand on his own two feet. Perhaps she had shown him an additional level of attention because of what had happened to Troy—Martina knew what it meant for a young black male to grow up in a society where terrible, unjust things can happen. But she had always wanted for De'Jaun to have as normal a childhood as possible. At sixteen, De'Jaun was an advocate and an activist in his own right, receiving many invitations to speak, but Martina also wanted to strike the right balance between exposing De'Jaun to human rights issues and making sure he wasn't being exploited in any way because he was Troy's nephew. She didn't want her son put on a pedestal only to find someday that the pedestal had been an illusion.

De'Jaun's teachers told Martina that his mind sometimes seemed to wander during days of assessment testing. He didn't seem to be paying attention, one teacher remarked in a parent-teacher conference. Of course De'Jaun's mind wandered during those long, silent tests—how could it not? As her son got older, Martina watched the straight As turn to As and Bs with an occasional C and witnessed the disappointment that De'Jaun exhibited on those occasions. Martina wished that De'Jaun would put less pressure on himself.

Martina knew that De'Jaun wanted to become a medical robotics researcher in order to find a cure for her cancer, and that he wanted to succeed in order to make his uncle proud. That was a big burden for a child. Troy wanted De'Jaun to do the best he could, but he didn't expect him to be the best in everything in order to earn his approval. Martina wanted her son to know that it was okay with her if he occasionally got a low grade or didn't live up to everyone's expectations.

Martina worried about how much De'Jaun held inside regarding the strain he was under. The past weekend, he had stayed mostly in his room, watching the Food Network and playing video games, rather than making plans with his friends. One day, Martina walked into his room and saw him watching a Disney movie.

"Aren't you a little bit old for that?" she asked him.

De'Jaun just shrugged. Martina didn't say another word—she realized that Disney was probably comforting to him.

Martina was glad when the Amnesty USA annual general meeting took place in mid-March. De'Jaun could be himself and feel supported among his Amnesty friends—but even in that environment, things could be difficult.

"Troy's at risk of his fourth execution date," Laura Moye said, introducing a panel of speakers that included both Martina and De'Jaun. "He has an appeal pending in front of the US Supreme Court. So we're very much trying to remain vigilant and continuing to get signatures collected on the petition, in case we need to go into a clemency campaign."

Martina knew that De'Jaun was aware that his uncle's fate would likely come down to the parole board's decision and that the sense of urgency that Laura was trying to convey was required to mobilize a massive campaign, but hearing it said aloud was difficult. Laura, Wende, Ben Jealous—none of them had to live the reality of a fourth execution date and possible clemency campaign the way her family did. Martina had not fully realized how deeply the series of execution dates had traumatized De'Jaun until she saw him break down and cry during a joint video interview at the conference. Martina tried to take over to answer the next question, but she began crying as well. It was awful.

What would happen to her child if both she and Troy died? As hard as she tried not to entertain that dark scenario, Martina could not eliminate that horrible, nagging question from her brain. Mama was elderly. Kimberly would step in, of course, but Kim had her own health issues to deal with. Ebony and De'Jaun bickered like siblings sometimes, but they were inseparable. She knew that Ebony would be there for him—and Lester as well. If only all this were not hanging over De'Jaun as he prepared to finish eleventh grade and enter his final year of high school. She wanted him to be able to enjoy his senior year. Troy and Martina spoke regularly about how they could help De'Jaun not to be overwhelmed, but the reality itself was overwhelming. More and more, Martina watched De'Jaun trying to step up to the plate and take charge, as if he were preparing to take her place. He directly said as much to her during the Amnesty video interview.

"Mom, now that you're kinda getting older—you're still young, but you're getting older—it's gonna soon be time for me to carry your burden."

She knew by *older*, De'Jaun really meant *sicker*.

Martina didn't want him to carry her burden. He had his own role to play, as a young person with a powerful voice. "You don't have to carry it for me, you carry it for yourself," Martina answered. "That's what I want."

What Martina really wanted was for De'Jaun to be a happy child. But it wasn't always possible to be happy with a mother who was in and out of the hospital and an uncle facing a possible fourth execution date.

✧

Even through the plexiglass that had replaced the iron grille, three-year-old Kiersten was determined to teach Uncle Troy what she had learned in her weekly ballet class.

"Lookin' good, Twinkle-toes!" the other men on visitation cracked at Troy as he grinned broadly, standing on his tippy-toes with his arms curved not-so-gracefully above his head, as Ebony's little girl scolded him through the phone for failing to twirl properly.

At the end of every visit, after the family's circle of prayer, Troy pressed his hand flat against his side of the plexiglass while Kiersten mirrored him on the other side. Kiersten's entire hand with fingers extended barely filled the length of Troy's palm. Hand-to-hand with his niece, Troy would squish his nose against the glass and make a silly face to Kiersten, who would squeal and giggle in delight as Martina and the rest of the family watched, smiling at their special ritual.

"What's that, TiTi?" Kiersten asked, as Martina held out an envelope to the little girl.

"It's your very own letter from Uncle Troy," Martina told her.

Kiersten eagerly ripped open the envelope and pulled out a piece of paper.

She looked for a moment at the outline of Troy's hand that he had traced on the sheet of notebook paper, then pressed her own little palm against the drawing and smiled. Hand-to-hand, their special ritual.

Kiersten proudly marched around the living room the rest of the evening, holding up Troy's hand outline for all the family to admire. "This is my letter from Unca Toy!"

"TiTi, where my crayons?" Kiersten asked Martina the next day. Martina handed the little girl a pack of Crayolas and watched with amazement as Kiersten placed her left hand in the center of a piece of paper and traced her fingers carefully with a crayon held in her right hand. When she finished, she folded the paper carefully, wiggly childish crayon lines and all, and asked for an envelope so she could send her hand tracing back to Uncle Troy.

✧

March 28, 2011

Martina lay in bed, listening to De'Jaun getting ready for school. It was exactly ten years ago to the day that Dr. Kim had told her she had six months to live. She had made it ten years, against all odds.

The phone rang as Martina was fixing breakfast.

"Martina. It's Jay." She knew Jay well enough by now to recognize the nuances in the tone of his voice. Her heart seized before Jay got out the next sentence. "Troy was denied by the Supreme Court. We're going to exhaust all legal means available to us." She detected just enough steely resolve in Jay's voice to know that, devastating as this news was, he was not done fighting.

Martina hung up the phone before asking Jay if Troy knew yet and how he was taking the news. Troy would be more worried about the family, especially about Mama, than about himself, Martina knew. Should Martina call Virginia, who was out running errands, to make sure she reached her before a reporter did? Or should she wait until Mama got home and tell her in person? How would her mother be able to survive a fourth execution date?

Martina's cell phone began beeping and ringing: Wende Gozan Brown; Laura Moye; Ed DuBose; Ben Jealous; Ledra Sullivan-Russell; friends and advocates wanting to confirm the news and encourage her that there was still hope; reporters asking for a statement. Martina worked to contain the rage she felt at the thought of Troy's imminent execution date and to channel that fury to fuel her fight. Martina was going to fight until there was not a single breath left in her body.

✧

Mama's eyes were tracking repeatedly back to the same place in the copy of the *Savannah Morning News* spread over her lap, her hands trembling slightly. Martina leaned over Virginia's chair to see what sentence Mama had been reading and rereading: "The Supreme Court has rejected an appeal from Georgia death row inmate Troy Davis, clearing the way for the state to resume planning for Davis' execution."

Martina logged onto the website to read the rest of the article online. Executions in Georgia were on a temporary hold since Georgia's supply of sodium thiopental, one of the three drugs that Georgia used in its lethal injection cocktail, had been confiscated by the Federal Drug Enforcement Agency. The Georgia Department of Corrections had obtained its stash of sodium thiopental from a British pharmaceutical company that operated out of the back of a London driving school, violating the Controlled Substances Act by not registering it with the DEA. If it were not for the unresolved lethal injection issue, an execution date for Troy might have been announced immediately.

Martina was relieved that Mama wasn't looking at the online version, which included horrifying comments:

—$.75 bullet is a lot cheaper and will do the job just as well

—No sodium thiopental? No Problem. . . . . . . just fire up ole sparky. He deserves it.

—Fry baby fry

The following morning, Virginia had the *Savannah Morning News* on her lap again, this time opened to the editorial: "It's time to stop playing the broken record known as the Troy Anthony Davis appeals process."

"The paper is saying to kill Troy and get it over with!" Mama said to Martina, aghast.

"Don't read that garbage," Martina answered firmly. "We're still fighting. We're not going to worry about all the negativity."

Martina admired how Virginia kept up a strong exterior, assuring every caller that no sir, it wasn't over, and yes indeed, the recent confiscation of Georgia's sodium thiopental was surely a blessing from God. But once again, Martina could hear Mama alone in her room at night, praying not to let them kill her child. Why, given all this evidence, did they still want to kill her child?

✧

April 11, 2011

Mama drove Martina to the hospital for a procedure that would allow the doctor to look inside her stomach to check on her ulcer.

"Don't worry about the ulcer," Virginia said, patting Martina's arm as they sat in the lobby waiting for the routine to begin. "I've already prayed about the ulcer."

Martina woke up in recovery and found Mama sitting next to her.

"What did the doctor say?" she asked her mother.

"You have no ulcer anymore," Virginia reported, smiling. It was the first time in two years that Martina was ulcer-free. "God answered my prayer."

Virginia had to go to her own doctor's appointment around the corner, so Kimberly drove Martina home. That night, Mama reported that her doctor had given her a clean bill of health.

✧

April 12, 2011

Martina was recuperating from the anesthesia used in her procedure the day before.

"I'll fix you some lunch," Virginia offered.

Martina didn't feel much like eating, but she knew she needed to build up her strength.

"OK."

Now that the ulcer was gone, she hoped eating would get easier.

Mama put Kiersten down for a nap in Martina's bed and prepared soup for herself and for Martina.

"I was reading that Georgia might switch soon to pentobarbital," Virginia said as they ate. "A lot of states already have. If they switch, then they can start executing again."

"You can't pay attention to that, Mama. We still have a lot of fight."

Virginia nodded in agreement, but seemed distracted.

"I'm going to go watch some television," Mama said, after washing the soup bowls and wiping down the kitchen table.

"Okay," Martina responded. "I'm going to go lay down."

Mama settled into her living room chair as Martina went to her bedroom. Little Kiersten barely stirred as Martina stretched out next to her and drifted off to sleep.

The sound of the garage opening registered faintly in Martina's brain, followed by the slamming of the door. De'Jaun must be home from school. He slammed the door almost every day to get a rise out of his grandmother. Martina waited for Virginia's usual response of *Boy, stop slamming that door before you knock my mirrors off the wall!* but the scolding didn't come.

"Grandma, I'm home," Martina heard De'Jaun say. There was no response. She heard him repeat it, again with no response. By the third "Grandma, I'm home!" Martina sat up. She was already getting out of bed when De'Jaun burst into her bedroom.

"Mom, please help me, I can't wake up Granny!"

"Dial 911!" Martina said to De'Jaun and made her way to the living room, unsteady, weak, but as quickly as she could.

Mama was slumped over in her chair. Martina put her fingers under her mother's jaw and her ear to her mouth. No pulse or breath.

"Help me get her to the floor!"

Together, Martina and De'Jaun lifted Virginia and laid her gently on the carpet.

Martina began administering CPR. "Don't leave, Mama," she whispered in Virginia's ear. "Don't leave, because Troy's going to be alright."

But as a nurse, Martina knew that God had come for her. Mama was gone.

One emergency vehicle after another pulled up as Martina sent texts to Ebony, Lester, and Kimberly, telling them to come home right away. Who else could she call? Who did she trust? Her oncologist was the first person who came to mind. Martina was hysterical when Dr. Negrea answered his cell phone.

"Calm down," Dr. Negrea told her. "I'll meet you at the hospital."

No heart damage, the doctor at St. Joseph's Hospital said upon the preliminary autopsy. No stroke or blood clot. Mama's death appeared to be from "natural causes." But there was nothing natural, Martina knew, about her mother's heart breaking from being unable to endure her son's fourth execution date.

One by one, each family member entered Virginia's hospital room to say a private goodbye. Martina waited until everyone else had had his or her turn before she took hers. Mama's eyes were closed. She looked peaceful. Martina stroked her mother's cheek. Her skin was soft and still slightly warm.

"God rewarded you with your wings, Mama," Martina said softly. "You're with Aunt Mattie now, looking down and protecting us." She bent over to kiss Virginia's smooth forehead. "I'm going watch over all us kids, Mama, and make sure we all stick together, just like you wanted."

✧

Troy was answering letters on his bed when he heard the footsteps. It didn't sound like a guard. He went to the bars and saw the prison chaplain walking past cell after cell. That was odd; the chaplain was not usually on the row this time of day. Troy waited for the chaplain to pass his cell as well, but instead of walking past, he stopped and stood directly before Troy, meeting his gaze through the bars wordlessly. Troy sank down to his knees.

"Not Tina?"

"No, it's not Martina," the chaplain said gently. "It's your mother. Martina called and asked me to tell you."

Troy stayed on his knees, covering his face in his hands. He could not bring himself to look at the chaplain. And he could not cry. It was the same when Daddy had passed—he had tried and tried to bring down tears, but he couldn't. On his knees at the entrance of his cell, Troy prayed for strength and for guidance. And he prayed for tears.

✧

"Will you read my letter to Mama at the funeral?" Troy asked Martina. Troy's letter had just arrived that afternoon and Martina had only opened it minutes before.

"Troy, there's no way that I can read that letter aloud without falling apart," Martina said. "Maybe Gemma would be willing to read it."

"I'll do it," De'Jaun volunteered after Martina hung up the phone.

"Are you sure, De'Jaun?" Martina asked him. If she couldn't handle it, how in the world would her child be strong enough to stand up at his grandmother's funeral and read the letter from his Uncle Troy?

"I want to read it. I can do it," De'Jaun insisted.

✧

Why was the warden choosing to display this extra, unnecessary cruelty when the whole family was suffering, Martina wondered? Warden Humphrey revoked Troy's phone privileges the day before the funeral, giving the excuse that it would be too emotional for Troy to hear his family members' voices. Like so much else, Troy was powerless to do anything about it.

It gave Martina some comfort that people filled the church from all over the country to honor Mama. Dressed all in white, in her white casket, Mama looked like the beautiful angel she now was, watching over them. Lester tucked a button into Virginia's casket. "Innocence Matters" was printed on the button with a photo of Troy wearing a golden, silky robe from his high school graduation, a half-smile playing on his lips and giving a big thumbs-up. The warden had prevented Troy speaking with his family today, but he could not prevent Mama taking something of Troy with her to the afterlife.

The Reverend Dr. Warnock from Ebenezer Baptist Church came to Savannah to deliver the eulogy, turning it into a powerful call to action. "The best way to honor Virginia's life is to fight for Troy's life!" he said passionately from the pulpit.

Martina had not been able to bring herself to plan in advance what she would say, but the words poured out of her.

My father Joseph was a spitfire. He spoke his mind and he was a hell-raiser. I always admired him for that, and prided myself for being like him, because everyone says, "Tina, you're just like your daddy." But the person with power in our family wasn't just my father. It was that gentle giant, my mother. She gave me what I needed to lead. We're going to miss her and we're going to cry, but we're going to celebrate her life and we're going to continue her legacy. She taught me how to fight, and she taught me how to be faithful. I love you, Mama.

Virginia had been deeply beloved and greatly respected in the community as a woman of God, and the church was full of Savannah ministers. Maybe now, the ministers would lead their congregations to action on Troy's behalf, Martina thought, as she encouraged everyone to sign the petition for Troy and to bring copies to their own churches. As she stepped down from the pulpit, Martina could see Virginia's earthly body laid in the casket below her, but she could feel Mama's soul in heaven, fighting for her son harder than ever.

Martina watched De'Jaun walk up to the pulpit, holding Troy's letter. Would he be able to get through it without breaking down? He smoothed out the paper and began to read.

To my Dearest Mama,

Who would have thought this would be the last letter between us? Surely not me! I feared this day would come before I came home to you, but now that it came to pass, we all will hold onto the millions of beautiful memories you gave us. . . . Mama it hurts deep through my Soul not to be able to see your beautiful smile again. I know you and Aunt Mattie are like two little girls holding hands while skipping through a field of roses. I'm happy for both of you to have no more stress and no more pain. Mama, everyone is here to say their final goodbyes, but I'll never let go. You weren't my rock, you were the mountain God carved every strong woman from.

De'Jaun read clearly and with poise, with no crack in his voice and with eyes that remained dry. Martina was amazed. How could he not be falling apart right now?

All I know is that I will walk out of here a free man very soon and keep the family strong just like you would expect me to. I pray it rains heavy on that day because I'll know for sure that you were amongst the Angels crying tears of joy saying "Praise God" and "Thank you, Jesus." Until then, just ask God to send His Holy Spirit to help all of us stay strong and get through this. I

love you, we love you, because to all of us you will always be MAMA.
Forever my love!
Your son,

Troy A. Davis

De'Jaun folded up the letter as mourners throughout the church wiped their eyes and, standing erect, walked down the pulpit steps. Martina already knew that De'Jaun got his compassion from Troy and his tenacity from her, but who had given him this profound inner strength? She stared at De'Jaun as he took his seat, and suddenly realized that she was no longer looking at a child but at a young man. And at the end of the day, it turned out that this young man, her son, was the strongest of them all.

✧

Martina's cell phone did not stop ringing. Virginia's death had had an impact.

Hundreds of people finally seemed to grasp what the family had been saying for years: the system trying to kill Troy was attacking the entire family. People all over, but most importantly in Savannah, wanted to know what they could do for Troy's campaign. Martina had distributed over one hundred of Troy's petition sheets at Mama's wake and funeral.

"I got four sheets filled out already with over one hundred signatures," one caller said just hours after the funeral. "You got any more you can give me?"

Martina was feeling ill, but this was energizing. She got up, put her shoes on, and went to Kinko's to copy more petition sheets.

Martina attended a meeting that night with Laura Moye and activists, some from Savannah, such as Solana Plaines and DeNise Chaney, and others who had driven all the way from North Carolina, such as Daniel and Donna Kroener. Laura had told Martina not to worry about the meeting, especially on the night she had just buried her mother, but Martina wanted to capitalize on the spark that was igniting Savannah to action. Fighting for Troy was what Mama would have wanted her to do.

✧

It was hard to get used to the quiet and emptiness in the house. Mama's clothes still hung in the closet; her bed was left with the sheets tucked in and blankets neatly pulled up as she had made it the morning she passed.

"We can't just let the room stay that way," Martina said once or twice to her siblings, but Kimberly, Lester, and Ebony were not ready to touch it.

Three-year-old Kiersten continued to insist on changing into her play clothes after day care in her grandmother's room, just as she always had with Virginia. Some days, Kiersten seemed to understand that Granny was an angel up in the sky with Jesus. Other days she asked for her Granny—sometimes upset, other times matter-of-fact.

"TiTi, this is Granny's chair," she said to Martina every day, patting it to make sure Martina knew.

✧

Martina dreaded that first visit to Troy without Mama.

"Sorry about your loss," one guard after another told the family, from the time they signed in and went through the security screening to the moment they were sitting down opposite Troy with a plexiglass window between them.

Martina and Troy had made an unspoken agreement to keep the visit light and filled with humor. There would be plenty of time for them to talk about Mama's passing. But now, what they both needed most was to feel the comfort of their brother-sister banter and playfulness. Martina cracked an off-color joke that first made Troy's jaw drop, then caused him to laugh his Pillsbury Doughboy laugh.

They had both promised Mama to keep the family strong—and that's what they were going to do.

✧

May 20, 2011

"The Georgia Department of Corrections will substitute pentobarbital for sodium thiopental," Martina read in the Associated Press report, after a flurry of text messages and phone calls alerted her that the switch had been announced. "The change in drugs should clear the way for Georgia to execute

Troy Anthony Davis . . .”

Pentobarbital was commonly used to euthanize animals. Martina thought about that day, years ago, when De'Jaun had asked if she was going to put their dog Egypt to sleep the way they were trying to put his Uncle Troy to sleep. And now here it was: Georgia was one step closer to killing its inmates using the same method that is employed to put an animal down. Martina was relieved that Mama didn't have to read this.

“ . . . Chatham County District Attorney spokeswoman Alicia Johnson said the office was 'not immediately' filing paperwork to seek an execution order for Davis,” Martina continued reading, before closing her laptop in disgust.

Martina had been ecstatic two and a half years before when Larry Chisolm, an African American man who had gone to the same high school, Windsor Forest, as she and Troy, had been elected Chatham County district attorney over Assistant DA David Lock. At least Chisolm wasn't a junior Spencer Lawton, who embodied Savannah's white old guard. The new DA would surely look upon Troy's case with some understanding of how the forces of racism and retribution had played into the SPD's investigation and Troy's conviction. Yet, after two years in office, Chisolm had shown no indication of doing anything other than following Lawton's party line. Martina's initial hope had hardened into cynicism.

And what did “not immediately” mean? Was it due to compassion after the loss of Mama? Or was it strategic? Chisolm would look as if he lacked any sympathy if he sought an execution order for Troy just five weeks after Troy's mother had passed. Martina wished she had some idea of how long “not immediately” was.

✧

Summer 2011

Her ulcer was gone and her tumor markers were still low, but Martina was losing weight at an alarming rate.

“The chemotherapy is preventing your liver from making the protein your body needs,” Dr. Negrea told her. She ate as much high-protein food as she possibly could, taking additional supplements, but her weight kept dropping.

Martina became unable to keep certain foods down, and soon she could keep no food down at all. After a night of particularly intense vomiting, her doctor checked her into the hospital and put her on a total parenteral nutrition (TPN) drip, a mixture given directly into her bloodstream that supplied the calories and nutrients her body could not absorb by eating. An infection in her abdominal wall spread and entered her bloodstream, so antibiotics were added to her TPN. Each time she was released, the vomiting would start again and she would land back in the emergency room and back on TPN.

She began to feel confused a few days after one release from the hospital.

"Mom, you weren't making any sense when you answered that lady's question!" De'Jaun remarked on their way home from a trip to the pharmacy.

The next day, she went to see her GI doctor.

"How are you feeling?" Dr. Hunter asked her.

"Extra large," Martina answered.

Dr. Hunter readmitted Martina immediately and a battery of tests were ordered. The test results showed high ammonia levels, which Martina knew were a worrying indication of liver dysfunction and explained her disoriented mental state. The doctors started her on lactulose to help draw the ammonia from her body.

But when she was finally able to go home three weeks later, Martina began to experience excruciating pain in her legs and arms.

"This is one of the most severe cases of neuropathy I've ever seen—I'm checking you in for inpatient rehab," the doctor told her.

The longer Martina was on the rehab floor, the weaker she became. It was normal for her function to deteriorate, the doctor told her. Her muscles had to break down in order to build back up. But soon Martina needed help bathing and getting out of bed. Eventually, she could not even brush her own teeth.

"Rehab is making me worse," she told the doctor angrily. "I'll do outpatient rehab—I need to get off of this floor."

But as Martina was checking herself out, she was struck by pain so severe that she nearly keeled over. A nurse took her temperature. "You're spiking a

101-degree fever," the nurse said. "We can't send you home like this—we're going to have to admit you to the inpatient unit." The fever came down with medication, but Martina's neuropathy continued to get worse and her functioning deteriorated further. When she was no longer able to walk, Lester pushed Martina in a wheelchair around the grounds of the hospital so she could get some sunshine. He frequently stayed with Martina in the hospital overnight.

Martina put all her energy into gaining weight and gaining strength so she could go home, but a few days after her doctors finally agreed to discharge her, her ammonia levels went back up and the vomiting began again. Once again, Martina was readmitted to the hospital.

"We're going to try a jejunal percutaneous endoscopic gastrostomy, or a JPEG," Dr. Negrea told her. Martina knew that inserting the JPEG—a feeding tube that would bypass her stomach and deliver the nutrients directly into her small intestine—would be painful. More painful than the physical suffering, however, was seeing how her condition impacted De'Jaun, who spent hours every day of his summer vacation at her bedside.

"De'Jaun, you don't have to come to the hospital every day," Martina told him. "As long as I talk to you on the phone, I'm okay."

Martina was relieved when De'Jaun went to Los Angeles for a short-term internship with Ben Jealous and the NAACP. Of course she ached to see him, but she realized what was best for her child.

Difficult, too, was trying to campaign for Troy from the hospital bed. Calls and texts continued to flood in from organizations and activists seeking her input. Some days she managed to push herself to be on conference call meetings and to answer questions, but on other days she wanted to shout at the world that she just couldn't do it. No matter how much grit and determination Martina had, she was not a cut-out in a pop-up book who could spring back up no matter what.

Most excruciating of all, however, was the knowledge that an execution date could be set at any time—and she had not seen Troy for months.

"I'm going to visit you as soon as I get out of this place," she told him each time they spoke.

"You have to take care of yourself first," Troy would answer in a soft voice. "You have De'Jaun to think about."

Dr. Negrea came to her bedside one day. "We've detected fluid in the lower lobe of your right lung," he told her. "A surgical pulmonary specialist for cancer is going to drain it." The specialist, Dr. Douglas Mullins, used a long, thin needle for the procedure that went through her back and between her ribs to access the fluid that had built up over her lung.

But the next day, after x-rays were taken, Dr. Negrea was back at her bedside. "Fluid is back in your system," he said. "Dr. Mullins is going to have to insert a non-invasive small port to drain it."

Martina took a deep breath and steeled herself as she asked Dr. Negrea what she really needed to know. "Am I coming to the end?"

"What are you talking about?"

"Every time I turn around, I'm back here with some other problem. If I'm coming to the end, I want to know."

No, Dr. Negrea assured her, she was not coming to the end.

If she wasn't at the end, then she needed to get herself better, so she could see her brother. Martina could no longer tolerate lying in a hospital bed worrying about Troy, painfully aware that Troy was sitting in his cell, worrying about her.

✧

September 6, 2011

A journalist called Martina on her cell phone at the hospital just moments after Jay had informed her.

"How do you feel now that there's an execution date?" the reporter asked.

How the hell do you think I feel? Martina wanted to scream.

The date was scheduled for September 21, two weeks away. She was curiously aware of not being frightened or anxious. A certain numbness had set in with the repeated execution dates. And with each new close call, the campaign to save Troy's life had grown in strength and organization. The number of people ready to mobilize on her brother's behalf was exponentially greater than in 2008, and that number had been significantly larger than in 2007. AIUSA, the NAACP, National Action Network, the ACLU, and other allies had been ready to spring into action for months now. The media truck would get rolling once more. The activists would be set into motion.

Martina had to concentrate on what needed to get done. The parole board chair, James Donald, had signaled that he would entertain another clemency hearing, and Jay would learn soon when the hearing would be scheduled. Given that there were three new members of the parole board since Troy's last clemency hearing, there was good reason to be optimistic about the outcome.

"Jay said that they're going to do everything they can, but that I've got to be realistic," Troy said to Martina when he called that evening. "He doesn't want me not to say goodbye to all of you, thinking that I'm going to walk away from this."

Martina had to get out of this damn hospital.

"I want to try to walk," Martina told Lester.

"You can't walk," Lester said, taking in her frail frame.

"Yes, I can."

"Try it," he said. "I'll be walking right behind you."

Exerting all her strength, Martina lifted herself off of the bed. One unsteady foot in front of the other, she slowly made her way down the long corridor to the nurses' station, turned around, and walked back to her room, sitting back on her bed triumphantly.

The next afternoon, she convinced Dr. Negrea to discharge her and went home, determined to get strong enough to visit Troy that weekend.

But the following morning, Martina was back in the hospital.

✧

Between supporters seeking marching orders, journalists clamoring for interviews, and friends wanting updates, Martina's cell phone rang without pause. It was impossible to get any rest. Difficult as it was, Martina had to relinquish control and trust Kimberly and De'Jaun to step in and be the voice for the family.

Her trust was bolstered when she got calls from friends after Kim had given an interview. "I heard your sister on the radio. She did a great job!"

Even if Martina had been willing to do an interview or two, she couldn't— Ebony had confiscated her cell phone for most of each day.

"How you doing?" Troy asked each time he called, concern ringing in his voice.

"I'm getting better. All I can do is lie here and take my medicine."

She could tell that he was not convinced. Finally, Troy confessed that friends had written him letters informing him that Martina was concealing details of her condition from him. Martina was furious. How dare they upset Troy at a time like this? It was her business and her business alone to tell her brother if there was anything to be worried about!

"I'm not hiding anything," she insisted.

"I believe you," Troy said, but Martina heard the doubt in his voice.

✧

After the execution date was announced, the warden limited Troy's writing material to one small notepad and one pencil, saying that he would be provided with another once he used it up. The prison also restricted his incoming mail. Troy would usually sift through the dozens of envelopes he received during the daily mail call, reading and responding first to correspondence from his family, closest friends, and others he deemed as highest priority. But now, he was permitted to receive only one letter at a time. When he finished reading and answering that letter, he would be given the next one. Martina had heard rumors that Warden Carl Humphrey had been serving on the Savannah Police Department at the time that Officer MacPhail was killed. Perhaps that was why he was treating Troy so harshly.

September 10, 2011

"I haven't been able to see Troy for three months," Martina told Dr. Negrea when he came to check on her. "I am not going to sit in this hospital with my brother facing execution in ten days." Troy called on her cell phone as Dr. Negrea was considering Martina's words.

"The family just left visitation," Troy said.

It had been a noncontact visit, Troy told her, but the guard had let Kiersten hold Troy's finger for a moment through the locked gate separating visitors from the bowels of the prison. Troy had stroked his niece's small hand through the yellow iron bars. "You tickling me, Uncle Troy!" Kiersten had giggled.

"How you feeling today?" Troy asked Martina.

"Troy, hold on a moment." Martina covered the mouthpiece with her hand, and then, to Dr. Negrea, "Would you like to talk to him?"

"Sure." Dr. Negrea took the cell phone. "Troy, this is Martina's oncologist. I've heard so much about you. I want you to know we're in your corner. Your sister is a strong woman and her cancer is still in remission. We're going to do everything we can. She's going to get through this."

Troy's phone time was up. Martina turned to her doctor. "One of two things will happen," Martina said to him. "Either you will release me, or I will bust out of here myself." Dr. Negrea met her gaze and repeated the words he had just uttered to Troy. "We're going to do everything we can."

Dr. Negrea, Dr. Hunter, and Dr. Mullins huddled in the hallway on Monday, trying to come up with a plan of action to release Martina. Fluid had started building up around her lung again, but a chest tube would help with that, they decided, though it would have to be inserted without her being anesthetized because Martina's blood pressure was too low to risk anesthesia.

"I'm not going to lie to you," Dr. Mullins warned before he began. "This is going to hurt."

Martina gritted her teeth against the agony of feeling each step of the procedure: cutting the bigger incision; removing the smaller catheter; scraping out the tubing with a wire apparatus; putting in the bigger shunt.

If this was what was required in order to be able to see Troy, then this was what she would endure.

✧

Friday, September 16, 2011

Martina lay in the hospital with Ebony by her side as De'Jaun and Kimberly boarded a bus filled with Savannah activists, headed to Atlanta for a march from Woodruff Park to Ebenezer Baptist Church, to be followed by a prayer vigil. The previous day, AIUSA, the NAACP, Change.org, Color of Change, and MoveOn.org had delivered nearly one million petition signatures calling for clemency to the Georgia Board of Pardons and Parole, followed by a press conference. High-profile celebrities had begun tweeting about Troy, including Kim Kardashian and Outkast rapper Big Boi, who was from Savannah.

De'Jaun had taken Martina's cell phone before leaving Savannah so that she would be forced to rest, but Ebony was receiving updates on her phone. "They're saying that 3,500 people are marching from Woodruff Park to Ebenezer Baptist Church!" Ebony said.

Martina tried to visualize that number of people taking to the Atlanta streets for Troy. That same march in 2008 had turned out three hundred supporters, and their first rally in Atlanta back in 2007 had turned out forty people. Now, just over four years later, there were too many supporters to even squeeze into the cavernous Ebenezer Baptist Church. The activists organically organized an impromptu second vigil outside the church to accommodate the overflow.

Friends inside the church texted to Ebony the words De'Jaun spoke as he and Kimberly addressed the rally, and Ebony read them aloud to Martina:

"People keep asking what my family is going through right now," De'Jaun told the thousands who had gathered. "I tell them that we're going through the same thing we've been going through every day for the last twenty years."

At the end of the service, Reverend Dr. Warnock invited the family to come up to the pulpit to receive a blessing. Martina tried to visualize the ritual that the messages on Ebony's phone described: De'Jaun, Kimberly, and Valerie's son (Aunt Mattie's grandson) Elijah stepping onto the pulpit as Reverend Dr. Warnock called for the laying of hands, a custom usually reserved for occasions such as the ordination of a minister. Dozens of people surrounded the family, covering them with outstretched palms while the reverend slowly, powerfully, invoked God's presence. Even from her hospital bed in Savannah, Martina could feel the strength that came from those outstretched hands, blanketing her family with love and support.

The next day, Saturday, September 17, Martina checked out of the hospital with Dr. Negrea's blessings. Early Sunday morning, she and her family began the long drive to Jackson to visit Troy. From there, they would continue onto Atlanta for Monday's parole board hearing.

Troy's execution date was just four days away.

✧

Sunday, September 18, 2011

Martina did not want Troy to know how much pain she was in, but they were too close for her to conceal it—he could see it in her eyes. And there was no way to hide the fact that she was in a wheelchair. Troy was equally unable to mask his fear in seeing her frail frame sitting in it.

The Southern Center for Human Rights had worked with Department of Corrections officials so that the family could have a contact visit. Just being able to see and touch her brother made Martina feel stronger than she had in months.

Troy scooted his chair directly in front of Martina's wheelchair and held her hand.

"How are you feeling, Tina? You doing better?"

"Yeah, I'm doing good. I'm only in this wheelchair because I'm still a little bit wobbly," she reassured him. The guards had let her stay in her own wheelchair, rather than making her transfer to one provided by the prison. "Other than that, I don't need it."

Martina lifted her shirt so that Troy could see her incision, where the tubes had been inserted and the catheter was draining. She wanted him to see for himself that she was not hiding anything from him.

Aside from a quick discussion of what actions the lawyers were pursuing, the family did not talk about Wednesday's execution date. Kiersten had Troy on his feet in order to teach him her latest ballet moves, and Troy asked De'Jaun about his upcoming SATs and college applications. It was not until the very end of visitation that the following day's parole board hearing was even mentioned.

"You ready to sit up there and say what you have to say, De'Jaun?" Troy asked his nephew.

Martina, Kimberly and Mama had all pled for Troy's life in the sentencing phase of the trial and previous parole board hearings. This time, it would be De'Jaun.

"Yessir," De'Jaun answered. "I talked to Jay, Danielle, and John and let them know what I was going to say. They told me what to expect. I have it written down. I'm ready."

The rest of the family had already sent letters to the board. *I don't diminish the MacPhail family's pain, but my family is going through a similar hurt*, Martina wrote. She wanted the board to know how much they loved Troy and what a central role he played in their family.

"I'm just tired," Troy said, alone with Martina for a few private minutes before visitation ended. Martina understood without him having to articulate further: Troy was tired from death and dying constantly hanging over his head. He was weary from being put on death watch for the fourth time, each time stripped of all possessions and issued a special uniform and flip-flops. He was worn out from the knowledge that his family was praying instead of sleeping at night, now that the countdown to his killing had begun yet again. He was drained from trying to prove to the state that his life mattered.

Martina wanted desperately to ease Troy's exhaustion, but what could she say to him? There were no adequate words.

"Troy, I'm trying. I'm trying everything I can."

Troy took her hand in his.

"I know you're trying."

She had done all that she possibly could. But sitting face to face with Troy, all Martina could feel was guilt that she had let him down. And all Troy could feel, sitting across from Martina, was guilt that she had sacrificed so much on his behalf.

✧

Monday, September 19, 2011

The parole board had announced that only ten people would be permitted inside the clemency hearing, including lawyers and witnesses. Martina suspected that the board did not want high-profile members of human rights organizations, such as Ben Jealous and Larry Cox, to report to the media what went on inside the room. Martina was frustrated that she and the family were being shut out.

Martina, Lester, Ebony, and Kiersten waited for three hours in a private room inside the Sloppy Floyd building with a handful of friends who had come to Atlanta, while De'Jaun and other witnesses testified on Troy's behalf.

Kimberly was the one family member inside the hearing with De'Jaun to give him support.

John Hanusz found Martina after Troy's half of the hearing concluded. He was animated. "The hearing was fantastic. I think we have the three votes we need." He briefed Martina on the details and showed her the clemency application that the legal team had submitted to the board the previous week.

Brenda Forrest, a juror at Troy's trial, took up nearly a third of the three hours allotted for Troy's side of the hearing. The new evidence, Brenda stated, would have had a great impact on her decision at trial. "I would never have sentenced Mr. Davis to death and I no longer believe, beyond a reasonable doubt, that Mr. Davis was the shooter. I feel, emphatically, that Mr. Davis cannot be executed under these circumstances. . . . To execute Mr. Davis in light of this evidence and testimony would be an injustice to the victim's family, and to the jury who sentenced Mr. Davis."

Affidavits from four other jurors had also been included in the clemency application. Those jurors had also expressed grave concern about Troy's execution, two of them clearly asserting, as had Brenda Forrest, that under these conditions, they would have had doubt about Troy's guilt.

Quiana Glover finally had the opportunity to tell the story that she had been prevented from testifying to at the evidentiary hearing: At a party, her friend had cautioned Redd Coles that he was drinking too much and to slow down.

"This [expletive] is killing me," Coles had responded.

Quiana had asked Coles what he was talking about.

"Man, looky here, I'm the one who killed that [expletive]. But if they want to hold Troy's [expletive], then let them hold him. Besides, I've got kids to raise," Coles had told her.

There had not been enough time for the oral testimony of Jennifer Dysart, a professor at John Jay College of Criminal Justice, who had conducted extensive research about eyewitness identification, but Dysart's affidavit had been included in the written application. The eyewitnesses had faced many obstacles that would have negatively impacted their ability to accurately identify the shooter, Dysart had asserted. Additionally, the state's faulty identification processes, including a suggestive photo array and a reenactment of the

crime involving a man (Coles) who should have been a suspect, likely con-
taminated eyewitness memory. And Reverend Dr. Warnock testified persua-
sively that mercy was required based on biblical teachings. According to John,
however, it was De'Jaun's appeal that had had the greatest impact.

"You can be very, very proud of him," John said. "The board seemed to be
genuinely touched. They asked him about his future plans, where he wants to
go to school. Terry Barnard made a beeline to him afterwards to shake his hand
and tell him what an impressive young man he is." This was important—
Barnard was the parole board member who was widely believed to be the
"swing vote."

Martina had seen the statement that De'Jaun had written out. She was
certain that he had spoken slowly and clearly, just as she had always taught
him to, as he delivered his plea:

> The word *uncle* doesn't even come close to describing the bond that Troy and
> I have. Troy has been like a father to me. Even though we are separated by
> many miles and thick prison walls, he has helped to shape me into the person
> I am today: I'm an honor student, I'm confident, I always work toward my
> goals, and I'm a person that wants to get the most of all the opportunities I
> have been blessed with. I feel like I owe that to my Uncle Troy.
>
> Although my uncle has always been a huge support to me, he's not
> afraid to challenge me or tell me about his expectations either. For my entire
> life, he has stressed the importance of getting an education and bettering
> myself. There was never a question about this. When Uncle Troy helped
> pay for my new car, he told my mother that if my grades slip even a little
> bit, she has to take the car away. Uncle Troy has always told me that as long
> as I have a good education, the world is mine. I always believed him—and
> still do.
>
> Uncle Troy always helped me work toward those goals. My mother was
> diagnosed with cancer in 2001, when I was six years old. She has spent a lot
> of time in the hospital and getting chemotherapy treatments. The treatment
> has often left her feeling weak and tired, and has been really tough on the
> family. When she got sick, my uncle stepped in and did a lot of the things
> that she would have done, like help me with my homework.
>
> For years, I spoke to my uncle every night and went over my schoolwork
> with him. He helped me with reading, spelling, and English—he was really
> good at those subjects. Because we spoke every night, Uncle Troy was able to
> track my progress and really work on those areas where I was having difficulty.
> It's almost as if he was right there with me. That feeling of closeness with

Uncle Troy is what helps me get by sometimes. I really need him in my life, and I know he's never going to stop being there for me, no matter what.

I used to get really afraid when it would come time to take a test. I would freeze up, even though I knew the material. I told Uncle Troy about the problems I was having. He told me, "You gotta face things head on, De'Jaun." He said that I couldn't run from difficult situations.

Uncle Troy came up with a series of drills that he thought would help me face my fears and get over that hump. We practiced them every night, and before long, my nervousness was gone.

"You gotta face things head on, De'Jaun"—it's a philosophy that I try to live every day—in everything I do.

Uncle Troy has also made sure that, above all else, I treat people with respect and dignity. From the time I was a little boy, he made me address people as sir and ma'am and to be kind to everyone I meet, whether it's a homeless person or someone who was powerful. "Everyone is a human being," he said, "and they deserve to be treated that way." The Bible says that we are all children of God, and my uncle—who is a student of the Bible—has taught me that lesson over and over.

I have seen him enough over the course of my life to know that this is the way that he treats people—even when things are difficult. He leads by example, and I have done my best to follow the example my uncle has set for me.

When I became a teenager, Uncle Troy sat me down and talked to me about girls. He told me that there would be a lot of changes for me in the next few years and that I shouldn't lose sight of what's important—my education. He told me that there are a lot of girls out there and that I shouldn't rush into anything or make decisions that I wasn't prepared to live with for the rest of my life. Most importantly, he told me that I should treat every woman the way I treat my mother, aunties, and grandmother—with nothing but respect.

Family is the core of Uncle Troy's existence. No matter what I have gone through, be it my mother's illness, my grandmother's death a few months ago, or other hard times, Uncle Troy has been my rock. Even in the toughest of times, he is strong and selfless. It is clear to me that he is more worried about how I am doing or how I might be feeling than about his own needs.

It's hard for me to imagine what life would be like without Uncle Troy. Losing him would mean losing my father, my teacher, my mentor—and my best friend. I love him so much. His death would devastate me. It would devastate my family.

Martina knew that De'Jaun would have looked up from his notes and made direct eye contact with each member of the parole board as he concluded:

On behalf of myself and my family, I ask you—I beg you—please spare the life of my uncle, Troy Anthony Davis.

✧

Martina saw bits and pieces of statements from the MacPhail family as she watched the media coverage from the Georgian Terrace Hotel, where her family sat waiting for the board's decision.

"We know what the truth is," Officer MacPhail's widow Joan said emphatically. "For someone to loosely say that Troy is a victim . . . we are true victims. Look at us. We have put up with this for twenty-two years and it's time for justice today. We need our justice."

Mark's daughter Madison, tears in her eyes, spoke about the future she would never have with her father. He was forever frozen at twenty-seven years of age, she said. In a few years, Madison herself would be older than her father was. She and her brother had never gotten to experience a life with their father.

"I'm not for blood. I'm for justice. When it's over, I will be able to finally close this book," Officer MacPhail's mother, Anneliese, said. "And hopefully get some peace. I will never get closure. I may get some peace."

What a travesty it would be, Joan added, if the board did not uphold the death sentence. "Not that we would relish the fact that someone is dying," she hastened to add. "We are not killing Troy because we want to. We're killing Troy . . . or we're trying to execute him . . . because he was punished. He was found guilty by a jury of his peers and we need to go ahead and execute him. And be done."

Martina, De'Jaun, Kimberly, Lester, Ebony, and Kiersten waited at the Georgian Terrace for the parole board's announcement until the board finally issued an update: no decision would be announced that night.

✧

Tuesday, September 20, 2011

Martina was talking to Wende in the lobby of the Georgian Terrace after trying to swallow a few bites of breakfast when Laura rushed into the hotel, looking grim. Laura saw Wende and stopped short.

"Wende, they . . ." Laura began and then suddenly noticed Martina, Ebony, and Lester. "Wende, can I talk to you for a moment?"

Wende and Laura stepped to the other side of the lobby, and then Wende was back by the family's side.

Martina knew before asking. "It's not good, is it?"

Wende confirmed Martina's instinct quietly. "We were denied."

Martina tried to wrap her brain around the news as Laura hurriedly left the hotel to mobilize supporters and media. Ebony began to cry softly. "Why do they keep doing this?"

Martina was numb as Lester wheeled her chair into the elevator and they all, including Wende, went up to the family's suite to deal with the news. Kimberly went into a bedroom with her cell phone to inform the list of friends that Troy had given to the prison the previous week, should it come down to the final two days of goodbye visits.

The rest of the family huddled in the main room on couches near the TV, as Wende took Kiersten to the back of the room to color. Whenever they had previously encountered a setback, Martina and her family had immediately sprung into action, cell phones and conversations buzzing. But this morning, the air of the hotel room was somber and thick with tension.

More information started trickling in from the lawyers and other informed sources. Apparently, it had been a 3–2 split. One more vote in his favor, and Troy would be being led out of the death chamber at that very moment. The board chairman, James Donald, on whose support they had been led to believe they could count, had done an about-face. It had to be politics, Martina thought. She wondered: Perhaps Donald had been threatened with losing his chairmanship of the board? Maybe he was worried that a vote for clemency would damage his political aspirations? But Martina couldn't sit and worry about why the parole board had ruled against them—she was too focused on her concern for Troy. How could they make sure that Troy would get the information from a compassionate source before hearing it on the news or from prison officials? Kimberly was able to reach documentary film maker Terry Benedict on the phone just as Terry was arriving at the prison for his final visitation. Terry would tell Troy.

Suddenly, Kiersten pointed with animation to the television where CNN was playing. "Look! That's Uncle Troy!"

Wende put her arm around the little girl. "You know why your Uncle Troy is on TV, sweetie? It's because thousands of people all over the world love your Uncle Troy."

Kiersten nodded sagely. "Jesus loves Uncle Troy too."

✧

"Jay and the lawyers are trying different avenues. Activists are petitioning Larry Chisolm to ask the judge to withdraw the execution warrant. Nobody is giving up," Martina told Troy resolutely when they arrived at the prison for the first of their two days of final visits. "But—if things don't turn out the way we want, is there anything in particular you want us to do?"

Troy paused for only a moment. "I want to make sure that people keep fighting to end the death penalty. Tell my friends around the world to continue to prove my innocence. And I want everyone to know how much I appreciate all they've done for me." If it came to burial arrangements, Troy had one request—he did not want his body on display.

Martina promised him. The world would know his name and what Troy Anthony Davis stood for. Then they stopped talking about it. They didn't want to dwell on death and dying. Troy did not want Kiersten and De'Jaun to see how shocked he was at the board's decision. Instead, he kept his faith pinned on receiving another miraculous reprieve.

Kiersten demonstrated her ballet moves, rubbing Troy's face whenever she felt that he was distracted, saying, "I love you, Uncle Troy!"

Martina watched De'Jaun closely as he and the guards teased each other back and forth, De'Jaun picking at them for being so muscular. "I bet y'all can't play no ball!"

Martina saw hope in De'Jaun's face, not fear, as if he knew with confidence that God would see Troy through.

Lester was quieter than usual; he, Kim, and Ebony were showing signs of exhaustion and distress. Martina channeled all her energy toward maintaining a strong, optimistic front. She could not allow Troy to see her break down and cry. She refused to put that burden on him.

✧

Wednesday, September 21, 2011

Martina buttoned her blouse with trembling fingers. She had been up vomiting most of the night. She wasn't sure how she was going to get through the day.

The family arrived at the prison at the same time as Gemma. They walked in together, as they had on September 23, 2008. After all these years of work and the swelling support for Troy, here they were, repeating the same journey into the prison as they had taken three years ago, almost to the day.

They went through security and walked down the tunnel, De'Jaun pushing Martina in the wheelchair, past the one-word inspirational posters. Opportunity . . . Achievement . . . the irony cut into Martina deeper than ever.

As in 2008, only a few people could go in with Troy at a time. Ebony, Lester, E.Red, Gemma, and Ledra went in first. Other friends and family rotated in and out.

"I'm afraid to go in," Elijah told Martina. "I'm afraid I'll cry."

Martina did not want overly emotional friends to upset or create stress for Troy, but because of the limitation of numbers, she could not be in the room with them to monitor what they said. She knew that Troy would be consoling and comforting everyone to the best of his ability. They were all just doing the best they could.

"Troy told me to make sure to carry on his legacy," one friend said to Martina as she left the visitation room, her voice cracking.

"Keep your head up and do what Troy wanted you to," Martina said. "We're going to keep fighting, and we need you to keep fighting too. No matter what happens tonight, this isn't the end for Troy. Troy Anthony Davis will live on."

Jay and Danielle were working the pay phone in the waiting area, making every possible last-ditch effort. Elijah was stretched out over several chairs, sleeping. Stress and exhaustion were on everyone's faces and in the slumps of their shoulders.

There seemed to be a lot of activity and preparation—more, it seemed to Martina, than there had been in 2008. Guards and prison officials crossed briskly through the waiting area into the interior of the prison and many of them seemed somber.

"Martina," a burly African American guard who De'Jaun had been teasing yesterday said. "I know it's hard for you and your family, but please don't cry. If y'all break down, I'm going to break down too."

"My mother told me she would be praying for Troy today," another guard, a white man, told Martina.

Martina had known some of the guards for years and she realized that witnessing the family's hurt shook them. Those same guards had known Troy for years as well and had their own relationships with him.

Jay was on Troy's list to witness the execution, as he had been on every execution date. Jay had lived through as many close calls with Troy as the family had and knew better than anyone that a last-minute miracle could still occur. But when he left the room from having just said goodbye to Troy, his face was drawn tightly.

"How is he?" Martina asked him.

"He asked me if I thought they were going to get him this time. I told him we were still fighting, but that he needed to be realistic."

Jay went back to working the pay phone as Martina prepared herself to go inside for her time with Troy. What could she say to her brother, a perfectly healthy human being who, barring a last-minute intervention, would be dead at 7 p.m.?

Troy arranged his chair next to Martina's wheelchair.

"How you doing?" Martina asked him.

"I'm all right . . . just really tired." All night long, Troy said, a guard had awoken him every time he drifted off to sleep and asked him, "Mr. Davis, you okay?"

De'Jaun brought Kiersten in, who immediately ran to Troy for a hug. Troy stood up and lifted Kiersten, placing his hands under her tummy and swinging her back and forth like an airplane.

"Again! Again!" Kiersten called out. Martina saw a small, grief-filled smile play on Troy's face as he swung his niece, who was shrieking and laughing with delight.

"Do it again! Again, Uncle Troy!"

De'Jaun took Kiersten out of the room so that E.Red could get some time.

It was a quarter to three before they knew it. Visitation would be over in fifteen minutes. Martina watched E.Red with concern as he walked out of the prison, head down, without saying a word to anybody in the waiting room. Martina knew that Troy had been a central, guiding figure in E.Red's life over the last three years, ever since he had reconnected with the family.

Gemma and Ledra hugged and kissed Troy quickly and walked out, passing Kiersten and Ebony entering.

"Why is she crying, Mama? What's wrong with her?" Kiersten asked, looking at Gemma.

It was just the immediate family in with Troy now and three guards who stood in the corner of the small, narrow room, doing their best to be noninvasive.

Troy took Lester aside for a few minutes, then De'Jaun. Martina did not try to hear to what he was telling them. These were their private moments with their brother and uncle.

Troy spoke his message to Martina in front of the rest of the family. "I want you to really, truly take care of yourself, Tina. Keep your faith strong, and keep the family together." Martina knew that these would be his words to her. It was what he always told her.

"It's time for you to leave," the guard said. The prison needed to prepare Troy for execution. One more hug each. Then, De'Jaun pushed Martina's chair and Lester, Kim, and Ebony, holding Kiersten, filed out behind them. They held their heads high, stoic. In 2008, there had been tears at this juncture. This time, there were none.

Gemma had been waiting for the family by the vending machines and joined them as they crossed the waiting room toward the double yellow iron bars. Martina looked back over her shoulder to see if the guards might bring Troy out for a final goodbye. They didn't. In 2008, they had heard the iron gates slam from inside the prison as they had exited the visitation area. This time, there was an unsettling silence.

"God bless you, Troy!" Gemma called out just before entering the first of the double set of iron bars.

Martina and Kim took the elevator and everyone else walked down the stairs. They met at the bottom and De'Jaun silently resumed pushing Martina down the tunnel, past the one-word affirmation signs.

A dozen CERT officers in black uniforms filed briskly past the family, moving toward the interior of the prison. The last officer in the line met Martina's eyes briefly and gave her a slight, somber nod, as if he were offering her a silent acknowledgment, before continuing his stride upstairs, through the visitation area, and into the bowels of the prison and the death house, to perform whatever his role would be in what was about to take place.

The guard at the prison entrance had a large, padded envelope for the family. Ebony signed for it, and picked up the package containing Troy's belongings.

✧

The press conference was already under way when Martina and her family entered the Towaliga County Line Baptist Church, just across the road from the prison. The church was packed with supporters and press. Camera operators tripped over each other trying to get the best possible shot. One bumped into Martina's wheelchair as he pushed his camera directly into her face.

"Back up!" mild-mannered Lester shouted.

"We have a right to capture the story!" a cameraman called out.

"You'll get the story, but you don't have to knock her over to get it!" Lester snapped back.

Martina feared that she might get crushed. "Put me up on the pulpit," she said. E.Red, Lester, and De'Jaun lifted her wheelchair and hoisted it the few steps up, but the press continued to swarm her.

"She's not going to give a statement if you don't back up!" Lester said.

Finally, the press settled down and the family members circled around Martina's wheelchair as the cameras started snapping away. Gathered around the immediate family were E.Red, Valerie, and Elijah. Behind them stood Ben Jealous and Ed DuBose of the NAACP, Larry Cox from Amnesty USA, and the Reverend Dr. Warnock.

Martina knew that the press wanted to hear from her and she was going to make sure that she delivered the message that Troy would want imparted:

"Our family is hurting, but we will not give up this fight. Troy said that this fight did not begin with him, and this movement should not end with him, because if we can amass millions of people to stand up and say, 'We will not stand for this,' then we can end the death penalty. And that's what we need to do. . . . We cannot go back idly, no matter what happens tonight, and say, 'Well, we marched down the street, we wore I Am Troy Davis shirts,' and that is it. We have to be the catalyst for the change that we want to see."

"Yes!" someone called out from the church pews. Martina felt a surge of strength and energy.

"Troy Davis has impacted the world. My brother never thought that people would know his name across oceans, across states, in places like Tanzania and Ethiopia, places where they kill people in the Middle East, and they're still saying, 'I am Troy Davis.' And they say it in hues of colors that my brother has never seen and languages that he can't speak. But when they say, 'I am Troy Davis,' everybody knows what that means. . . . That means that we can all be Troy Davis. And if we don't stand up for the Troy Davises, then we are no better than the people who put him there."

"Amen!"

"That's right!"

"Our lives, and my son's and my sisters' and brother's lives and my niece's life, have been richer for knowing Troy. Anybody who's met Troy has come away with an imprint of him on their soul. . . . So I just would like to say that I am Troy Davis."

The crowd took on the chant without Martina having to lead it.

"We are Troy Davis! We are Troy Davis! We are Troy Davis!"

"I've been battling cancer for ten years," Martina continued, as Kiersten leaned against her arm. "I don't have cancer, but I'm reaping some of the effects of the medicine."

"Amen."

"Several months ago, I was doing fine. And after that, I couldn't get up out of the chair. But I'm here to tell you . . ." Martina heard her voice crack. De'Jaun put a protective hand on her shoulder, rubbing it gently. Martina did not care that she was weak and highly medicated—she was not done fighting. She took a deep breath. "I'm here to tell you that I'm going to stand here for my brother today."

Martina handed the microphone to Lester, and slowly, unsteadily, rose from her wheelchair as supporters in the pews burst into applause. Martina was standing up, straight and tall. She was standing for Troy and for every victim of the criminal justice system.

De'Jaun took hold of her from behind to steady her as Lester gave her back the microphone. No matter what happened tonight, Troy was going to live. "I am!" she called out to the crowd.

"Troy Davis!" they roared back in support, their voices filling the church.
"You are!"

"Troy Davis!"

"We are!"

"Troy Davis!"

"Now let's get to work, and let's tell Georgia that we will not stand by, and we will defy them."

✧

Lester attempted to push Martina back to the private rooms that the NAACP had organized for the family as the entire church swarmed over her.

"We love you!" people in the pews who had come from all over Georgia called out to her as flashbulbs from cameras nearly blinded her.

"We love Troy!"

"We're sticking with your family!"

Martina knew the hugs she was covered with were offers of support. But she could also feel hurt transmitted through those hugs. Martina was in no position to absorb other people's pain.

Jay, Danielle, and Steve Marsh were in the back room, making calls. Kitty Behan, who had stayed in contact with the family after leaving Arnold & Porter, brought a spread of food for everyone. The lawyers, family, friends, and activists were running in and out and back and forth, either giving information or trying to get information.

Shortly after 5 p.m., Steve popped in with an update about the eleventh-hour appeals that the Resource Center had filed to stay the execution, alleging claims of innocence and prosecutorial misconduct involving evidence that had emerged at the evidentiary hearing. "The Georgia Supreme Court denied us," Steve said. "Now we're going to the US Supreme Court."

Jay made silent eye contact with Martina briefly before leaving the church. Martina knew he was heading back to the prison to undergo a security check before waiting to enter the death house as Troy's witness.

It was time to go to the prison grounds. The hundreds of supporters spilled out of the church as the sky darkened and walked two by two in a silent procession, led by De'Jaun, Ben Jealous, and Larry Cox, up the hill toward the road that separated them from the prison grounds.

Two vans waited at the end of the road. Martina looked around for her son as Kimberly, Lester, Ebony, Kiersten, E.Red, Gemma, Kitty, Ben, and Larry squeezed into the vans.

"Where's De'Jaun?"

"There he is." Lester spotted De'Jaun leading a group of university students and pulled him into the van just as it was driving across the road.

Martina was stunned to see state troopers and SWAT team officers clad in full black riot gear and face masks charge from the prison driveway toward the road and form a line, leaving a gap for their vehicles, with rows of CERT guards behind them. After the family's cars went through, the troopers closed off the line, blocking off the prison entrance, and started moving forward in formation, pushing the students back across the road. Supporters lined the road, unable to get any closer to the prison grounds. Thank goodness Lester had gotten De'Jaun into the van when he did or De'Jaun might have been separated from the rest of the family.

✧

It was just after 6:30 p.m. The family showed their IDs to the CERT guards and the cars continued down the embankment to the protest pen. There must have been 150 additional protestors in the pen on top of the hundreds across the road, many of whom had come with buses provided by the National Action Network and who had been there since early afternoon without food or water. Dozens of the press were lined up on the other side of one length of the thick rope, running live feed.

There was a sprinkling of CERT officers around the perimeter of the pen, and more troopers stationed deeper in the woods, where Martina suspected that the K-9 cars were. Lester helped Martina out of the van and into her wheelchair. A SWAT chopper hovering overhead almost drowned out the protestors' angry chants, but she could still make out the refrain of:

"No justice!"

"No peace!"

A few protestors spotted the family and the outraged crowd gathered at the entrance of the protest pen. Suddenly, and seemingly without direction, the protestors transformed into a human corridor and the angry chanting morphed into fervent prayer. Martina could feel deep sorrow and profound respect rippling down the lines as De'Jaun pushed her wheelchair through the human corridor, the rest of her family following. Kiersten, in Ebony's arms and overwhelmed by the intensity, began to cry, "I want to go home!"

The prayerful song grew more pitched as the receiving line closed into a circle, wrapping itself tightly around Martina and her family, hundreds of hands raised to the heavens as the prayers were sent upward.

✧

7 p.m. The gospel songs and prayers rose in volume and intensity at Troy's scheduled execution time, peaking in pitch and fervor as the supporters blanketed the Davis family with faith and love. Martina saw Kimberly quickly brush a tear off her cheek.

At 7:04 p.m. a rumble began from across the highway. Before Martina had the chance to wonder what caused it, the rumble spread into a low, guttural roar and then exploded into a shout: TROY GOT A STAY!

The cheering, jumping, and shouting overpowered Martina. "Hallelujah!" was mingled with "Allahu Akbar!" People grabbed each other in jubilant hugs. Others dropped on their knees crying in relief.

"Hold on, wait, we don't know if it's a stay yet!"

The tension was too great to bear. Ebony erupted into tears, clutching a supporter standing next to her. "Oh Jesus! Oh Jesus!"

Martina sat quietly in the chair, trying to keep her focus. She couldn't celebrate until she knew definitively what was happening.

"No stay," someone called out minutes later. It was merely a delay, until the US Supreme Court ruled. There was no knowing when that might be.

The tight knot of tension dissipated throughout the prison yard as supporters and activists broke off from the circle and huddled in small groups, sitting, talking, as Vizion Jones, vice president of Atlanta's chapter of NAN, continued to lead others in prayer and song.

Martina was numb and weary as 7 p.m. slipped into 7:30 and then to 8. She sat silently in her wheelchair with Gemma standing by her side, praying for God to give Troy life and monitoring Steve and Danielle's postures at the far corner of the pen, still working their cell phones nonstop. Martina would know from their body language if news arrived and whether it was good or bad.

"Poor Troy," Gemma said to Martina. "What they're putting this man through."

"Gemma, Troy's tired. He's just really tired."

But Martina, too, could not stop thinking about what Troy might be going through. Had he already been strapped onto the gurney, and did he remain there as minutes stretched into hours? Was he in pain or discomfort? She didn't want the Supreme Court's delay to give him hope, if that hope was just going to be snatched away from him.

A light drizzle began to fall and Martina pulled her brown sweater up around her shoulders. She had to avoid infection at any cost.

Ben Jealous, Ed DuBose, Larry Cox, and Laura Moye were making their rounds up and down the media rope, speaking to reporters on the other side. Martina did not want to give interviews, but made exceptions for press who had come all the way from Europe and for Amy Goodman from *Democracy Now!*, who had been covering the twists and turns of Troy's case longer and more consistently than any other reporter.

8:00 p.m. Kathryn Hamoudah and Sara Totonchi from SCHR showed Martina the text of a letter to the parole board from six former wardens of death rows around the country, including one from Georgia, imploring that the board reverse its decision. SCHR had collaborated with the National Coalition to Abolish the Death Penalty to release the letter. Martina scanned the text quickly:

> We write to you as former wardens and corrections officials who have had direct involvement in executions. Like few others in this country, we understand that you have a job to do in carrying out the lawful orders of the judiciary. We also understand, from our own personal experiences, the awful lifelong repercussions that come from participating in the execution of prisoners. While most of the prisoners whose executions we participated in accepted responsibility for the crimes for which they were punished, some of us have also executed prisoners who maintained their innocence until the end. It is those cases that are most haunting to an executioner. . . . Living with the nightmares is something that we know from experience. No one has the right to ask a public servant to take on a lifelong sentence of nagging doubt, and for some of us, shame and guilt. Should our justice system be causing so much harm to so many people when there is an alternative? We urge you to ask the Georgia Board of Pardons and Paroles to reconsider their decision.

Under other circumstances, Martina would have been celebrating these un-likely allies. But all she could do was pray that the letter would have some impact—and quickly.

8:30 p.m. Martina's eyes constantly darted around the pen, tracking her family members. De'Jaun and E.Red sat near the edge of the rope together in silence, heads bowed. Kimberly and Ebony sat on a wooden bench, surrounded by supporters. Lester hovered nearby. Worry whirled in her head—how were her sisters and brother holding up? How was this impacting her son?

9 p.m. Kiersten began to entertain a group of college-aged young women, pretending that she was the mama and they were the children. Before Martina knew it, Kiersten was leading a train of twenty supporters around the prison yard. The train disintegrated after a few moments and Kiersten, tired from staying up late for evenings upon evenings, began to get crabby. De'Jaun scooped his little cousin up and held her high over his head while Kiersten laughed in delight.

Martina looked up at them from her wheelchair and smiled. Even now, amidst sorrow, pain, and tension, her son knew that there was a little girl who needed to laugh, and to play, and to feel safe and protected.

9:30 p.m. What was taking the Supreme Court so long?

"Every minute that Troy stays alive is a miracle," Ben Jealous said to the supporters gathered around him. A miracle perhaps, but every passing minute was also torture.

10 p.m. Supporters were singing Bible verses. Martina sat and waited. People swarmed around with "I Am Troy Davis" T-shirts and signs. Martina waited. Those holding vigil across the road got louder and the troopers and police became more aggressive, with sirens wailing and lights flashing. She waited.

Danielle approached Martina, leaning over and talking quietly into her ear. An unknown individual from inside the prison had just called on Danielle's cell phone. Troy was in his cell and was not afraid. His main concern was that his family knew that he was okay, and he wanted to know how they were doing. Danielle made sure the caller would communicate to Troy that the family was all together and surrounded by hundreds of people, in the prison yard and lining the road across from the prison, and that they were all supporting him and them.

Martina permitted herself a moment of relief. Troy had not been in the death chamber all these hours, strapped down to the gurney.

✧

10:20 p.m. Steve Marsh made his way toward Martina across the prison yard. His head was down and his posture, just ever so slightly, was hunched. Martina knew what Steve was going to say before he reached her side.

Brian Kammer at the Resource Center had taken the call from the US Supreme Court just minutes ago, Steve told Martina, and then called Troy to let him know that the execution would proceed. Brian and Troy had prayed together and then Brian told Troy that he had changed the world.

"How did Troy take it?" Martina managed to ask.

"He told Brian that he'd really like to stay in the world."

Ben Jealous called for everyone to gather around the Davis family and broke the news to them. Stunned supporters hugged wordlessly and cried silently as Laura Moye got in the center of the circle and put her hand on Martina's shoulder.

"It's been a privilege and an honor to stand by this family!" Laura said fiercely and lovingly, as she encouraged the activists gathered there not to give up the fight. "Remember that Troy himself made this fight bigger than him."

Everybody melted away to different parts of the protest pen, as Martina was thrust into a new, grim phase of waiting. Had the IVs been inserted into Troy's veins yet? Was he saying his final words?

A young African American woman approached Martina. Her name was Monica, she told her, and she was a law student in North Carolina. She had driven all the way from San Francisco for two days to be in the prison yard. It was a testament to Troy's impact on young people around the world.

"You could become a powerful activist," Martina told Monica. She did not want this young woman's dedication to get lost. "Long after I'm gone, it'll be students like you who will have the power to create change."

Laura Moye was standing a few feet away.

"Laura, come over here," Martina called out, though her voice was weak and her throat sore. "I have to tell you something." Laura approached quickly. "I want you to meet Monica. She drove all the way from San Francisco to be here tonight. I want to make sure you help her get connected with activists in California so that she can stay plugged into the movement."

Laura pulled out her Blackberry and Monica opened her notebook as photojournalist Scott Langley snapped a photograph. As Laura and Monica exchanged contact information, Martina glanced up toward the prison, just down the long driveway, past the ponds, the groves of trees, and the cement walls and barbed wire that masked the execution chamber.

What were they doing to her brother at that very moment?

The prison spokeswoman, an African American woman wearing a black blouse and glasses, came out shortly afterward to make the announcement.

"The court-ordered execution of Troy Anthony Davis has been carried out. The time of death was 11:08 p.m."

Everyone around her was weeping, but Martina's eyes were bone dry. She just wanted to get out of there as quickly as possible. De'Jaun pushed her wheelchair out of the protest pen and helped her back into the van. The cars slowly drove up the incline, where they were confronted again with more than a hundred armed SWAT team officers in black riot gear making a corridor for the vehicles to pass through. This corridor was so different from the human corridor that had embraced her family upon entering the prison grounds just hours ago.

The SWAT chopper continued to hover overhead, its blades loudly slicing the night air. Hundreds of protestors, many of them sobbing, were crowded onto the embankment of the road, lining the drive all the way to the church. The door of the van was open and supporters shouted into it, extending their arms to her, "We love you, Martina! We love you and we're gonna keep fighting!"

A group of students were huddled on their knees, crying. Troy would want for her to encourage them. "Hold your head up," Martina told them through the open door. "You fought for Troy, and we're going to continue to fight. It was not in vain."

Outside the church, Elijah was weeping uncontrollably. AIUSA and NAACP staff sat hunched over on the church's front steps, eyes rimmed red with grief and exhaustion.

Dozens of friends and supporters wanted to express their outrage and sorrow. But Martina just wanted to leave. The rest of the family climbed back into the vans, and, wordlessly, pulled away from the church, past the truck stop, past the entrance of the Georgia Diagnostic and Classification Prison, and on toward the highway.

Martina had been coming to this prison nearly every week for twenty years, but she would never have to come back to this godforsaken place again. No more would she have to talk to Troy through plexiglass or see him led by guards through yellow iron bars in a white prison-issued uniform or hear about abuses and indignities that he had no choice but to endure. She would never return here again.

Yet deep in her bones, Martina knew that a part of her would always be on Georgia's death row—because that was where her brother had been killed. She would continue to hear those gates clanging in her dreams.

Dear Kiersten,

I wanted to thank you for your beautiful drawing and your letter. You sure made your Uncle Troy smile.

I love you and pray that God will always Bless and keep you safe. Give your mother a hug for me and tell her that I love her too.

See if your hand can fit inside of mine.

Love
Uncle
Troy

Troy's letter to his niece, Kiersten, including his handprint, to remind her of their special "hand-to-hand" ritual. Courtesy of the Davis family.

The laying of hands at Ebenezer Baptist Church at a prayer vigil on September 16, 2011. Courtesy of Jonathan McKinney.

September 21, 2011: Martina stands from her wheelchair to lead supporters in the rallying cry "I am Troy Davis" at a press conference just hours before Troy's execution. Surrounding her, from left to right: Edward DuBose of the NAACP, E.Red, Lester, De'Jaun (helping her stand), and Kimberly. Courtesy of Scott Langley, deathpenaltyphoto.org.

De'Jaun leads a procession of students and supporters from Towaliga County Line Baptist Church toward the prison on September 21, 2011. Courtesy of Jonathan McKinney.

September 21, 2011: De'Jaun looks to the sky at 7:03, just minutes after the execution is scheduled to begin, before the delay is announced. Courtesy of Scott Langley, death-penaltyphoto.org.

Supporters wrap the Davis family in a prayerful circle shortly after 7 p.m. on September 21, 2011. Courtesy of Scott Langley, deathpenaltyphoto.org.

September 21, 2011: A demonstrator is arrested across the street from the prison for breaking the police line. Courtesy of Scott Langley, deathpenaltyphoto.org.

September 21, 2011: While waiting for the US Supreme Court to rule on whether or not the execution will proceed, De'Jaun plays with Kiersten, as Lester, Martina, and Ebony look on. Courtesy of Scott Langley, deathpenaltyphoto.org.

Afterword

Troy was buried on October 1, 2011, at a closed-casket funeral. Nearly two thousand people attended the service at Jonesville Baptist Church in Savannah, Geogia, after which his body was interred at a private ceremony for family and close friends in a cemetery plot next to his mother. Just before Troy's casket was lowered into the grave, twenty-two white doves were released from cages—one for each year Troy had spent in prison. There was a rushed, frenzied flapping of wings and then the birds soared in a single formation in the sky, finally free.

Exactly two months afterwards, on December 1, 2011, Martina Davis-Correia passed away, having gone into renal failure. Martina was laid to rest next to Virginia and Troy on December 10, 2011, which was, fittingly, International Human Rights Day.

Martina and Troy sometimes referred to themselves as twins, and, though they were seventeen months apart, their lives and their fights were intricately intertwined.

"Twin struggles," Martina said to me. "Twin souls."

Martina spoke often of the imprint Troy left on those he befriended; as one of those friends, I can confirm the truth of this statement. But there are also hundreds, if not thousands, of us who have been profoundly touched and changed by Martina as well. Laura Moye, AIUSA's death penalty abolition campaign director emeritus, has called Martina a modern-day prophet for human rights. For those of us inspired by Martina, she will always be reflected in all aspects of our struggle for a more just world.

Human rights photojournalist Scott Langley captured many searing, poignant moments in the Georgia Diagnostic and Classification Prison yard on September 21, 2011. Among them is an incident described in this book: Martina gazing toward the prison as Laura and Monica, the young law student, exchange contact information after Martina asked Laura to connect Monica with death penalty abolition activists.

The photo was taken at 11:08 p.m., capturing a look of anguish on Martina's face as she wonders what they're doing to her brother at that moment.

We learned later that 11:08 p.m. was the exact time that Troy had succumbed to lethal injection.

What was Martina doing at the moment that Troy passed?

She was enlisting another recruit in the fight to bring down the system that killed her brother. That was the essence—and the indomitable spirit—of Martina Davis-Correia.

The Davis family lost three warriors for justice in 2011, but those they left behind—Kimberly, De'Jaun, Lester, Ebony, and Kiersten—are continuing Troy, Martina, and Virginia's struggle, knowing they are empowered and protected from above by three angels.

And what of the MacPhail family? Six months after the execution, Officer MacPhail's mother, Anneliese, was interviewed by CNN. The article described a woman still haunted by loss. "I don't have the peace yet that I was hoping for," she is quoted as saying, though she remained convinced that Troy had committed the crime.

Though the MacPhail family wanted Troy's execution to go forward, Mrs. MacPhail's sentiment reflects one reason why a growing number of family members of murder victims have been speaking out against capital punishment: the "closure" that families so desperately seek remains elusive. The death penalty offers the false promise that the taking of one life can be answered by the taking of another. The hole that Mark MacPhail's loss brought to his family is every bit as gaping now, I dare venture to guess, as it was before September 21, 2011.

Troy himself hoped that the MacPhail family would consider the following, as he spoke his final words to them from the gurney:

"I'd like to address the MacPhail family. I'd like to let you all know that, despite the situation, I know you are all still convinced that I'm the person that killed your father, your son, your brother. But I am innocent. The incidents that happened that night, it was not my fault. I did not have a gun that night, I did not shoot your family member. But I am so sorry for your loss. I really am, sincerely. All that I can ask is that each of you look deeper into this case so that you will really, finally see the truth."

Troy and his family always understood that the struggle was much bigger than Troy Anthony Davis and that, though Troy never wanted to be a martyr for a cause, his execution would be part of sparking a much larger, stronger movement.

"When I see death row exonerees, I see the face of hope," Martina said at Troy's wake, looking directly at Darby Tillis, exonerated from death row in 1987. "We can abolish the death penalty."

Troy told his supporters from the gurney:

"I ask my family and friends that you all continue to pray, that you all continue to forgive, that you continue to fight this fight."

To his executioners, he said:

"For those about to take my life, may God have mercy on all of your souls."

His last words: God bless you all.

At Martina's funeral, Laura Moye spoke about the day when the United States will terminate its practice of killing its prisoners.

"When the book is written on how the death penalty was abolished in this country, there will be at least one chapter about Troy and Martina," she said.

Troy and Martina are no longer here to lead the death penalty abolition movement that they galvanized, but their spirit remains at its heart. They placed in our hands the responsibility to continue their struggle.

I look forward, as does the Davis family, to our movement growing in strength and numbers as we work together, as Troy and Martina both asked of us, to continue to fight this fight.

Jen Marlowe
April 24, 2013
Seattle, Washington

September 21, 2011: Martina introduces a law student (Monica) to Laura Moye from
AIUSA, so that Monica can get involved in the death penalty abolition movement.
Monica and Laura exchange contact info as Martina glances up at the prison. It is
later learned that this exact moment—11:08 p.m.—was Troy's time of death.
Courtesy of Scott Langley, deathpenaltyphoto.org.

"The family that prays together stays together." Clockwise from the top: Martina, Kimberly, Ebony, Kiersten, De'Jaun, Lester. Courtesy of the Davis family.

Acknowledgments

There is so much gratitude that is due, not only for assistance in the writing of *I Am Troy Davis*, but for the love, support, and solidarity shown to Troy and the Davis family over the years. We wish we had the space to adequately acknowledge everyone, both within the pages of the book and here—but no amount of space would be sufficient.

There are many without whose incredible generosity of time, background information, documents, and recollections this book simply could not have been written. Chief among them are John Hanusz and Laura Moye. You played a central, indispensable role in the writing of this book.

Scores of other people also provided critical information and insight and/or checked sections of the manuscript for accuracy, and to them we offer deep gratitude. They include Jason Ewart, Wende Gozan Brown, Gemma Puglisi, Earl, a.k.a. E.Red, Wanda Jones, Beverly Youmans, Sara Totonchi, Kathryn Hamoudah, Randy Loney, Mary Sinclair, Kim Manning-Cooper, Rosanne Fabi, Laura Tate Kagel, Jeff Walsh, Jared Feuer, Ledra Sullivan-Russell, Bob Nave, Kalonji Jama Changa, Scott Langley, Rob Freer, Terry Benedict, Carolyn Bond, Lynn Hopkins, Bill Marks, Brian Kammer, Stephen Marsh, Edward DuBose, and Emmet Bondurant.

Katherine Long jumped into her role as research assistant with energy and great skill. Doreen Shapiro provided astute editing during the initial draft and

Ruth Baldwin's acuity brought the manuscript to a new level. In addition, special thanks are owed to Ruth (along with Marissa Colón-Margolies) for believing in and supporting this book and ensuring that it came to be. And it could not have found a better home than that provided by Haymarket Books—much appreciation to Anthony Arnove and to Julie Fain for their enthusiasm for the project and for the wise guidance (and endless patience) that they have exhibited, as well as to Dao X. Tran, Sarah Grey, and Rachel Cohen for bringing it to the finish line.

Many others have helped the book in so many ways. The project was conceived in Megan Thomas's backyard. Marc Reiner generously provided a legal review of the manuscript. Scott Langley offered use of his powerful photographs.

Those are just a fraction of those who supported and assisted in the book's creation. There are countless more who shared different pieces of Martina and Troy's journey, and whose support and love is deeply felt and appreciated. You will always be close to our hearts.

—Jen Marlowe and the Davis family

Tina and Troy: I am my brother's keeper.
Courtesy of the Davis family.

Index

About the Authors

Jen Marlowe, a human rights activist, writer, and filmmaker, is the author of *The Hour of Sunlight: One Palestinian's Journey from Prisoner to Peacemaker* and *Darfur Diaries: Stories of Survival*. Jen's award-winning documentary films include *One Family in Gaza, Rebuilding Hope: Sudan's Lost Boys Return Home*, and *Darfur Diaries: Messages from Home*. Her website is: www.donkeysaddle.org

Martina Davis-Correia, the sister of innocent death-row prisoner Troy Davis, was Amnesty USA's Death Penalty Abolition Co-Coordinator for Georgia. She served on the boards of Georgia's NAACP branch, the Campaign to End the Death Penalty, and Georgians for Alternatives to the Death Penalty. Martina was also a leading advocate for women with breast cancer. She was twice named Savannah's "Unstoppable Woman."

Troy Anthony Davis was executed on September 21, 2011, for the murder of a Savannah policeman, despite an international outcry due to his strong case of innocence. Troy worked tirelessly while on death row to prove his innocence and to abolish the death penalty. *TIME* magazine named Troy one of 2011's most influential people.

Sister Helen Prejean wrote the internationally acclaimed book *Dead Man Walking*, describing her experiences as spiritual advisor to Louisiana death row inmates, now a major motion picture starring Susan Sarandon and Sean Penn. Sister Helen's second book is *The Death of Innocents*. She educates about the death penalty by lecturing, organizing, and writing.

Right to left: Jen Marlowe and Martina Davis-Correia with Troy Anthony Davis (on the poster).